The Stepfamily

Living,

Loving,

and Learning

The Stepfamily

by **ELIZABETH EINSTEIN**

MACMILLAN PUBLISHING CO., INC.

NEW YORK

Macmillan Publishing Co., Inc.
866 Third Avenue, New York, N.Y. 10022
Collier Macmillan Canada, Inc.

Library of Congress Cataloging in Publication Data
Einstein, Elizabeth.
  The stepfamily.
  Bibliography: p.
  Includes index.
  1. Stepparents—United States. 2. Stepchildren—
United States. I. Title.
HQ759.92.E36   306.8   81-19353
ISBN 0-02-535100-1   AACR2

10 9 8 7 6 5 4 3 2 1

Designed by Jack Meserole

Printed in the United States of America

For BEN,

    My stepfather, with love and gratitude.

For CYNTHIA and LYNN,

    My first stepchildren.

And for BEVERLY, BRENDA, and KURT,

    Whose lives as my stepchildren changed

    my own forever.

The bond that links your true family is not one of
blood, but of respect and joy in each other's life.
—RICHARD BACH

Contents

Preface

One of the most complex of family relationships is the stepfamily—a configuration resulting from remarriage with children. Its very existence is a product of death or divorce. No one forgets this; fear of its recurrence is part of the stepfamily's fragile foundation. This family faces a challenging task. Yet few people understand its special dynamics, and this lack of knowledge can lead unsuspecting stepfamilies into chaos.

This journalistic account of the stepfamily was intended to help fill an information gap. But with each question I asked, each interview I conducted, each page I wrote, I was forced to explore my own life as a stepchild and as twice a stepmother to other people's children.

So this account has become a report of growth, a report of sharing. Through talking with many other stepfamilies I learned that one way to gain perspective is to share experience. From my personal story, readers can know they are not alone in this complicated situation.

Although I did not know this would be so, the sharing started early in the interviewing phase with a black family in Washington, D.C. Concerned that I gather the information outlined in my publishing proposal, I came armed with questions. But well into the interview the talk felt strained. Some of the family members were defensive, others angry. One adult refused to talk of his stepmother. I knew the feelings well. I put away my questions and began to share my own memories and mistakes from being a stepchild and stepmother for thirty years of my life. As they responded to my sharing, the style unfolded for talking with forty-five other stepfamilies.

Three criteria guided me. First, the interviews with other stepfamilies provided a spectrum of experiences in this complex family form. These experiences often make stepfamily members feel inadequate; talking about them revealed that they are normal and predictable variations on a theme of family life in which millions are involved.

One truth emerged from these interviews. No generalized pattern for success exists—nor do generalized solutions to problems. These families were in diverse developmental phases of the stepfamily experience and viewed events and feelings from different perspectives. While their experiences revealed patterns, each stepfamily had to work out its own survival as relationships and feelings from the past were entwined with those of the present.

Because stepfamilies believe in family life and strong relationships, they want to understand what makes living together in a stepfamily so difficult. Most realized it was what they did not know that hurt them; certainly, that was the case for us.

Living in a stepfamily need not be as difficult as it was for us. To make it easier, people need information about what makes the stepfamily different and what relationships affect its survival. In many ways, our family is an example of how not to approach stepfamily life and our mistakes reflect those of millions of other stepfamilies.

My deepest gratitude goes to those necessarily anonymous stepfamilies who shared their experiences. They opened their lives to me in the hope that sharing their pain and joy might help other step relationships become happier. Most said they wished someone had told them how it would really be. This did not mean they would have avoided remarriage; it meant they would simply have had more realistic expectations.

From my own experiences as a stepchild, a part-time stepmother, and then a full-time stepmother, I knew why stepchildren feel afraid, abandoned, and rebellious as well as why stepparents feel angry, guilty, and resentful. To share this knowledge meant explaining away my own feelings and behaviors or trying to make some sense of them. Facing my own fears and guilts forced me to examine destructive patterns and perceptions.

In *The Survivor*, Terrence DesPres explains why many survivors of the death camps relive the anguish of their past as they recapture the Holocaust's atrocities in writing: "The survivor's aim is to let the world know." Without DesPres's book and his sensitivity to what I was trying to do, I might have lacked the courage to finish what I started. As he suggested, my greatest fear was that of being judged.

Many authorities helped me sort out the underpinnings of the stepfamily experience. Without the time and concern of these professionals, this book would not have taken the form it has. My deepest gratitude to:

Roger Bach, psychologist at Bach Institute in Beverly Hills, California.

Richard Ellison, professor of law at Syracuse University in Syracuse, New York.

Irene Goldenberg, psychologist and director of psychological services at UCLA's Center for Health Services in Los Angeles.

Frank Halse, Jr., marriage and family therapist at the Child and Family Service Agency in Syracuse, New York.

Jerome Kagan, research child psychologist at Harvard University in Cambridge, Massachusetts.

Janet Levine, case worker at the Franklin Hampshire Community Health Center in Northampton, Massachusetts.

Jeannette Lofas, executive director of the Step Family Foundation of Manhattan in New York City.

Harlan London, associate professor of human development at Syracuse University in Syracuse, New York.

Lillian Messinger, principal investigator of Project Remarriage at the Clarke Institute of Psychiatry in Toronto, Ontario, Canada.

Janice H. Nadler, clinical psychologist at Cedars Sinai Hospital in Los Angeles, California.

Robert Pickett, professor of child and family studies at Syracuse University in Syracuse, New York.

Alvin Poussaint, professor of psychiatry at Harvard Medical Center in Boston, Massachusetts.

Leah C. Schaefer, psychotherapist and president of the Society for the Scientific Study of Sex in New York City.

James Sicherman, pediatrician in Syracuse, New York.

Joseph Steinberg, attorney in Hartford, Connecticut.

Emily B. Visher, psychologist and president of the Stepfamily Association of America in Palo Alto, California.

John S. Visher, psychotherapist and board member of the Stepfamily Association of California in Palo Alto, California.

Marcia Wrytzen, counselor at the Center for Creative Living in Allendale, New Jersey.

Of these, Irene Goldenberg, Emily Visher, and John Visher gave extra measures of help.

Now I understand why typists are mentioned. Jane Frost prepared perfect manuscripts and even took phone dictation in tight spots. Her sense of humor was appreciated. Tippy Crouch transcribed the interview tapes.

After a frenzied introduction to the pinwheel of publishing, I had the good fortune of having senior editor Jane Cullen at Macmillan inherit my manuscript. Her sensitivity to the importance of my subject truly made the difference. I owe Jane a great debt.

Several people read portions of the manuscript and offered suggestions and encouragement. I wish to thank Terrence DesPres, Dinah Eng, James Geis, Arnold Goldstein, Nancy Rubin, Constance Warloe, Richard Wilson, and Geoffrey Wolff. Through eyes made sensitive and critical in thirty-five years and more as a social worker with families, Gertrude Einstein critiqued each first draft (such as some of them were), encouraging and alerting me where I went astray. My deep thanks to this loving role model and mentor.

My gratitude to Joyce Halse, who, when the going got really tough, held us all together with her good humor and strength.

As I wrote this book, my husband Walter and sons Chris and Jeff were exceptionally tolerant of my moods and my long absences, as well as of the change and confusion this project added to our already complex relationships. Their love and support gave me the courage to share our story.

Throughout the writing of this book, one person was a tower of strength. As a mentor he worked with me on every draft, even helping me conquer the split infinitive. As a professional counselor he guided me through examining myths and illusions that tied me to my past and kept me from becoming all I could be. As a friend he encouraged me when I felt I could not go on. He said I taught him about stepfamilies; but what he helped me learn about myself gave me the courage to attempt to understand my life. For this great gift of love and life, I wish to thank Frank Halse, Jr.

Chippewa Bay, New York

The Stepfamily

Prologue

A love poem Walter wrote me before we were married was titled "Sand Castles." While it wins no literary prizes, it captured my heart with its dream of rebuilding our lives and it beckoned me to come and see what life with his family would be like. Both of us were divorced and had custody of our children; both of us were doing the best we could with our single-parent families.

But both of us were traditionalists and wanted marriage and total family life. And so the three of us and the four of them became what family therapist Virginia Satir called a *blended family*—a nice term for what is legally a stepfamily.

Like many who remarry, we thought: "We've been through this before; this time we'll do it better." First of all, I had lived in a stepfamily before, but my husband had not; neither of us understood its complexities. Second, the we'll-do-it-better thinking set up unrealistic expectations that added to our problems. Our family never measured up to the poem's image of the sand castle, and I wondered what was wrong with us.

Recently the old poem resurfaced, and its irony ten years later startled me. What clearer analogy for the unaware stepfamily, for our family, than the sand castle. Like the vulnerable beach structure, our stepfamily was built on an unsound base and without an understanding of the tides that can sweep it away. On this fragile base, with forces and relationships that shape it into complex configurations, people who are vastly different not only in appearance but in values and goals end up trying to hold together this complex configuration we call a stepfamily.

Once remarriage creates a stepfamily, its members cling together and hope they won't become another broken family. Yet despite everyone's eagerness, their diverse backgrounds generate vastly different ideas about how to make a family work.

With no plan and no architect to serve as coordinator, the structure is built on the sand of unrealizable hopes and dreams. Most new stepfamilies do not understand the dynamics of the tide sweeping them into a sea of chaos and complexities. Few realize that this different kind of family must build new family relationships for the future, and retain ties to past ones. Most people do not lack the stamina to build a firm foundation for their new families; they simply lack the information and skills to carry it out.

Stepfamilies must be built with more than good intentions, dreams, and hopes. Awareness, skills, and realistic expectations can provide a stable structure that permits the stepfamily to achieve its potential.

1 Meeting the Clan

Outside the door, the teenager stood among her be-longings—clothing jammed in tied-up boxes, a red plaid bag, a grocery sack stuffed with high school keepsakes. Between nibbling her nails and twisting her red hair, she glanced toward the road, hoping her boyfriend would come soon to pick her up.

In yet another act of defiance, she had not come home the night before and had not let her father know of her whereabouts. When she finally arrived, he kicked her out. Stunned by his reaction, she turned to her stepmother and tried to apologize. But the stepmother screamed, "No more. I've had enough apologies. I am not your mother and I don't want to be. Don't ever call me Mom again. Never."

She never did.

That woman was me, and the youngster was my stepdaughter—once a favorite child. That day I felt callous and cold and empty. And relieved. After six years of unfulfilled expectations and promises, I was willing to cast this eighteen-year-old from my life. Things would be easier with her gone, I told myself. No more triangles and deceit. Maybe no more guilt and anger. I walked away. But deep inside I knew these were more false dreams about our life as a stepfamily. Knowing I could have stopped her from leaving, knowing this crisis was turning her life in a direction far from her goals and dreams, I wondered what crueler thing I could have done to this young woman whom I had helped to rear.

First her biological mother left. Now I told her I no longer wanted to be her mother. I knew the rejection she must have felt, for I am a stepchild, too. Since my parents divorced, fear of such a rejection has been my companion.

After my stepdaughter left home in this tumultuous way, much of my guilt was rooted in my belief that my being a stepchild should have prepared me to deal with all the problems facing a stepmother. And since for six years I had been a part-time stepmother to my former husband's daughters, I should have been experienced enough to avoid such turmoil with this second set of stepchildren. But the deepest guilt I felt came from

3

the contradiction between reality and the illusions in which I had shrouded our mother-daughter relationship. Because I dreamed of having a daughter of my own, I took on my husband's two daughters as though they were mine, as though they were products of our relationship. In reality, they symbolized his former marriage.

The indelibly etched scene of Bev's departure sometimes caught up with me in my dreams or during long solitary walks. The last time was in a sunny living room overlooking the East River in New York City as I waited to interview Leah Schaefer, a psychotherapist who helped writer Nancy Friday unravel some of the mysteries of the mother-daughter relationship in *My Mother, My Self.*

Friday's book helped me understand my relationship with my own mother. But because it also raised many questions about my relationships with my daughters (really my stepdaughters, I kept explaining defensively to Dr. Schaefer), I had come to talk with this expert about the value of writing a book. Would others want to read of my experiences as a stepparent? Could I help others avoid the pitfalls when I had not yet discovered all the secrets myself? And could I handle exposing events that I wished had never happened?

Deeper questions about our stepfamily plagued me. How could our family have fallen apart, despite our dream of making it better than the ones we had left? Bev had been the favored child. How could the father who promised her the moon turn on her and then, within a year, repeat the scene with his younger daughter? Why was the blame heaped on me, and why did I accept it so willingly? Were our children damaged by being forced to leave the house? Had our relationships with them ended? After this, would our marriage hold together? Should it?

By the time Dr. Schaefer welcomed me, my professional poise as an interviewer was shattered. When she asked me why the memory of my stepdaughter's exodus upset me, I said I felt guilty whenever I thought about it.

"But why?" she asked again. "Why does it bother you so?"

"I'm not sure. She looked so alone, so afraid and rejected."

"But why should that bother you?" Dr. Schaefer continued to ask the same question, over and over, and I answered around it. But she pursued, repeating it.

As I responded, my throat tight, my mouth dry, I began to realize that the replay of the blowup with my stepdaughter had aroused long-buried memories of my own worst childhood fears.

"What if your stepfather had kicked you out of the house?"

"I think I would have died," I told her between sobs. "Already my heart was broken when my daddy left. If a second father had rejected me, had shown me I was unwanted, it would have been too much to bear."

"That is probably why you feel so badly about having rejected your stepdaughter," Dr. Schaefer suggested. "What you told her recalled your own fears of having such a thing happen to you. Maybe what you said didn't bother Bev as much as it bothered you. Still, you feel you let her down in a way that would have devastated you. But she is not you, and the past does not have to dictate your life, or hers."

THE REALITY BEHIND THE NUMBERS

Dr. Schaefer's insightful advice altered my writing plan. Instead of merely presenting the stepfamily journalistically, I decided to include my attempt to understand my feelings about my life as a stepperson. After talking with many stepfamilies I began to realize how common my emotions about being a stepperson were. As these feelings were shared, and as common patterns emerged, it became obvious that all of us were experiencing social relationships and situations that were unique to stepfamilies.

The statistics alone are staggering. Of the children born during the seventies, half of them will experience broken families and most of these will eventually become stepchildren. Today 80 percent of divorces are followed by remarriage, making more than 25 million adults stepmothers or stepfathers. Most are stepfathers, because women have traditionally been granted custody of the children. But this is changing; and as more fathers gain custody of their children, more stepmothers are rearing other women's children. It is estimated that more than 15 million children now lived with remarried parents. Five years ago one of every eight children was a stepchild; today the figure approximates one of every five.[1]

The poignancy of these figures came alive for me during one of my first interviews, with a family in Rockville, Maryland. The husband and wife were both stepchildren. The woman was stepmother to the teenage boy sitting cross-legged on the sofa; the boy's mother and stepfather lived several states away. In this Rockville family the twenty-two-year-old morally adopted daughter also was home; she was a stepchild. And I was stepchild and two-time stepmother. In that room all five of us were stepchildren; both of us married women were also stepmothers.

In my own biological family three out of five brothers and sisters, all of us reared as stepchildren, have since become stepparents to other people's children. One brother died as a teenager and never experienced marriage. My sister, although not herself a stepparent, is entwined deeply in the stepfamily networks we have created. Of five stepchildren in the two separate families that I have had a hand in rearing, some of them will inevitably become stepparents.

The romantics say love is better the second time around. When applied to remarriage, this idyllic notion of songs and movies fails to mention the leftovers from former family relationships: children, former spouses, child support and alimony, anger, guilt, jealousy, and fear.

Nor is it mentioned that the people who jump into remarriages are themselves often the same. Only the partner has changed, and they have a much more complex family situation in which to repeat past mistakes.

The romantics fail to mention that most remarriages include children, and stepparenthood places a special stress on the new family unit. Rather than simply building the marriage, the couple's energy must be directed immediately toward childrearing.

When touting remarriage, no one explains that the emotions and interactions of the stepfamily are far more complicated than those of the first families. Furthermore, society not only provides little support for the stepfamily, but may undermine the stepfamily's chances for success by assuming it will behave like the nuclear family.

CHANGING IMAGES OF THE FAMILY

The idea of family is dying, say the cynics. Families are not dying; but they are changing their shape and purpose. Although nearly one-third of American families can be labeled nuclear, only 16 percent of them still fit the traditional nuclear family model—a working father, a homemaking mother, and dependent children.[2] The forms are changing, but the tradition of families remains strong. *Families* writer Jane Howard's glimpse at alternative family styles, ranging from nuclear to gay to step, reveals that in many ways a sense of family is more critical than ever.

Many people run from it. But no sooner do people escape from one family than they find another—often much like the first. "The trouble we take to arrange ourselves in some semblance of families," Howard writes, "is one of the most imperishable habits of the human race."[3]

Definitions of a family differ sharply. Some writers focus on the physical unit made up of kin and others living together day by day. Legal experts stress biological relationships. Some scholars look at kinship and family as an attitude, "a self-defined identification with or among a group of individuals who exist for each other psychologically and socially, however geographically remote that may be."[4] All these definitions are acceptable alternatives that provide healthy places in which people can love and work and grow.

Statistics show that although 96 percent of all adults eventually marry, 38 percent of those marriages end in divorce.[5] These broken families include millions of children who for part of their lives may live in single-parent families. Yet despite the growing prospect that the strain of divorce or the sting of death will create a loss, marriage persists.

"People are not disillusioned with the idea of marriage and families," explains Robert Pickett, professor of child and family studies at Syracuse University, "because within three years most people plunge into remarriage, hoping the first time was just a bad combination of partners, immaturity, or inexperience." He goes on to say that as people leave marriages disillusioned and hurt, they carry leftover feelings into new marriages—along with one or two sets of children.

These remarriages create a new genus: the stepfamily, in which one or both partners have children, and ties to first families must be retained.

Stepfamily structures vary with child custody; visiting and live-in stepchildren create part-time and full-time stepparents. There are also couples with children who have long-term relationships but are not legally married. The common denominator is that at least one adult has children by a former relationship. These adults help rear children that biologically belong to the spouse and the former mate.

A DIFFERENT KIND OF FAMILY

Like the traditional family, the stepfamily's members are committed to one another emotionally as well as economically; they work together and they play, fight, share, laugh, and cry together. But the stepfamily is not an imitation, a carbon copy, a replacement for the nuclear family.

The stepfamily looks like the nuclear family—mother, father, children. But its differences are striking, and part of the magic of melding the new stepfamily into a cohesive network is recognizing and acknowledging them. The major difference lies in the structure of its relationships. A host of extra people and pressures push and tug at the stepfamily, making the determination of its own destiny difficult.

Some of the relationships that make it different are directly within the family unit and between the two joined nuclear families—former spouses, the other parents, stepparents, stepbrothers, and stepsisters. The stepfamily's success is determined largely by the quality of these old and new ties.

Less obvious, but no less real, are the unresolved feelings from the past and fears about the future that gnaw at family members until a crisis forces either resolution of the feelings or dissolution of the family in order to lower the stress. As a product of the death or divorce of a parent and mate, the stepfamily is based on loss. As each family member deals with this loss, anger, guilt, jealousy, misperceptions, and fears pervade the new group. While these emotions exist in all families, they are intensified in stepfamilies because the members have experienced deep personal loss. Remarriage does not ease the pain of that loss—not for adults or for children.

External relationships also make the stepfamily different. A large outside cast of people and pressures support or detract from the stepfamily's stability and survival chances. Critical roles may be played by the extended family or by society's institutions. Divorce does not cut the ties with grandparents, aunts, and uncles. What is their role in the stepfamily? And what role will the law, the school, the church, and the media play to support or undermine the new family's efforts?

What people learn in their first families may limit their ability to be realistic about living in a stepfamily. Stepparents may themselves be stepchildren, a pattern that becomes more common as families reorganize after divorce. For such people, misperceptions about their own lives in stepfamilies and illusions about this family style may complicate the already difficult task of being a stepparent.

The changing roles and rules for marriage partners create yet additional pressures for the stepfamily. How mature people are determines how well they can function as stepparents or adjust to being stepchildren. Pressures that are common to all families today have to be understood for what they are and not confused with stepfamily stresses.

THE INVISIBLE STEPFAMILY

Poets and philosophers write of the family. Artists paint it. Musicians write songs about it. Historians study its roots and social significance and predict its future. Social workers devise programs to make it stable. Psychologists counsel its members. Lawyers work to protect it or dissolve it. Demographers count it. So when I began preparing a magazine article in 1978, I expected to find a great deal of information about the stepfamily.

Historically, stepfamilies formed when one parent died—usually the mother, in childbirth—and the other parent remarried to provide the children with some semblance of family life. At the turn of the century almost 90 percent of stepchildren had been orphans; by 1970 the figure was down to 30 percent. The remainder are products of divorce.[6] As divorce rates doubled in the 1970s, the chances of living in a stepfamily soared.

How astonished I was to find so little about stepfamilies in the library. Computers churned out references, including one that irked me—"Public Relations: The Stepchild of Journalism"—but little that was pertinent to stepfamilies. What is more, college courses on children and the family discount the stepfamily. One 432-page textbook covers the stepfamily in two pages.

There were a few articles and books, but why so little? My questions began with academics because most information that finally reaches the public is rooted in formal research. Ventured Dr. Pickett, "The family touches the life of every human being, yet even the traditional family was not well studied until the late sixties."

Popular and scholarly writings described how family relationships changed, and academic studies delved into every aspect of the family's values and attitudes. "But family research lacked unity and a common sense of direction," explained Dr. Pickett. "It also left gaps. Traditionally there was little awareness of the stepfamily's difference, and it was lumped with general family research statistics."

Tradition. Was this the culprit? Dr. Pickett took down from his shelf a dusty toothpick model that a family sociology student had constructed to illustrate evolving family relationships. On the left, three toothpicks formed a simple triangle—the nuclear family. On the right was a complex architectural affair. Wooden picks representing biological parents, stepparents, aunts, uncles, and grandparents stuck out every which way, nothing seeming to hang together. This intricate structure represented the stepfamily.

Today, although the stepfamily is an emerging area of academic interest, historians, sociologists, and scholars in the field of children and the family still remain less concerned about this kind of family than the enormous population merits.

As social forces nipped at the traditional family's foundation and it had trouble determining its own destiny, the stepfamily remained unrecognized as a family form. Uncomfortable with its status and identity, many stepfamilies masked as nuclear families, reinforcing their invisible status and stresses.

Such masking leads to denial and failure. Pretending to be like the nuclear family creates unrealistic expectations, and when the stepfamily expects the masquerade to work, others also have the same expectations.

One remarried upstate New York couple with nine children said, "Everyone kept telling us, 'What you're doing for those children is great.' We felt the pressure to do better, to live up to what they expected, but it was chaos. Our neighbors and friends, even a counselor we saw, had no idea what our problems were, and they kept urging us to do more. And when we couldn't be what they expected us to be, we felt like failures."

Pretense also produces denial. Should discussing problems make them worse, many people resort to denial as a defense. Insecurities about family identity and ambiguous roles as stepparents and stepchildren can bring on denial—not by what is said but by what is left unsaid.

There is a reason behind stepfamily denial. Being in the minority is difficult, and stepfamilies are the focus of an unpopular and negative image, part of it painted in fairy tales. Even today, many believe that to be a stepchild is to be neglected or less than the best (as the library printout indicated about the status of public relations).

Legally the prefix *step-* refers to a relationship by marriage rather than by biology. It comes from the Anglo-Saxon *āstēpan*, "to deprive." From this came *stepchild*, "a bereaved child or orphan."[7] Part of the stepfamily's difficulty lies in this historical meaning. And when the word is used to debase, it preordains the stepfamily's second-rate status.

The term carries such a negative feeling that sociologist Jessie Bernard avoided saying stepchild, stepmother, and stepfather in her classic study of remarriage, referring to them as smear words.[8]

Professor Bernard substituted the term *acquired.*

Other researchers have come up with *blended, recoupled, reconstituted,* and *refamilied* to refer to the stepfamily. But blending means combining so the separate parts cannot be distinguished. In the successful stepfamily this rarely happens because the biological parent without custody lives in a separate household and is never blended into the family unit. Recoupled conjures up images of freight trains hooking up. Reconstituted means rebuilt by putting together the parts in a different form. The meaning may fit, but the word seems more apt for frozen orange juice. One researcher coined *binuclear family* to describe the two households but one family of divorced parents who have each remarried.[9]

One writer distinguishes between stepfamilies (products of death) and synergistic families (a result of divorce and remarriage).[10] While the assumption that synergy—cooperation between two parts that produces a greater effect together than separately—is a stepfamily trait that has merit, new labels are merely new masks. The key lies in changing attitudes, and this involves education, inside and outside the stepfamily.

NO-WIN ROLES

Most adults are unprepared for one of the most crucial tasks in life—parenthood. Although there are no lessons and no licenses, writers such as

Gesell and Spock offer advice and warn of the conflicts. As I reared my own sons, these books reassured me that my conflicts and fears were normal. But when I became a stepparent my only guides were trial and error and intuition.

Even knowing that the stepfamily is different, and knowing something of how it works, is not enough to keep stepfamily members out of difficult no-win situations. Sex, money, and discipline cause big trouble for the stepfather. Although he may support as well as help rear the children of another man, to avoid problems with his wife he must think twice about disciplining her children. As a youngster I wondered if my stepfather let me get away with so much because he didn't care about me. I recall clearly when he finally carried out a threat. At seventeen I had failed to do some job, so he told me to cancel a date with a boy named Ed (that I remember the boy's name reflects the importance of the event). I assumed that the threat could be ignored, and I never called the boy. That evening I dressed for the date as though nothing had happened, but this time my stepfather held his ground. He greeted Ed, telling him that I had been a bad girl and could not go out. He elaborated that I had known of the punishment in the morning and should have called him earlier.

I was furious and started to bolt out the door, but something stopped me. Despite the anger and embarrassment, I felt loved and cared about. But I never told my stepfather that. Instead, I ranted and raved and pouted. Today I understand the precarious position my stepfather and others like him are forced into. I sought boundaries; he feared overstepping his.

Money is a source of power between a man and his former wife, no matter how much child support he pays. Money also assuages the guilt of absent parents. It was no wonder my sons loved weekends with their father. Just as we did for his daughters twenty years ago, to make up for his not being able to be with the children he loved so much, my former husband provided a three-ring circus of entertainment when our sons visited him. For others, as guilt increases and relationships become too painful, the fathers see less and less of their own children. That guilt may filter down to the stepchildren as resentment, and it takes the shape of over-indulgence and overcompensation toward his natural children. Or, as my own stepfather was finally forced to do, sometimes men stop supporting their own children to meet the economic demands of the stepfamily.

Sexy adolescent stepdaughters can create tension for the most guarded of stepfathers. To compensate for their sexual feelings toward their stepdaughters, and to avoid having their wives misinterpret these feelings, stepfathers walk a fine line. Not knowing what to do, often they stand aloof emotionally, making their stepdaughters feel rejected. Thus, whether dealing with discipline, money, or sex, stepfathers are caught in a double bind.

Stepmothers, plagued by centuries of fairytale stereotypes, live in the shadow of an idealized mom, dead or alive. To build the kind of happy family they dream of, many attempt to outdo their stepchildren's mother or, worse, to replace her.

As nurturers, stepmothers want to make up for the past havoc in the children's lives. To compensate and help the youngsters forget their pain, women become supermoms, often forfeiting their own needs for the needs of the children. But the past cannot be erased, and such martyrdom arouses anger, exhaustion, and frustration, breeding grounds for resentment and conflict.

Because women have been taught that fulfilling a family's emotional needs is their responsibility, the stepmother tries to take on that burden for the entire family. She may think she has married a man who will give her a good deal of attention, but she soon realizes that much of her energy and attention is directed toward rearing his children.

Research reveals that women are far less likely than men to achieve a good relationship with their stepchildren.[11] This may stem from the fact that women have traditionally spent more time at home with the kids. As new patterns of parenting evolve and both parents take an active role, this will change. But until now, stepmothers have been the first to jump on the guilt bandwagon when stepfamily relationships falter.

Like many stepmothers, I took the blame for everything. What was I doing wrong? I reared my own children well; why were things not working out in our new family? Since I was in charge of the house and kids, it must be my fault. I tried harder—and created more tension. Nearly all the stepmothers I interviewed shared this experience.

Choices that affect the stability and emotional needs of stepchildren are made by others, yet these decisions weave in and out of their lives. Too often they are confused and hurt about their broken family, and they carry this confusion into the new stepfamily. As a youngster I often wondered whether my father would have stayed if I had been a better child. The divorce was probably my fault, I concluded, and too much of my adult life has been dedicated to gaining approval and avoiding rejection. If I am good enough and can please people, I reasoned, I won't be left again.

This loss that children of divorce face pervaded my youth. I was close to my father and missed him terribly; but because we had fun together as a family and my mother was happy again, I grew to respect and like my stepfather, too. Most stepchildren face such divided loyalties. Not daring to let their feelings show, they vent their anger on the interloper: the stepparent. I did just that to my stepfather, and years later my stepchildren did the same to me. As a stepchild I did not understand my rebellion; as a stepparent I assumed my stepdaughters' rejection and rebellion reflected a flaw within me.

Children may be touched by the confusion of belonging to two families more than by the positive aspects. Visitation can become a guilt-producing seesaw of patterns and rules and of right and wrong ways of doing things—unless children are helped to understand what is good about their stepfamily.

Variations of stepfamily structures create diverse living arrangements. Some stepchildren live full time with a parent and stepparent. Others visit the parent without custody and new stepparent. Where does the visiting stepchild fit? As one psychologist put it, treating the visiting children as full members of the family doesn't work because they aren't; treating them as visitors also doesn't work because they aren't. Not knowing where they fit in either family, yet holding membership in both, can create inner turmoil that results in unpredictable behavior.

The saddest role for children is that of pawns, as the parents vent their anger toward each other. The children see themselves as the trouble source and assume the friction is their fault.

In a stepfamily some children have different names. Since children need to feel a part of a group rather than set apart, different names can heighten insecurity. As a stepchild I hated having a name that was different because it set me apart from friends who were part of *real* families. The problem of names can be solved through adoption, but its implications run deep, severing family ties and creating identity problems.

Children's sense of family ties is also threatened if they are unable to visit their grandparents regularly. Being unable to maintain the satisfying relationships of the past may make stepchildren feel as though they belong to no one. Many stepchildren I interviewed echoed this gnawing feeling from my childhood.

These are only some of the problems that confront stepfamily members. The implications of these problems, as well as ways of coping with them, are explored in the pages that follow. As couples get deeper into new relationships that will make them a stepfamily, exploring the problems and possibilities of this different kind of family provides a head start on positive stepfamily living.

2 Getting in Deeper

The first time I reached out to hug the tiny blonde who would become my stepdaughter, she flung up her arms to protect her face and backed away. Her fears were the first indication of trouble. Less than two years later, laden with other clues, I became a stepparent to my new husband's children—but without examining their needs or my own.

The role of stepparent has few rules and the rewards are mostly long-term—a challenge not to be taken on lightly. Having their heads and hearts in the clouds while dating is one thing for the young; their relationship centers on each other. When people with children fall in love, they have to consider what it would be like to live together as one family. Before they decide to marry they must look at issues as obvious as values and childrearing differences, as well as at those as obscure as unmet personal needs and childhood scars.

The courtship time prepares the way for the new stepfamily. A romantic relationship for people with children is no carefree courtship in that hopes for the future weave in and around a phase of mourning the past. It requires serving up harsh realities along with the candlelight and wine. But above all, a remarriage courtship includes the realization that the children's needs will often come before those of the couple.

Two adults can use their courtship to build a sound foundation for their future stepfamily. Or, if they emphasize romance and fail to face reality, they can set the stage for disaster. As the two begin to consider remarriage, seeking serious answers to difficult questions can help avoid future problems. Are they where they want to be in their personal development? Have they resolved relationships with former spouses? Do they agree about childrearing? Do some of the children have special needs or problems?

RESOLVING OLD RELATIONSHIPS

A clean emotional slate is one of the best ways to start stepfamily life, and achieving this is a task of courtship. To have dealt with the emotional business of the former marriage—as a couple and as individuals—means relieving the new stepfamily of some of the hostility, fears, and jealousy that can keep it tied in knots. To be sure, the past cannot be erased or forgotten, but dealing with it openly permits hurts to begin to heal.

As society's attitude toward divorce has become more tolerant, friendly divorces have become commonplace. Couples have learned that although they cannot live together, they can respect and admire one another as people. Such an attitude reassures children that both parents love them and welcome them. But many divorced persons harbor anger, jealousy, and bitterness toward former mates. When remarriage occurs before such feelings are resolved, the children's loyalties may be torn between parents.

Legal divorce is no guarantee of emotional divorce. Most former marrieds need three to five years to reach the stage of feeling nothing more than indifference or friendship toward one another. Closing the gap between the legal and emotional divorce can be accomplished only through hard work, communication, and perhaps even counseling.

People who are legally divorced can check the progress they are making toward emotional divorce by answering such questions as these: Have we stopped blaming our former spouses? Have we stopped dreaming of a reconciliation? Have we stopped phoning over less-than-urgent matters just to have a reason to talk? Are we involved in healthy new relationships? Emotional divorce nears closure when people begin rebuilding their own lives, including new relationships with other people to love or remarry.

Preparing for a successful remarriage also includes looking inward to examine personal contributions to the marriage failure. Immaturity and false expectations end many first marriages. Others flounder because of personal inadequacies. Men might ask themselves whether they placed their work before their families, or whether they stopped romancing their wives after the wedding, or whether their involvement with their children was satisfactory. Women might examine whether they devoted all their attention to the children and overlooked their husbands' needs, or whether failing to face their unmet personal needs skyrocketed their anger.

DESERTION BY DEATH OR DIVORCE

There was a time when most people who remarried had been widowed. Today most people who remarry have been divorced. In either case, the stepfamily forms in the wake of a loss, and mourning follows a similar pattern of denial, anger, despair, and acceptance.[1] One myth that surrounds stepfamily life is that things are easier if the loss resulted from the death of a mate and parent. But often it is *more* difficult. As painful as divorce is, the former partner is still around, and feelings about the loss can be vented through anger, relief, or jealousy. For children, a continuing relationship with a divorced parent provides them with relief by providing opportunities for reducing these feelings. But when a parent dies, both the children and the surviving parent feel abandoned and betrayed, their anger and guilt unresolved.

The widowed who remarry too soon are asking for trouble—for themselves and for their children. While some may think it urgent to provide a new parent for their children, unfinished grieving results in problems that ultimately may be released into the new stepfamily. In a family still bewildered by its loss, new stepparents can be overwhelmed by the anger and resentment of children who feel deserted. As hard as they may work to make the family a unit once again, new stepparents may succeed only in reaping the rejection of the children they are trying to help.

An upstate New York woman with four grown children left a good job to marry a widower with four younger children. Her new husband insisted she stay home to care for the family in his beautiful house in the country because the children were used to it. She missed her work and her contact with people but stayed home for the children's sake. After four years, she was still living with the ghost of the dead wife and mother, whose portrait hangs in the living room. Whenever she changed anything in the house, the husband restored it.

"I feel like a maid," she confided. "I don't know how much longer I can take this. I was a successful person in my own right, but it's getting harder to remember that."

Frustration with her new life led this stepmother into depression and counseling. With her identity eroding, she is trying to decide whether to stay or leave. She has become attached to her new husband's children, and she worries about putting them through yet another loss. But she can do little until her husband and stepchildren finish mourning the dead wife and mother.

The divorced mourn too. But this breakup leaves a legacy of guilt, hostility, and insecurity. What could I have done better? Have I damaged my kids? What's the matter with me? Can I do better if I have another chance at marriage? The blow to one's self-esteem is compounded when friends and acquaintances ask why the marriage failed. And they do ask.

More important than whether death or divorce ended a former marriage is whether the unfinished business of that loss has been dealt with.

As Dr. Pickett put it, when two people share the bond of children, a relationship is altered, not closed. "Caring for those children continues. Whether through joint decision making, sporadic visits, or child support, nourishing of children between former marrieds eventually affects the stepfamily and its ability to do well by those children."

Of course, Dr. Pickett was right. In no way could I forget the relationship with Bill, my former husband. I take pride in my young son's ability to think abstractly and my older son's love of reading and self-teaching skills. These traits are rooted in their father as much as are their expressive eyes and small stature. My love for him as a person will never die, but altering our relationship and accepting the loss of our marriage provided the catalyst for me to move ahead. For me, our emotional divorce came after I was remarried.

PARENTS—THE REMARRYING KIND

People used to jump into remarriage, but today they are making valiant efforts to learn and to transform themselves into stronger, better people, writes Leslie Aldridge Westoff in *The Second Time Around*, a book about remarriage in America. Most people she interviewed were surprised at what they had learned between divorce and remarriage.[2]

Of the stepfamilies I interviewed, some had devoted time and energy between marriages to understanding themselves better. But for many others, especially those who remarried about the time Walter and I did, the pattern resembled ours. So did the problems. Too many couples who move toward stepfamily life think, "It'll be better this time around."

Researchers find that many youthful marriages fail because of high expectations. Often remarrieds carry higher ones. When desires for another chance at family life run high, so do expectations. And when expectations are high, so are disappointments. One stepfather told me, "You're so sure you've learned from the past that you refuse to believe you would go on repeating the same dumb mistakes. But I did."

When Walter and I met over the bridge table we were both still mourning our old relationships. But as we began dating, we were in different stages of the divorce experience. When a friend introduced us, Walter had been a single parent for well over a year. He had tired of juggling parenting, working, and dating, and he was seeking a wife. As for me, my husband Bill had been gone only a few months and I was still hoping he would return.

Our dating became serious too soon. As we talked of our marriages and how we had failed, we discovered that his former wife and I shared more in common than our interest in cooking. To combat depression and the loneliness of deteriorating marriages, both of us had turned to another man. According to Phyllis Chesler in *Women and Madness*, wives are conditioned to think themselves at fault and often fall into depression.[3] I fit right in. Therapy and an affair were my way of filling the void.

When we met, Walter was angry and I was consumed with guilt. Anger at his former wife reflected his damaged ego over her involvement with someone else. Staying angry at her also helped justify his refusal to acknowledge his own failings or his responsibility for her turning to another man. That unresolved anger kept them at war for years, and their hostility later spilled over into our stepfamily.

As for me, I accepted much of the blame for the failure of my marriage. I had married young, and Bill was fifteen years older than I. His children visited us summers and he paid a large child support. Then a career change meant his continual absence, and I reared our toddlers nearly alone. The deep void in my life that caused a severe depression after the birth of our second son led me to the affair with another man. My pleas for us to see a counselor remained unmet.

Even after Bill and I separated and I took a job, and later as Walter and I dated, I hoped Bill would return. This hope, this fantasy, kept me from telling our sons we were getting a divorce. My deception in turn nurtured the children's fantasy about seeing their parents reuniting. Yet children can handle the truth well when they know what is happening between their parents and how it will affect their lives.

It became clear that unless I took responsibility for our failing marriage, Bill would not return. I could not feign remorse; we let our marriage slip into the divorce courts with barely a whimper.

As my relationship with Walter accelerated, I began to notice that, like my former husband, he, too, rejected all responsibility for the failure of his marriage. I detected familiar themes in the breakdowns of our marriages and wondered whether my feelings were similar to those his wife must have experienced. Those echoes kept me on edge. Would this relationship be different?

Walter had put aside his concern for his family and begun to dream of becoming an air force general, burying himself in his work to achieve it. In quest of his own dream, Bill had abandoned me emotionally with two toddlers as he built an advertising agency. Both men were convinced that their efforts were only for their families. While neither ultimately achieved his professional goal, both men lost their families to divorce—a common plight in the 1960s, when men were socialized into striving toward successful careers as females were into marriage and motherhood.

Neither of our first marriages should have failed. But in the social climate of the sixties, as divorce became more acceptable, instead of working at marriage we simply quit.

For the divorced or widowed parent, dating is a time for repairing egos, practicing skills, renewing hopes. In *The Divorce Experience*, Morton and Bernice Hunt compare this period to the old German *Wanderjahr*, a year in which an apprentice traveled and improved his skills before settling down to practice his trade. For the formerly married, the *Wanderjahr* is a time to travel from date to date, before getting in deeper with one person to practice loving, and rebuild a family life.[4]

Since stepfamily life will be different and challenging, parents who date must arrange relationships like chess pieces to create the most winning situation possible. And once dating becomes a commitment, adults must make a place in their courtship for their children. The time when remarriage is in the wind is a time to share and a time to shield.

SEX AND THE SINGLE PARENT

One of the first casualties of divorce is sexual confidence. One of the strongest needs of newly separated adults is to prove themselves attractive sexual human beings as well as parents, explains Jane Adams in *Sex and the Single Parent*. She argues the case for sexual frankness with children. She believes that more difficulty stems from a lack of frankness than from an awareness of parental sexual activity.[5] But leave the children out of it until the relationship has moved from casual to committed.

Children of loss may worry about being replaced. A parade of bed partners may erode the child's respect for the parent with custody and at the same time arouse feelings of jealousy and insecurity. A study of 127 middle-class Boston fathers revealed that when fathers brought another woman into their children's lives, a number of conflicting emotions emerged. Father and children could not avoid the recognition that the new woman could become wife and stepmother. Fathers became anxious to protect their children from the pain of another separation from someone they might become attached to. Children, wary of becoming dependent on an adult who might be temporary, often did not allow the woman to care for them.[6]

The same study showed that single fathers, eager to spend more time with their children on weekend visits, also wanted time alone with the new women in their lives. Although the men in the study started sleeping with women quickly, most couples saw each other for four to six months before the woman slept over when the children visited. Children can make parents self-conscious about changing sex partners too often. One man's young daughter walked into his bedroom one Sunday morning, looked at the sleeping woman by his side, and asked, "Which one is that?" After that he limited his dating to one woman and moved toward a more settled relationship.

For months after we met, I avoided sex with Walter, no easy task since he was a handsome man and I was lonely. But the payoff did not seem worth it. Regardless of what my single acquaintances said, playing musical beds failed to enhance their self-esteem. But after sex became a part of our lives we had to decide how to handle it with our children. Because we often took weekend holidays away from the children, we did not hide the reality of our sex life from them. But we did not sleep together when they were around until a few weeks before our marriage. By then our future together was a certainty.

Morton Hunt, author of *The World of the Formerly Married*, writes that even now, few single parents whose codes of behavior and sexual values were shaped before the sixties can involve themselves in sexual relationships without serious concerns about their partner or their children. While 20 percent of the men and women in Hunt's survey say their children know of their sexual behavior, parents remain concerned about their children, whose values and morals are still being formed.[7]

Adults should keep two issues in mind when deciding how to handle their sex lives around their children. Youngsters should be shielded from casual and short-lived relationships, and parents should confront their children in sexual situations only with partners they love and respect. The gap between prudence and propriety is immense.

The children's jealousy can become a problem. Assuring them that the love between a man and woman is different from love between parents and children helps to eliminate their fear of being replaced by the new mate.

After experimenting with casual relationships or serious love affairs, four out of five divorced people remarry within five years. The Hunts' survey of formerly marrieds revealed that people harbor diverse expectations of remarriage. But among the formerly married there is a strong agreement as to why they again seek out marriage. The chief reason cited for remarriage was companionship. Emotional needs ranked second and sexual needs third.[8]

How long people wait between divorce and remarriage affects the future stepfamily's adjustment. When the single-parent family continues for a long period of time, a special bond develops between the parent and child, making a new stepparent feel like an intruder. An adult Sacramento stepchild recalled how angry she had been when her mother remarried five years after the divorce. "I was five when my father left, and after I got over being angry at him, my mother and I had a wonderful life alone," she says. "When this new man intruded into our world I resented him." This woman had a tumultuous relationship with her stepfather that persisted into her adulthood.

How the children were cared for between marriages offers another clue to stepfamily adjustments. Some children are reared by a grandparent or other relative who is too permissive or too harsh. Others are watched by a succession of housekeepers—some who keep a tidy house but neglect the emotional needs of the children, others who care too much. A leftover housekeeper who stays on with the new stepfamily can wreak havoc. At one upstate New York house a twenty-year-old housekeeper, who had cared for the divorced man's young sons, stayed on when he remarried—until the rivalry between stepmother and housekeeper became unbearable. The housekeeper had to go, but this adjustment caused more emotional problems. Within eighteen months the youngsters had lost their mother and the housekeeper to whom they had become attached. From their confusion and insecurity, the trust tests they set up for the new stepmother were difficult.

A FAMILY ROMANCE

When people with children fall in love, it is especially important to heed attitude and behavior clues that signal problems or major differences. With few rules, confused roles, and many extra players, and without understanding its dynamics, the stepfamily's chances of survival are poor—as evidenced by a remarriage divorce rate of 44 percent.[9]

Couples whose courtship is limited to restaurants and getaway weekends avoid making the critical discoveries that can provide a firm foundation for their stepfamily. In contrast, a family-style courtship can give the new stepfamily a head start.

As my relationship with Walter evolved, most of our weekend dates became family outings reminiscent of my parents' courting days, when the five of us accompanied my mother and Ben nearly everywhere. Even now, we think back with pleasure to the Sunday-afternoon rides in the gray Studebaker. At the start of the trips, each of us was given a comic book, and we stayed calm as long as it took us to read them all. When the cramped car caused too much jabbing and arguing, the courting couple headed for a place where we could work off our energy.

Like my parents, Walter and I packed our crew of five children into the car for outings and picnics. When seven of us were too many—at the drive-in movies, for example—we went in two cars, one for us and one for the children. During treks between the two vehicles, they scribbled initialed hearts on the steamed windows, another reminder that our romance was a family affair.

We became specialists at tracking down free or inexpensive events we could all enjoy together: festivals, sailing regattas, outdoor concerts, fairs, field days, museums, historical spots. Most Sunday newspapers list such events.

Many stepfamilies that I interviewed had similar dating patterns. Sitter costs were one reason. But most said family outings—camping, swimming, picnicking—offered the best way to get to know one another as potential family members. A day cramped in a car or a weekend of camping is much like a weekend encounter session, where progress begins when people are tired or relaxed enough to be themselves. This much exposure may reveal incompatibilities that break up a romance, but if the relationship breaks under this strain, the stepfamily would never survive. And breaking up a stepfamily is serious. Adults and children have already experienced one family loss; another can affect trust and self-esteem levels more deeply.

From the beginning our children got along well with each other. His Kurt and my Christopher, called Hopper, were seven. His ten-year-old Brenda mothered my four-year-old Jeff, and his twelve-year-old Bev fit in with both pairs and with us. We liked each other—a good beginning, I thought.

CHILD THROUGH THE CRACKS

As our relationship deepened, I began to dislike one of Walter's children. What made me uncomfortable about the boy was difficult to detect. He looked like his mother, but so did his older sister, my early favorite. Kurt was the promised son for the macho father. Baby-sitters took care of him as his mother finished college and the marriage came apart. When she left, Kurt was five. Walter took custody of the children and juggled both parental roles. He learned the practical matters of housekeeping, became a fair cook, and indeed, once collected a Mother's Day card from a colleague. But during the day, the children were cared for by one housekeeper after another. As Walter's evenings and weekends began to be taken up by a social life, and the older girls went on with their own activities, Kurt was lonely.

Young children have the greatest troubles over losing a parent, research shows. They wet beds, cry, regress to preschool behaviors, remain grief-stricken and fearful, resort to denial and fantasy. Older brothers and sisters can grasp the consequences and eventually overcome the family disruption, but seven- to ten-year-olds may continue to have trouble adjusting.[10] Kurt's response was typical of the helplessness researchers are now identifying in children of divorce in his age group.

Because my feelings toward this child affected our adult relationship, when Walter began talking marriage I said no, giving my fears about Kurt as the main reason. We talked with a counselor, who suggested that the youngster most likely missed his mother and our remarriage might stabilize him.

One of the wisest paths people contemplating remarriage can take is to deal with such feelings as they emerge. It is not easy to tell the person you love about your negative feelings toward his or her child. But as it is discussed and dealt with, guilt and anxiety do lessen. Communication is the key. Talking with your partner about how you feel is the beginning of understanding why you feel that way.

Keeping such delicate issues secret until after the marriage only adds to the strain. "When difficult feelings and relationships are not worked out before the stepfamily forms," says psychologist Irene Goldenberg, "the times ahead will be troublesome. When you dump strangers, extra in-laws, and former spouses into a remarriage while balancing a job, being a parent, and trying to master the challenges of stepfamily living, things get chaotic."

SUBTLE CLUES AND NEON-LIGHT WARNINGS

Some future stepparents ignore the signals that surface. Coming from broken marriages, they prefer to dwell on having another stab at happiness. Maybe the problems will disappear after the wedding, they reason. That's what the counselor suggested to us about Kurt. Whether the clues are so subtle as to barely merit attention, or whether they ring bells and flash lights, none should be ignored.

Getting to know one another as families is important, but for the couple time alone is necessary, too. Before the remarriage is the time to uncover differences in childrearing attitudes and to discuss how two parenting styles can be melded into one. Lucile Duberman's research with what she calls *reconstituted families* reveals that in first marriages the most serious marriage troublemakers are sex and money. But in remarriages, the sociologist found, most problems center on childrearing.[11]

Somewhere in the transcript of every interview I did was the admission that the conflict or crisis revolved around the kids in some way. Even the stepchildren who talked with me were fully aware they were the center of most of the battles. Some children related it sadly, fearing they might be responsible if this marriage broke up; others mentioned it smugly, aware of the power they wield over their parents' relationship.

How the kids will be raised is a major issue that needs settling. Clues that surface during courtship reveal differences that may be intolerable. When Walter was in my house for an evening visit early in our courtship, rather than stay in bed my older son Hopper decided to check out the competition. He plodded into the living room in his bunny-sleeper, grinned sheepishly, and asked for a drink of water, which he was perfectly capable of getting for himself.

After Hopper had made several more trips out of bed, Walter asked my permission to intervene. I nodded. As I yielded authority, my son looked panicky. "I don't have to mind you," he shouted at the intruder. "You're not my father. He's coming back." He began to cry.

"We'll see who's boss," Walter said, then picked him up and stuck him upside down in a nearby empty wastebasket, feet wiggling helplessly. After extracting a sobbing promise that he would stay in bed, Walter lifted him out and carried him to bed, reminding him who was on top.

My youngster stayed in bed. But I did not like what I saw. This man's fathering style centered on power and control, vastly different from the way Bill and I had reared our children. He had no doubt done similar things with his own children, but somehow that was different. I closed my eyes to such clues signaling what would become a grave issue between us.

In the year and a half that we dated, other clues surfaced that warned of future trouble. One evening I was at Walter's house for dinner with the children. After clock watching, suddenly he announced that he had to go on an errand to a neighbor's house. Soon the telephone operator rang to ask permission to charge a call Walter was making to his former wife. I felt threatened and angered by his secretiveness. Why didn't he trust me to understand? What were they planning? We were to be married in two months. Should I break our engagement?

Later that evening, I asked how long it had been since they had talked. "Several weeks," he said. I confronted him with his deceit, and we discussed it. It hurt that he could not trust me enough to understand, and I disliked deceit as a means of dealing with issues. She wanted to come back, and he was torn between what he felt he should do and what he wanted to do. We worked it out, but the incident bothered me. A serious character flaw, which would later mar our relationship, had revealed itself. More important, my husband-to-be had not resolved the relationship with his former wife.

Closing their eyes to future discord is common among women who think they have no option but marriage as a way of caring for their children. Rather than risk the relationship, many put on blinders and cross their fingers. Redivorce rates are higher among those with low income and little occupational skill, research indicates, because they have fewer resources for carrying out marital roles.[12] Low-income stepfamilies face a tougher situation the second time around and have fewer resources to pull it off.

Yet research on remarriage by sociologist Jessie Bernard shows that low-income parents are more likely to remarry than parents with more resources. These families need special counseling to make them aware of stepfamily pitfalls before they remarry.[13]

CHARTING THE COURSE ON EXPECTATIONS

Unrealistic expectations are among the stepfamily's greatest stumbling blocks. Expectations are built on hopes and daydreams about how things will be. When they are spun from fantasy rather than reality, life results in disappointments and complaints. Although no research has been reported in support of this, expectations are probably linked to awareness levels that emerge from education. Of course, education is linked to socioeconomic class. The stepfamilies I interviewed ranged from those having the most loving and harmonious relationships to those whose relationships were characterized by hostility and fighting. I've concluded that the difference between the extremes hinges on the stepparents' expectations and their ability to come to terms with reality.

Sometimes a father with custody expects his new wife to stay at home, whereas the woman expects to continue the fulfilling job she developed as a single parent. Sometimes the stepmother has to work to help pay alimony and child support when she really wants to stay home. Several stepmothers told me they left jobs because their new husbands wanted them to, and that soon their resentment was directed at their new stepchildren.

From the beginning, I did not intend to stay home to housemother our crew. I liked my creative work at a print shop, and we agreed that if we married I would keep my job, even though most of my salary would be used to pay a housekeeper.

But other expectations remained unexplored. One of mine centered on the myth of instant love. As soon as we married, I would of course love these children and they would return my love. But already I felt unloving toward my future stepson. How could I mother him if I harbored such feelings?

Just loving a person is no guarantee that you will feel the same about the children. There's nothing wrong in that. Indeed, as new stepchildren work out their own pain over what has happened to them, they may become quite unlikable, let alone lovable. Too many stepparents think something is wrong with them when they cannot instantly love their new stepchildren or find themselves rejected by the children soon after the remarriage. Building trust, which can evolve into love, takes time; and not succumbing to the myth of instant love will alleviate the guilt.

A STEPPARENT'S CONCEPT OF SELF

Narrowing the gap between expectations and reality helps prepare people for stepfamily living. Since expectations are harbored within the individual, dealing creatively with stepfamily dynamics also requires that stepparents have a clear understanding of themselves as people. When individuals remain uncertain about their identity or what they want from life, it is no time to take on the responsibility of becoming a stepparent.

As valuable as it is for the two families to get to know one another, and for the couple to spend private time together, each adult also needs alone time—that soul-searching time when thoughts and feelings no longer need be carefully controlled. It is a time to confront those signals that storms lie ahead. Facing them can be unsettling, yet the future of the marriage depends on it.

Though Walter's way of dealing with my son and of deceiving me sent prickles up my spine, and though I was overwhelmed at the prospect of raising five children, I evaded such issues.

Values and childrearing differences bothered me far less than something I could not easily pinpoint, an obscure and ambiguous feeling I failed to understand and did not even try to unravel then. But had I spent enough moments alone, I would have come to recognize the urgency of those feelings.

What about me?

During my former marriage, the magic formula of marriage and motherhood yielded less than I expected. I adored my sons, and while they were young I gave my all to being a good parent. But as my sons grew and demanded less of my time, something was missing. I filled the void with crafts, bridge games, luncheons, cooking, volunteer work, but the feeling did not go away. Avoiding these feelings drove me into depression, and ultimately ended my marriage for the wrong reasons. I lacked fulfillment—the core of what the women's liberation movement has been about, but during the sixties that awareness was just beginning.

When I was twenty-nine, and entering another serious relationship that included responsibility for three more children, the same feeling persisted. Only now—with years of stepfamily living experience, a college degree, and Gail Sheehy's *Passages* to help explain the phenomenon—have I begun to understand how critically the unexplored feelings affected my perception of myself as a stepparent.

The task of exploring the subtle signals cannot be undertaken in a candlelight and wine scenario with the man or woman you love or on a beach with two sets of happy kids running about. It can only be undertaken alone.

What is best for me? Is remarriage really what I want now, or is it simply a safe alternative to trying my wings now that my youngsters are in school? How did unmet needs affect my former relationship? These are not indulgent, selfish questions; they are critical ones that must be explored before remarriage with children. What developmental stage of life people are in as individuals affects all their relationships. A person whose own identity remains unclear cannot be an effective parent figure in a situation more stressful than that of the first family.

Since many of the rewards of being a stepparent are long term, people who take on this role need to have other sources of good feelings about themselves. This may require developing one's potential. Like many who remarry too soon, I remained unaware of the importance of knowing myself, and since I could not identify the feelings, I buried them. Once, I nearly dealt with it. During a holiday weekend I told Walter that our getting in too deep, too fast frightened me. I needed time alone. Since my former husband was moving back into the house for the summer to be with the boys, and I was taking an apartment, it would be a good time for us to separate and sort out our relationship. But it did not work. Without the children I was lonely, and whenever Walter would call, I'd relent and he would come over.

We drifted back together. Living alone was not as glamorous as I thought, and I missed the children—his and mine. By now they had all seen the movies *With Six You Get Eggroll* and *Yours, Mine, and Ours*, and the "Brady Bunch" had just hit TV screens. Stepfamily life looked like such fun. Our relationship continued, and soon what I call the propelling experience moved us closer to the altar.

THE PROPELLING EXPERIENCE

Many couples reported the same way of coming to the decision to remarry. Somehow the relationships move from just dating into remarriage plans before the couples realize what they are getting into or, in some cases, against their better judgment. In spite of warning signals, the propelling experience happens. This is because once relationships gain a certain momentum and reach a certain level of comfort and commitment, it simply takes more effort to stop them than to go on.

Some remarrieds said their courtship with children was such a circus that it seemed simpler to marry. "We'd put all the kids to bed at my house or his house so we could spend the evening together," one stepmother recalls. "But then they had to be rousted out in the middle of the night so they could be in the right house to get to school on time the next day." One stepchild said she was happy when her father decided to remarry, "just so we could all be living in one house instead of between the two."

"We blew into it," a Syracuse stepmother said. "We had been friends even before dating. But the agreement to marry came about by default. The kids did the proposing—in steps, little things. One Sunday afternoon we were both looking for apartments and the kids said, 'Why don't you two get married and then we need only one place to live?' He said, 'That sounds like a good idea.' Later, on a picnic, when he carved our initials into a tree, the kids said, 'I guess that really means you're going to get married, doesn't it?' His response: 'Well, if your mother will.' And that's kind of how he proposed."

Their marriage has endured for ten years. But to this day they disagree on how to rear the children. Their children manipulate them, get their way, and leave the adults to battle it out. The stepmother admits she recognized these differences while they dated. "But the kids had become so close, I couldn't bear to break it off. They wanted me to remarry. I thought we could manage better; we had no idea it would be so hard."

Another stepmother told how they had dated for over a year, often taking family trips and meals together. At supper one night the children asked their father, "Can't we marry Cathy, Dad? Please?" They felt like a family. Yet as individuals each had left much self-examination undone, and he was still emotionally tied to his former wife. After the marriage, their first year of stepfamily life was a disaster.

People who seek parents for the children and another chance at happiness for themselves tend to assume they're in love as soon as they find someone they feel good about. Armed with love, they think they can survive anything. The closer a couple comes to the altar, the stronger this conviction becomes. Decisions have been made—a different house, a school for the children—and once a wedding is announced, most people feel obligated to follow through.

TIME FOR COMMITMENT

Our courtship lasted more than a year. The final plans were sealed on my birthday when, with flourish and ceremony, Walter presented me with a tiny box. I held my breath. Please don't let it be a ring, I thought. Not yet. It was not a ring, but it was an engagement gift—an exquisite diamond pendant, presented with a speech matching in eloquence the "Sand Castles" poem. "I'll take the diamond, but I'm not so sure about getting married," I teased. "No wedding, no diamond," he said.

It was not a bribe, but time for a commitment. I was scared. I felt anxious about taking on the responsibility for other people's children, and the situation with Kurt had improved, but not much. Other uncertainties had surfaced, and I had not taken the time to explore other relationships or my own needs. I felt overwhelmed, but having a father for my children seemed better than single-parent living, which in the sixties was less acceptable than it is today. My desire for remarriage was not simply a callous search for a father for my sons. I felt I was in love with Walter. But I had not dealt with the problems that people with children must consider before remarriage, and neither had he. As we courted as a family, it became easier and easier to think of becoming one and more difficult to consider breaking off the relationship.

But on the other hand, I reasoned, I could certainly make a difference in the lives of these children. After all, I was experienced. I had become a stepchild at the age of ten, and for six summers I had been a part-time stepmother to my former husband's girls. Being a part-timer has its own problems, so any optimism seemed justified. This would be easier because the children would live with us full time, I told myself. Since I yearned for a daughter, and the package included two of them, the approaching marriage seemed doubly exciting.

Such unfinished business and unrealistic expectations were of course a mistake. But I did not know that then. After assurances to each other that we knew some problems existed in merging our families, I let Walter hang the pendant around my neck to seal our commitment to creating a stepfamily.

3 Hooking Up

As a youngster, being unable to attend my mother's remarriage ceremony hurt. Ben became my new stepfather while we five children attended an afternoon movie. My only memories of the event that made me a stepchild are those culled from snapshots.

The wedding pictures show my pretty mother aglow, no doubt relieved to have another chance at happiness. Since the divorce, she had struggled to keep us together and worked long hours at a five-and-dime. When she moved back into her parents' house, my sister and I had gone to live with an aunt and uncle. Now that we had a new father, we could all be together again.

The wedding pictures show Ben in a serious pose, perhaps reflecting how he felt about taking on the task of rearing five children who belonged to someone else. My aunt and uncle went with them as witnesses, and the snapshots show both women in navy blue dresses, reflecting the view of remarriage propriety in the fifties. Everyone was smiling. But each time I saw those pictures as a child, I wondered why, if it was a happy event, we could not have been there, too.

A childhood friend used to tell me stories about going to her mother's wedding: a pretty new dress, flowers, a party later. Her tales were not meant to be cruel; she was simply proud and happy that the ceremony included her because it made the new relationship special for her. I always felt left out of my mother's wedding.

When I was a child, we just slipped into becoming a stepfamily. Walter and I did it differently—but not without insecure feelings about challenging tradition. While most remarrieds of the past might have preferred a joyful celebration shared with family and friends, it was easier to follow tradition and keep their remarriage weddings low-key, simple, and private.

CHALLENGING CUSTOM

On the theme of remarriage, custom has lagged behind social reality. Stepfamilies represent a different order of things, and how they celebrate

30

their ceremonies is on the cutting edge of tradition. For most couples, the desire to be accepted now yields to personal desires and the kinds of weddings they really want.

Convention does not fit the stepfamily because it includes children. The wedding ceremony provides a chance to acknowledge that difference to family, to friends, and to community. Today many stepfamily weddings are joyous events, heralding the decision to the community and providing a building block for the new families. Some couples still slip off to a justice of the peace. Others have church weddings and gala parties. Most plan a creative ceremony and share their vows in a summer garden, or in a favorite park where they had courted, or in the family room before a blazing fire. But wherever they hold the ceremony, more and more couples include their children in the event that will make them a stepfamily.

Whatever the fuss that is made over flowers and food and guests, the wedding ceremony is important to the stepfamily's beginnings. Some trappings of the first wedding may be out of place, but to downgrade the event and its celebration undermines acceptance—inside and outside the new family. A joyful head start on building relationships in the family and the community is a first step toward changing the stepfamily's image in society. And, free from society's gloomy view of remarriage, the stepfamily can use this rite of passage to form a strong foundation on which to build a new life.

Ceremonies create memories, those precious storehouses from which people draw strength, warmth, and joy. No collective memory bank exists for new stepfamily members because each has a separate set of memories from the past. The remarriage ceremony is the first important memory that all the family can share.

After an at-home ceremony in Corning, New York, where dressed-up children served guests and enjoyed their parents' wedding, one happy couple packed the car and bade good-bye to their guests. Their children hopped onto bicycles and led the newly married parents through the streets of the subdivision to send them off on their honeymoon.

"Ours was probably the only bicycle-escorted 'just married' car in town," the stepmother says. "We were laughing so hard that my new husband forgot his luggage, which we didn't discover until we were two states away."

Ceremonies give events a stamp of approval, society's sanction. Ceremonies help us make transitions. And they remind us of our uniqueness and universality. As a dear friend once wrote me, "Weddings, funerals, and graduations punctuate all our lives, recalling times that were better, or at least seemed so. But they have an important function: to remind us as a group that living follows common themes. Pain and celebration, though individual in flavor, touch many lives the same."

Anthropologist Arnold van Gennep studied ceremonies that he paired with life crises. Citing marriage as a crisis, at the very least a social disturbance involving more than just the two people immediately involved, he explains that future family problems are linked to the devices a society offers its people for coping with such adjustments. In all cultures, rites and rituals such as weddings serve as the means for integrating people into a new group status.

In all the cultures that van Gennep studied, for those who remarry the wedding feasts and celebrations were a banal formality of interest only to the couple.[1] Ordained by society's attitudes, such an injustice wastes an opportunity for the new stepfamily to announce its presence to the community—openly and proudly. And it fails to help the new family accept its new status. This evidences a certain irony: Society expects the stepfamily to replace the traditional family but denies it the richness of the rite of passage given to first marriages.

My parents' secluded afternoon ceremony was typical of the times. Its lack of ceremonial sanction seemed to strip our new stepfamily of society's approval, and it kept me from accepting my new stepfather and my status in a changed family life. As an adult I have come to understand Mother's explanation that there was no money with which to outfit five children for the wedding. But through my child's eyes, our exclusion from the ceremony said something was not quite right.

When children think of weddings, they envision parties, presents, ceremonies, receptions, honeymoons, a joyous gathering of the clan, and heaps of good wishes. Not so for most remarrieds of the past. A study done at about the time of my mother's remarriage confirms that her wedding to Ben was what society expected it to be. Data gathered from 900 Connecticut couples revealed that second weddings were simple, especially if the woman was the one who had been married before. Dating and engagement periods were short. Few of the women had received engagement rings, and these few rings were less valuable. Few of the women were given showers. In general, there were fewer formal weddings, more single-ring ceremonies, fewer guests and attendants.[2]

Sociologist Jessie Bernard suggests that age and social status may account for some of the differences. She found that remarriage occurs more often in the lower socioeconomic class and that many remarrieds are older. They may not be able to afford, or may not want, a large wedding.[3] But beyond her explanations, the Connecticut study shows that a community's emotional response to remarriage ceremonies was no different in America from the cultures van Gennep studied.

Each wedding symbol shorn from the remarriage ceremony reinforces a negative image, wrote Anne Simon in *Stepchild in the Family*, the only popular book available on stepfamilies when Walter and I were married. "No long, white dress, no orange blossoms and no veil, society dictates to the second-time bride," she reported.[4] Simon's positive view of remarriage ceremonies gave me the courage to defy tradition and avoid doing what my mother had done.

Even today, attitudes that surround remarriage need updating. The change can begin when parents who remarry use the ceremony to symbolize brave and powerful statements. We know this will be difficult, couples with children are saying. But in spite of the pain of broken families, the fears we harbor, and the extra people tugging at us, we believe in marriage and the family. We want to make this work.

A FAMILY CELEBRATION

As they make their own rules and take creative license toward their wedding ceremonies, many about-to-be-stepparents include their children in the celebration. Youngsters help arrange flowers, address invitations, make decorations, prepare food. At the reception, dressed-up children serve guests and truly feel a part of what is happening to their lives.

In Horseheads, New York, three years after a six-year-old boy gained a new stepmother in an at-home ceremony, he proudly recalls his responsibility of holding the rings.

In Washington, D.C., another boy says, "It was fun when Mom and Papa married. My sister and I got dressed up and I got to serve the wine for the rabbi and minister. I also got to be in charge of the lights." His parents had wanted a small wedding in the presence of the people they loved, and that meant including the children.

Toward the end of the ceremony for a couple in Hyde Park, New York, all their children joined them at the altar to receive a special blessing. The woman's three-year-old daughter tugged at her new stepfather's trousers. He bent to hear her whisper. In his first official fatherly act, the new husband picked up the beruffled youngster and gingerly carried her to the baby-sitter waiting in the congregation. In the excitement of the ceremony, the child had wet her pants.

The involvement of children takes many forms. On the arm of her father, a ten-year-old walked down the aisle in a New Jersey garden. The youngster's new stepmother followed them. Although this may be difficult for many young, first-time brides to accept, being upstaged was less important for this stepmother than making the little girl feel a part of the ceremony that would join them as a family.

One psychiatrist cautions about carrying such involvement too far. "A bride, whether remarried or not, should be first at her own wedding," says Dr. John Visher. "Children should be of secondary importance. Arrangements where little girls are miniature brides might arouse fantasies that the girl has won the Oedipal struggle for her father's love." Enough of that will occur without the symbolic statement to intensify it, he says, and suggests including children in the ceremony in such a way as to keep the emphasis on the couple. "A clear generational boundary must be kept so no doubt exists that it is the couple being married," explains psychologist Emily Visher.

The role that children should play in the wedding ceremony is a sensitive one. More than simply appendages of old relationships, children are critical parts of new ones; they are not guests at the ceremony, but part of the celebration. But while they are not guests, neither should children take part in the wedding vows. Vows are an intimate promise between two adults to care for each other, and although the couple relationship will be the pivotal point of the stepfamily, it is also separate and deserves its private side. Yet while pledging faith to each other is a private commitment between two people with children, their vows also include the commitment to their new family. Some people write their own vows. If we were to merge our families today, I would have the children step forth to receive a special blessing, along with an injunction to help work at keeping family life happy.

Our children did not take part in the ceremony, but sat in the front row. Later, Walter's girls greeted reception guests and invited them to sign the guest book. The boys ricocheted between stuffing themselves with meatballs and snitching fingertips of icing from the pink-tiered cake, circled by mounds of camellias they had gathered earlier in the day with Walter. After the reception, my former husband picked up all the children to deliver them to their sitter.

When children can see that their other parent is accepting of the new marriage, they too can accept it better. Sometimes before giving in and letting their children attend or be a part of the ceremony, the parent left behind stirs up loyalty conflicts. How can a child experience joy at his father's wedding if he feels guilty about his mother, who makes it clear she is bitter and unhappy?

Parents who set up emotional tugs-of-war in their children actually hurt the children they love more than the former spouses they are trying to antagonize. Parents who create loyalty conflicts over whether their child should be part of the stepfamily wedding should look ahead to the time when their own wedding bells may ring and imagine how they would respond if the situations were reversed. How the other parent fits into the new stepfamily's life will be crucial to its stability, and how he or she reacts and helps the children adjust when the former spouse remarries presents one of the first tests of this relationship.

REMARRIAGE CEREMONY—A SUPPORT SYSTEM

Unlike the heralding of first marriages with a formal announcement to the community, remarriage engagements usually are no more than a private understanding between the couple. But Walter and I were excited about our coming marriage and wanted to share our excitement. In handwritten notes we invited our six best friends and their mates to celebrate with us at a dress-up dinner party, complete with flowers and French wine. At that time we enjoyed formal parties, but a picnic, brunch, or barbecue also would be a delightful way to announce to friends the intention of making a stepfamily.

Once couples decide on the kind of remarriage ceremony they want, things become hectic. To avoid my left-out childhood feelings, I wanted our children to be a part of these important beginnings. We wanted a chapel wedding at the air force base where Walter was an officer, and we wanted guests to share in the joy and celebration. But what would people think? A chat with the man who would marry us revealed that our anxieties were tied more to our concern at what others might think than to our desires. He encouraged us to do what we wanted.

We mailed formal, traditional engraved invitations for a Valentine's Day evening ceremony and champagne reception. In contrast, one New Hampshire couple with children asked a calligrapher to design their invitation. The groom had been married twice before, the bride once; between them they had eight children. The invitation depicted the couple and their children in caricature, the kids clad in baseball uniforms sporting the logo of the beauty salon the couple owned. The whimsical headline read, "2 strikes—1 ball—3 and you're out."

The wedding guest list sets up the stepfamily's future social and support group. Families are of course invited. The altered network of the extended family will affect the new stepfamily, and the wedding provides a chance to welcome extra kin into its sphere. Excluding some family members may eventually create alienation problems.

In a study about altered kinship patterns, researcher Donald Anspach found that when a woman remarries, her former husband's family tends to become more distant—geographically and emotionally.[5] But people do not become ex-relatives to the children, and in the happy encounter that a wedding provides, even the most cynical or reluctant relatives can be more accepting of the new in-law and new stepgrandchildren.

Intimate friends of the remarrying couple can share their joy in the new relationship, especially when they have been aware of the pain of old relationships. Friends often find such weddings more delightful than some traditional weddings. One of the happiest weddings Dr. Robert Pickett recalled attending was that of two university colleagues whose marriage made them stepparents to each other's teenagers.

"These two special people were so excited, so exhilarated over finding each other that we were all happy for them," he says. All five of their children kissed each other in acceptance as part of the ceremony, and each set of children invited friends to the reception. "The ceremony and celebration represented a passage for them, a resolution. As a friend, it felt good to be a part of it."

Acquaintances from work or clubs could in some way later be drawn into the struggles of the stepfamily, and they, too, might be asked to the wedding. All these people could later provide some level of emotional support for the new stepfamily.

TWO MORE TASKS

As ceremony dates near, preparations for all weddings become harried. Arranging a wedding that includes children can keep a bride- and bridegroom-to-be frantic, but two more tasks should also be completed in order to ease the early days of stepfamily living. They are finding a place to live and attending an education workshop to learn about the dynamics of stepfamily living. Taking time to do both will pay dividends during the first year.

The decision as to where the family will live is important because a house represents tangible evidence of the stepfamily's new identity. New surroundings can provide fresh perspectives on new relationships, and when couples can manage a new environment for the family, dealing with the ghosts of former relationships becomes easier.

Remarried couples who have chosen to move into one or the other's house have found that relaxing in another man's recliner or concocting a casserole in another woman's kitchen is not easy. The difficulty goes beyond insecurity or immaturity: It hinges on identity. Who we are is reflected in the clothes we wear, the car we drive, and the way we arrange our belongings in our own environment. Moving into someone else's domain requires a blurring of the intruder's identity.

When a new stepparent must accommodate the ghost of a former relationship in the new spouse's home, resolving identity problems may take energy that should be directed toward building relationships. A New York state stepmother resented living in *his* house because it really felt like *their* house rather than *ours*. In frustration she shouted, "This is nothing like my taste, and each day I have to look at that ridiculous red-flocked wallpaper I get angrier. My husband says we should wait to redecorate in case we move, but it's been a year now and her ghost still lives here."

This woman left a fulfilling job to stay home to care for her new stepchildren, and she spoke of feeling trapped. As she talked it seemed obvious that her husband had not ended his relationship with his ex-wife, who retained power over her ex-husband from three states away by placing constraints on selling the house and by challenging any change of its contents "for the sake of the children."

In these surroundings, daily remainders of the past increased the new wife's feeling of powerlessness and raised her anger level. Yet because she considered her feelings immature or silly, she kept them from her husband and directed the anger inward.

Competition and jealousy? Petty? Common only to women? One man moved into his new wife's apartment "because things were nicer there and it seemed easier than starting over." The convenience price tag was costly. "I couldn't put my feet up and relax without feeling like an intruder. I never felt comfortable until we moved." Who will wield the power in the new family? Whose house rules will be followed? Rather than forcing one group to adjust to the rules of the other's household, moving to new surroundings makes it easier to establish new house rules to fit the new, enlarged group.

If the children are unprepared for the change, moving can backfire. The sense of roots that children derive from friends and from familiar rooms may be critical to their sense of belonging and identity. While adults must make the decisions about such moves, informing the children of how events will affect them eases their shift into the new family surroundings. One compromise is to move within the same school district or church community, thus providing a new base for the family, yet retaining the old ties that children need to feel secure.

Before Walter and I were married, each of us had a house and at first the easiest solution seemed to be simply to sell one and move into the other. His neighborhood was near to both our jobs and had a better school. Mine was nestled in a country setting. Each had pluses. But both were filled with memories, and neither of us wanted to live in a house we had shared with another spouse. We found a large house near his old neighborhood so his children would not have to change schools. Since only one of my sons was in school, this was the best solution.

After choosing the house, we took the children to see it. We claimed our own bedroom, then let the children divvy up the remaining sleeping quarters according to their needs and desires. They bounded from room to room, discussing the pros and cons of each, who should have which, and how they would fix the rooms up with their own belongings. Later they switched rooms, but at the time they relished having some say in what was happening to them. As they handled this first brother-sister test, we could begin to see who would be the leaders and how they would solve future sibling problems.

Whatever the virtues of starting out in new surroundings, some new families will not be able to give up old quarters. For them, creativity can make staying put tolerable. Fresh paint, wallpaper, and a few carefully selected pieces of furniture, whether from antique shops or rummage sales, can give a fresh new look to old rooms. Changing bedrooms— especially the master bedroom—to suit new family members can also make everyone feel more comfortable.

Sandwiched in with working, dating, shopping, and house hunting, another important prenuptial task is to talk with a counselor or attend a stepfamily workshop. Too many would-be stepfamilies deny that anything might be wrong or that they have any uncertainties about their life together. Or worse, some know something is wrong but close their eyes to the problem, hoping—as we did with my stepson—that a new family life will solve it. The problems usually get worse.

Before walking down the aisle, more and more people are heading to counseling. As hectic as the period before the wedding becomes, putting off this investment of time is easy to rationalize. But because stepfamily life gets so complicated, counseling or education workshops make life after the ceremony somewhat more predictable. Especially if people have had bad first marriages, they should not expect good remarriages unless they understand what mistakes they made and have learned how to avoid them.

"If more couples headed for counseling before the altar, many might decide not to marry at all," says William Swingly, a counselor at the Family Service Agency of Rochester, New York. He helps couples work out geneograms—elaborate charts detailing each individual's roots, patterns, and relationships. Sometimes members of the extended family join in, thus learning to see their family as a system, identify styles that their families use to resolve conflicts, and discover what each person needs from the new marriage.

This process is helpful to divorced parents who are considering remarriage, Swingly explains, because unresolved conflicts from former marriages can be played out in the counseling, rather than in the remarriage. "If this deep exploration reveals that the couple's beliefs and behaviors lie at different ends of the spectrum, it's better they discover it now than put their families through another divorce."

Stepfamily counseling and workshops are burgeoning throughout the country. Much of it grew out of two statewide stepfamily foundations, one in New York and one in California. Because workshops pose little threat, people who avoid counseling will attend them. "Let's just go and see," they say, one to the other, secretly hoping they can learn why they hold negative feelings about stepfamily life. For many people, to enter a counseling situation implies that something is wrong; and if there is anything that stepfamilies become expert at, it is denial. No matter how bad things get, most close their eyes and blame the troubles on external forces. There is nothing wrong with their family, they contend. To admit distress is to acknowledge the possibility of another failed relationship—a possibility no stepfamily wants to face.

Such an implication before the vows have been sealed is too threatening for some people to handle, and even educational workshops intimidate them. "Many people show up once but don't return," says Marcia Wrytzen, who leads stepfamily workshops in Allendale, New Jersey. "Everything seems rosy during the dating period, so even couples who are aware of problems are reluctant to dig deep and shake up the relationship. But people can avoid a lot of hurt and upset if they do not go into stepfamily living blindly. I know that because my own remarriage nearly broke up over typical stepfamily problems. Our whole first year was a catastrophe, and I felt angry, guilty, and frustrated." In the workshops Mrs. Wrytzen shares those feelings to help other steppeople understand that it is normal to experience them and that there *is* something they can do about them.

TOWARD THE ALTAR

With or without this awareness, the courting couple moves toward their marriage ceremony. During interviews with stepfamilies, the happiest moments came as they recalled their weddings. Some dug out albums and mementos of the day and reminisced about the joyful event. One child retrieved the dress she wore "the day we got married." A Syracuse husband smiled nostalgically at his wife as he told me that as part of a garden ceremony at his parents' house, he sang a love song to her. Doing what feels right and comfortable, without worrying what others think, should provide couples the courage to be creative with their wedding plans.

Existing guidelines about stepfamily ceremonies belong to the past. In her revised *Etiquette*, although recognizing that times have changed, Elizabeth Post suggests small and private remarriage ceremonies. The bride can wear a street-length dress, she writes, but never white. And no veil or orange blossoms.[6]

I found the perfect dress for our wedding, street-length and simple. And white. I checked on tinting the dress. When I learned what kowtowing would cost, practicality beat out tradition. I would wear the white dress and a tiny veil. For us, white would symbolize joy.

As Valentine's Day approached, our children's excitement grew. Everyone was helping to make the day special. The girls filled tiny squares of tulle with rice, tying them with red ribbons and putting them into wicker baskets that the boys had spray-painted (for years afterward the children used them as Easter baskets). At the wedding they passed the rice bags to guests to shower us—bespeaking tradition rather than fertility, we decided.

Outfitting five children in wedding duds meant some mixing and matching between the two family closets. Shopping filled in the gaps. The potpourri of new clothes, expectant grins, and crooked corsages and boutonnieres has produced chuckles as, throughout the years, many a family supper ended with one of the children saying, "Let's look at our wedding pictures."

The celebration provided an important beginning for our new stepfamily. As the children reminisced about the rice bags they had made and the champagne they had sipped, always referring to the event as "our wedding," we realized our decision had given us a happy start that would provide solace in trying times.

Amid reminiscences of the joy of their wedding, some couples admitted they had harbored fears over having left emotional work undone. Our wedding rehearsal was the time of my last confrontation with such feelings. As I went through the motions, I was filled with apprehension— not so much over what I was doing as over something I was failing to do. I chalked up my fears to prewedding jitters and exhaustion.

About to walk down the aisle at our wedding, I was once again overcome with anxiety. But it was too late. The church was full of friends and acquaintances. Walter and the children were waiting. I brushed away the feelings, took a deep breath, and set out on that walk. I had permitted myself to be propelled into stepfamily living without understanding its realities, without sorting out my own attitudes about being a stepchild, and without acknowledging that my expectations were unrealistic.

The pomp and ceremony surrounding our remarriage was unusual a decade ago; today it is not. Yet for steppeople the ritual of weddings will continue to pose problems that demand creative solutions. For example, when the children marry, who sits where? Who gives away the bride? A young Maryland woman said it would be her biological father because she cannot hurt his feelings. "But my stepfather was the one who put up with me and my problems and raised me. All my father did was send the checks. If I could do as I wanted, I'd like both my father and my step-father to walk me down the aisle—one on each arm."

Stepfamily weddings can create uncertainties and tense times when former relationships remain unresolved. But they can also become mend-ing times. One California stepmother gave a rehearsal dinner party for the stepson with whom she had had a difficult relationship and invited his mother to the party. The young man raised his glass to toast his step-mother, thanking her for the effort she had put into the party—and into their relationship. "Before this, anything from him that included me was directed toward his father," she said. "But this toast was for me alone, and that he felt comfortable toasting me with his mother in the room was a very special reward."

The ceremonies that surround graduations, weddings, and funerals— the rites of passage—give stepfamilies a chance to enlighten friends and community as well as to show how old relationships can fit into the scheme of new ones.

4 Setting the Stage

We spent our wedding night in a military terminal waiting to catch a free hop to Hawaii to honeymoon at the grand old pink hotel on Waikiki Beach. After two hectic months of house hunting, sorting, moving, and planning, we looked forward to ten days of sun and sand.

Two days later Walter's father died and we flew home. One week after the funeral, my new husband left for a ten-day business trip. The day he left the sitter called me at work to say the garage was flooded and water was pouring from the roof. While building a fort in the rafters, the children had driven a spike into the main water pipe. Kurt had cut his foot. That same week I discovered some rings missing, and after the police questioned the sitter she quit. Brenda, my ten-year-old stepdaughter, had gouged her leg while bicycling. When I took her to the hospital for stitches, they asked me for a medical history, which I did not have, and a signature from a parent, which they informed me I was not.

Welcome to the world of stepfamily living.

After the wedding, many stepfamilies are overwhelmed at the confusion that merging two families yields and wonder what they have gotten into. But order and a sense of family identity *can* emerge—if stepfamilies take control and make things happen, rather than reacting in panic to events.

The first year in the life of a stepfamily is much like the first year of any marriage. These months can seem defeating unless family members are aware that the confusion of blending two families into a stepfamily is normal. A new kind of family will emerge, but it takes time and patience. The chaos of integrating so many relationships scares many stepfamilies into breaking up before they have barely begun—many within three years of the marriage.

Setting the stage effectively centers on some basic tasks. First, from the start stepfamilies must give up stereotypes, myths, and unrealistic expectations. Acceptance of the family's differences can work for the family rather than against it. Second, accepting reality about roles in the new family and resolving the way old relationships will fit into it are critical. New bonds must be built as old ones are restructured. Third, to build internal relationships, the daily business of names, patterns, and habits requires clarifying and compromising.

With perseverance and patience the new stepfamily must decide what stays, what goes, and what blends—whether values, traditions, pets, or people. Slowly its members begin to feel they are part of the same team, working toward the same future.

To set the stage realistically one bit of knowledge is essential. The point comes clear in a simple remarriage manual written by two step-mothers who came to recognize that from the beginning their families were different. But until they did, they thought themselves inadequate and at the root of the chaos they soon encountered.

One paragraph from their slim volume should be emblazoned on the minds of everyone whose life may ever touch that of a stepfamily. "The most pervasive myth in a stepmarriage is that the family should function as does a natural family. It doesn't. Classic mistake number one is to think that it will. It can't."[1]

Because we believed that myth and made that classic mistake, most of our energy has had to be directed toward crisis solving to keep our family from falling apart.

MIMES AND MYTHS, ATTITUDES AND ASSUMPTIONS

A natural tendency of the stepfamily is to imitate the nuclear family (consisting of parents and children) because people are comfortable with what they know. Until they understand that these roles will not work in the stepfamily, remarried people simply repeat what they did before.

Even after this approach failed and stepfamilies turned to counselors for guidance, they got little help. The helping professions have tended to view any family pattern other than the nuclear model as deviant, indeed pathological. Their solution to the stepfamily's problems lay in patterning it after the nuclear family. Finally, in 1966, two researchers recognized that attempts to make the stepfamily a duplicate of the nuclear family were doomed to failure. In a journal article they urged professionals to recognize this tactical error.

They identified three problems that directly related to ambiguous roles: (1) stepfamilies denied that any problems existed; (2) stepparents were hypersensitive to every event in which they were not seen in the parental role; and (3) the main source of trouble usually was the couple's inability to present a united front to the children. To help counselors overcome problems in dealing with these nebulous roles, they suggested that the stepfamily be likened to the kibbutz in Israel, the working-class family in France, or the extended family (parents, children, grandparents, aunts, uncles, cousins, and so on) of the United States.[2] Even though these professionals were on the right track, this alternative was barely mentioned in the journal again until 1978.

A professional couple who are themselves stepparents wrote about the conflicts inherent in new stepfamilies. Psychologist Emily Visher and psychiatrist John Visher noted common mistaken beliefs: (1) Stepfamilies are the same as nuclear families. (2) The death of a spouse makes stepparenting easier. (3) Stepchildren are easier to deal with when they do not live in the home. (4) Love happens instantly between members of the new family.[3] When new stepfamilies are aware that these are myths, they can develop realistic expectations for their lives together.

Remarriage is the last phase of accepting the old family's demise and beginning a new one. The wedding ceremony is the symbol. Early during the transition, the stepfamily serves as a prop to family members who are still trying to resolve negative feelings and adjust to broken relationships. Like any fresh wound, these take time to mend, and feelings are vulnerable.

Because the attitudes and assumptions about stepfamily living that family members bring to the new unit can influence their behavior, how they feel about themselves and their new family style can affect their relationships with one another. Viewing the stepfamily as a positive alternative, rather than a replacement, is a realistic attitude that will yield healthy behavior from its members.

As a youngster, what caused me problems was not the fact of my being a stepchild; it was how I viewed my status, how I felt about being a stepchild, and how I thought others felt about me because I was a stepchild. While I nurtured my anger at having to grow up in what I perceived as a second-best family, I kept myself from appreciating my good fortune at gaining a stepfather who provided us with a stable family life. As children do, I thought only of my own needs, and often my anger at my parents for breaking up my home spilled over onto my stepfather.

Like attitudes, assumptions can be destructive. To assume that the myths about stepfamilies are true will certainly create trouble for the new stepfamily. Likewise, assuming the stepfamily's success is a *fait accompli* may cause its defeat, whereas knowing that its evolution takes time will increase its survival chances. Ideally, courtship is a time to probe each other's goals, values, likes, and dislikes. But merging two families from different backgrounds into one cohesive unit is another matter.

Too often the impact of ready-made families on remarriages is understated. In a first marriage the couple has time to explore each other's values and goals. Even parenthood allows time for adjustment.

Not so for remarrieds with children. From the moment they turn from the altar, on the sidelines waits a crew of children with their own expectations and needs. Although they had no choice in creating this family, each child has ideas and hopes about it. Their presence is a reminder to the couple that the new relationship will often have to yield to the needs of the children.

Remarriage honeymoons are nonexistent or brief or accompanied by children. (My parents packed all five of us into the Studebaker to visit an aunt and uncle as their honeymoon.) As instant parents it becomes impossible to settle in slowly to plan childrearing tactics and get acquainted. That critical business should already be discussed and must be worked out immediately because the children are here now. Or, if they live with the other parent, they will arrive soon—weekends, summers, or maybe even later to live full time.

BUILDING FAMILY RELATIONSHIPS

To establish and maintain relationships within the stepfamily calls for a three-pronged approach: (1) The adults need to relate to the children as individuals and define their role with them; (2) the adults need to present a united front on priorities and discipline to provide security for the children; (3) the adults need a tactical plan that will ensure the survival of their relationship. And all these must be simultaneous.

BOUNDARIES AND ROLES   As bonds within the new stepfamily form, boundaries and roles between the old and new family must be dealt with and delineated until a workable situation is found. These concepts help family members to work cohesively.

Both physical and psychological *boundaries* contribute to group identity and make one family different from another. Physical boundaries include shared space, property, and activities; psychological boundaries define the degree of intimacy, authority, and affection that family members share. These are fairly clear within the nuclear family, but when the new stepfamily forms, the boundaries change. First of all, since biological family members now live in two families, the boundaries between them are blurred. Second, parental authority and economic subsistence must be shared, which causes the affections and loyalties of the children to become divided. Third, the stepfamily lacks a shared history of rituals and traditions.

Likewise, *roles*—the rights and duties that determine relationship behavior patterns—become ambiguous. In the nuclear family each person knows who does what and when. Although social roles have changed in the traditional family, the lines of responsibility and authority are basically understood. Regardless of abilities, roles are assigned or *ascribed*; a mother is a mother because she bore a child. But in the stepfamily, roles must be earned through individual effort; they are *achieved*. Stepparents must earn parental authority or affection. This takes time because no family member can be forced to accept a role. Like boundaries, roles must be clear. When they are in jeopardy or overlap with those of the old family, confusion results.

Boundaries and roles begin to shift in first families when one parent leaves and a single-parent family forms. As a parent who formerly shared responsibility for the family takes on full responsibility, the job of balancing the family's emotions, finances, and tasks is learned. And as the children take on responsibility for helping to make the family work, their roles change, too. A son may become a surrogate father, a daughter a confidante. After a time everyone adjusts to the changes and the family works well.

When a stepparent enters the picture, again the boundaries and roles shift. What role does this new person play? Where do former family members fit?

Each family member has expectations about the new family. Each makes plans, most of them unspoken, about continuing old roles or assuming new ones. Facing reality and lowering expectations includes exposing what anthropologist Paul Bohannan calls *hidden agendas*, those private hopes each family member harbors for the new union.[4] A mother who has managed alone for some time may expect her new husband to take over as disciplinarian—or she may resent his interference. The new stepfather who is unaware of the role other family members already have formulated for him may not measure up. In both cases, the expectations are the cause of friction.

The children's hidden agendas center on how much they will allow the new stepparent to assume the parental role. According to Bohannan, children respond in several ways. Genuine dislike may make a child stand aloof from the new stepparent. Or a child's closeness to the biological parent may make the stepparent seem a threat to the love and attention the child gets from the biological parent. Or a child may be aloof at first, but if the stepparent proves worthy, the child can be won over. Some children accept the new stepparent as a father or mother figure immediately—especially young children and those who have no parental figure in their lives. More mature youngsters tend to think of the new adult member of the family as mother's husband or father's wife, rather than as a parental figure. Understanding how they will relate to their new stepchildren can help new stepparents to produce compromises rather than clashes.

Roles and boundaries in the new family have to be spelled out as those from the former family are relinquished or redefined. Who attends school functions? Who gets the kids for which holidays? Who is invited to ceremonies and who is left out? Uncertainty breeds power struggles and manipulations.

"Clarifying such confusion is paramount to a stepfamily's ability to stabilize," says social worker Lillian Messinger. In working with remarrieds at the Clarke Institute of Psychiatry in Toronto, she recognized that roles and boundaries are central troublemakers in new stepfamilies. Ties to former spouses widen the sphere of people affecting the children's lives; and agreeing on roles, responsibility, and authority lines becomes difficult but critical, she explains. The stepparent wants the responsibility of a new child and expects the other parent to let go; but the parent without custody is unwilling to yield parenting decisions. This permits children to play one family against the other and perpetuates the emotional instability.

For some frustrated stepfamilies, the solution is to close the boundaries, cutting off certain family members. Because family life with fewer people is less complicated, this approach may lower day-to-day conflict; but ultimately it intensifies problems. Closing off family relationships is a grave mistake, warns Messinger. If not the beginning of the end for the stepfamily, it is the start of problems for individuals within it. Children are not divorced from the important people in their lives who continue to exist within these boundaries. Closing stepfamily boundaries can generate long-term emotional conflict. It did for me when, as a stepchild, I felt alienated from my father; and it did for me when as a stepmother, I tried to replace my stepdaughters' mother.

Most stepfamilies work best, Messinger found, when parents and stepparents keep in mind that their children are members of two households. She calls this concept *permeable boundaries.*[5] This is not to be confused with living in two families, such as split custody provides. Nor is it like co-parenting, where biological parents continue to make joint decisions. Children need the security of one home where they have a predictable base, belongings, and guardians, she believes. While basic decisions and authority lines should come from the household where they live, children need to know they are loved by both parents and accepted in both homes.

The permeable boundary concept is based on the idea of the family as a system, an approach developed by child and family therapists several years ago. This natural social system has roles, rules, communication patterns, and a power structure. As a system, a family operates on a transactional pattern of how, where, when, and to whom its members relate. Such patterns and roles regulate behavior; they also establish boundaries in which these patterns operate.

Children who are considered to be members of two households can feel free to move between the two families without loyalty conflicts. "Interactions with both families means the families of both biological parents, as well as the new stepparent, accept the fact that the stepfamily's boundaries remain open to the attitudes and affections of the former family ties," explains Messinger. "An attempt to close past relationships is to deny the reality of the biological parent. It also encourages the stepfamily to play the 'nuclear family game,' and trouble brews when feelings are inconsistent with that notion."

Such an arrangement means that children must be flexible. But experts say that children are resilient and can adapt readily to new situations—if they are not burdened by their parents' unresolved problems. When parents can adjust to their divorce, the children can, too. Released from the guilt and fears that loyalty conflicts arouse, children become free to grow. And having rights and responsibilities in both families teaches stepchildren to become flexible and responsible adults.

The stumbling block to such an idea? The adults, of course. A grave responsibility of parents and stepparents alike is to understand the critical need of children to maintain a relationship with the missing parent. From a recent study of California's children of divorce, psychiatric social worker Judith Wallerstein and clinical psychologist Joan Kelly found that the most influential factor in the positive adjustment of these children was a stable, loving relationship with both parents. And what counted most was the *attitude* of the parents. When adult friction had dissolved and regular contact and visits were encouraged by the parent with custody, the children thrived and were happy; when the parent without custody disappeared or was clearly indifferent, the children were depressed and their self-esteem suffered.[6]

Contact with both biological parents is stressful, to be sure. But closing out the other family breeds emotional hang-ups that the children carry to adulthood. As the stepfamily balances old and new relationships, permeable boundaries also allow children to develop trust and security. When such a stepping-stone is provided for children, respect for the adults in their lives grows. And it is this trust and respect that form the basis for love.

Once the adults agree about leaving the boundaries open between the two families, both must decide how they can best parent the new stepchildren. Little research has been done on this, and most decisions are at the gut level. The choice may depend on whether the stepparent has been a parent, on how much involvement is sought, on whether the child will live with the couple or the other parent, and on instincts about parenting.

Those who fake their feelings are destined to fail. One Syracuse stepfather said he didn't like kids much, but when he fell in love with a woman who had custody of her four children, he decided to pretend to an affection he did not feel. His deceit made him feel guilty and affected his relationship with the children. It was only when he finally decided to stop pretending and instead act as a friend toward his new stepchildren that the relationships warmed into very special ones.

Margaret Draughon suggests three possible ways for new stepmothers to approach their role: as other mother, as primary mother, or as friend. The choice could be based on the child's way of mourning the loss of the biological mother, regardless of whether she is dead or merely without custody. If the mourning is incomplete and the mother is psychologically alive, being a friend works best; but if the mourning is complete, stepmothers who adopt the role of primary mother have fewer problems. The other-mother model has no special advantage.[7] As for the primary-mother role, the trick lies in defining it. If the stepparent interprets the term to mean primary caretaker, rather than replacement for the biological parent, problems should be minimal. With no such data available for me to ponder, I reacted from instinct and my experience as a stepchild in defining my role. My first stint as a stepmother began when I was twenty years old—and before I was a mother. Problems were few because Bill and I shared similar values and attitudes about childrearing.

Reflecting on my part-time stepparenting, I vacillated from one to another of the three mothering styles that Draughon describes. Bill's daughters were eight and ten when we married, and although there was too little difference between their ages and mine, I was eager to practice mothering. Because we planned to have children, and because I wanted to prove myself to my new husband, I played the other-mother role, trying to outdo Bill's ex-wife. But his daughters only summered with us, and my effect as a parent was brief, so my role was often limited to that of their friend.

When one stepdaughter came to live with us full time for a while, I put on the mantle of the primary mother; but to avoid being cast as the wicked stepmother, I tried also to remain her friend. This swinging like a pendulum between making each day a holiday and maintaining a parent-child relationship is ineffective for any child. But for an adolescent stepchild with additional insecurities, it is a mess. I felt resentful because I was making an honest effort, as I believe most stepparents do, but it did not work.

Fairytale myths had so pervaded my thinking that I had been treating her in a special way as compensation. The day when I began to attach less importance to her liking me than to her respecting me, I began to treat her more as I would my own child. From then on, when she broke the family rules, failed to tidy her room, or abused her privileges, I reprimanded her just as I did my sons. Our relationship then began to improve. But most important, although I acted as her primary mother while she lived with us, I never tried to replace her biological mother.

The second time I became a stepmother I did what I now believe to be wrong: I attempted to replace the girls' mother, who had all but disappeared from our lives. The decision came from my wanting daughters, but into it filtered my unresolved childhood feeling that my stepfather should have made me his daughter.

As a youngster it remained clear to me that I was Ben's stepdaughter, and I managed always to interpret my status as second best—until that was how I began to think of myself. Not until years later would I find out what my low self-esteem stemmed from—not from being a stepchild, but from my attitude about it and from my alienation from my biological father. But the second time I became a stepparent I thought that by claiming the girls as my daughters and replacing their mother, perhaps I could help them avoid my childhood feeling of belonging to no one.

Such reasoning represented a grave mistake. Until writing this book, what I never unraveled was that one of the reasons for respecting my stepfather was that he fathered me, and well; but he never attempted to replace my father. My plan to make the girls mine pivoted on my needs, not theirs; but it was rooted in misperception and ignorance, not maliciousness.

The paradox about parental roles creates a dilemma for unaware stepparents. A stepchild may encourage one parenting style, consciously deliver one message, yet seek—or need—another course of action. With all good intentions, the stepparent follows the cue and takes over as the parent without permitting the child to acknowledge freely the biological parent. But when stepchildren get what they think they want, their hearts may not be able to handle the divided loyalties that may ensue. Both the child and the stepparent ultimately pay a heavy price.

Introducing, rearing, or treating the girls as my daughters was not the problem. To ease social situations, many stepparents introduce their stepchildren as sons or daughters; and in rearing these children they mother or father them. When taking on a full-time responsibility for raising other people's children, treating them as you do your own makes it easier to keep family order.

But treating biological children and stepchildren alike is different from feeling the same about them. What bred trouble for us was my unwillingness to accept that they were not my children, that they belonged to another woman. My silence about their mother (after all, *I* was their mother) left the girls without a comfortable arena in which to resolve their feelings about her; and when they did speak of her, my jealousy made me defensive.

I am not alone in this. "She is my daughter," other stepmothers told me. "I feel about this child exactly as I do about my own." During interviews two stepmothers shared photos that ostensibly proved how much the stepdaughters resembled the stepmothers. And in response I pulled out a similar snapshot of Brenda and me. "Yes, they even look like us," we affirmed desperately, nodding and agreeing.

Mirroring my thoughts and feelings of the past, a New York state stepmother who was twenty-nine years old (exactly my age when I began stepmothering for the second time) cried, "I want the children to be mine. I've had the little one since he was an infant. I raise them, care for them, worry about them. Why shouldn't I consider them mine? Except by phone, their mother is nowhere around."

ACCEPTING THE REALITY OF ROLES   Like me when I tried to replace the girls' mother, this young woman has not yet accepted that she is *not* their mother and never will be—biologically. We are stepparents. But that term is so loaded with negative emotions and images that we do anything to avoid it—even lie to ourselves.

By accepting reality about roles, stepparents can avoid costly mistakes and direct their energy where it really matters. Since children need parental figures, a stepparent can parent in many ways.

Some stepparents already know this. Marcia Wrytzen, who now counsels stepfamilies in New Jersey, explains why she did it differently from the beginning. "I introduce Christy as my stepdaughter because the truth of the matter is that she is not my daughter. I can be a buddy or friend, but I can never be her mother. Besides, I could never feel the same about her as I do about my own sons, whom I love in an unconditional way. At times I have very warm feelings for her, which even surprise me. But while I can say 'I love you, I love you' to my son, I cannot yet do that with Christy. Still, I care about her, I'm concerned, and I let her know that."

When one day her young stepdaughter asked why she was introduced in that way, Mrs. Wrytzen explained that she could not be dishonest with herself. Had I only asked my own stepfather that question, I might have gotten a similar answer. And with that honest answer, I might have grown up feeling very different about myself.

"What about stepmothers like myself, who call them our daughters?" I asked Mrs. Wrytzen. "Are we kidding ourselves?"

"Much depends on the child's relationship with the biological parent. If you can really be comfortable with it, then it's okay. But stepparents must be careful, because emotional feelings that result from how the relationship is approached must be faced, too. I think Christy would feel scared and angry if she thought I was trying to move in and push her mother out. I will never do that. But at the beginning of my marriage I was terribly confused about the way to play it."

The role that is chosen must feel comfortable emotionally for the new stepparent. For many who will rear their new mate's children on a full-time basis, the comfortable choice may be to become a primary parent. But any consideration of replacing the biological parent should be hastily abandoned. The biological parent can never be replaced—*never*. Even a parent who is dead or one who has abandoned the children retains an important place in the children's lives. As I learned only recently, the secret in being a stepparent is, do not cajole or claim. That is the most likely route into your stepchildren's hearts.

PARENTING AS A TEAM   The adults must learn to relate to the stepchildren as individuals and define their role with them; however that bond works, the stepparent is also part of the child's discipline team. What happens in the new family depends to a great extent on how the adults take charge.

Taking command requires identifying and melding the differences in day-to-day living habits as well as in childrearing ways. Before my remarriage, *we* were super tidy, kept rules flexible, relaxed at mealtimes, and had pets that lived in bowls or aquariums; *they* tossed clothes and belongings anywhere, used mealtime for problem solving, and had a house dog.

Turning these *we* and *they* living patterns into *ours* was a matter of compromise.

But we never agreed on the most important couple issue of all—disciplining each other's children. Walter and I had different values and ideas about bringing up children. For two years before we married, he raised his children alone, as did I. His military background influenced his fathering style—discipline from the diaphragm. He set rigid rules, expected conformity, yelled, punished severely. Believing that obedience and conformity were not conducive to independence in children, I was permissive, encouraged individuality, was forgiving and quiet-spoken.

Out of habit, as well as out of our failure to understand that childrearing was the major issue in beginning as a stepfamily, we continued to use our own parenting styles, each of us forever undermining the other. When he punished a child in what I thought too severe a way, I interfered, hoping to soften the blow—hardly good parenting practice. Then we tried his way, then mine. But we were uncompromising and inconsistent so neither way worked. Because parenting each other's children was our critical task, we should have worked out these differences beforehand; because the differences remained, uproar ensued. Soon the kids were in control, manipulating us through guilt, jealousy, and triangles.

Adhering to a single childrearing system ensures that stepchildren get what all children need—consistency, concern, and boundaries. While unity and consistency are important to all families, they are doubly so in stepfamilies. Without them, children from diverse backgrounds can use their differences to pit parent against parent—whether those in the household or those without custody who influence this new household.

As two stepfathers made plain, those entering stepfamily living with any other notion ask for trouble. "If I could do one thing over again," a Syracuse stepfather lamented, "it would be to work out the big stuff in advance. And that means values and kid raising. The way we went at it, nothing was ever solved. The kids got between us, and then I'd blow my cool. Then she and I'd fight. What a mess."

And a stepfather in Rockville, Maryland, warns, "Once a couple decides what to do to raise the kids, I don't believe it makes any difference whether a child is yours or hers or one you plucked off the streets. Our problem was that we were not raising them, but merely caretaking, keeping them in line so we could do what we wanted to do. We were excited about our relationship and the kids were just in the way most of the time."

A major adjustment problem centers on discipline. Phyllis Stern, a nurse and a stepparent who studied how stepfamilies integrate and develop a sense of family, identified five discipline patterns. "Discipline can be handled so that conflict is manageable," Dr. Stern explains, "or so that differences can blow the group apart."[8]

Her study included only stepfather families, but the patterns are similar for stepmothers. The pattern she calls "not my kid, or stepfather left out" occurs when a new stepfather enters the picture, and the mother and children must grant him co-management privileges or he remains an outsider. If the stepfather makes a friend of the children first, and assumes the disciplinarian role slowly, the family integrates without severe problems. But when he moves too quickly, or his new rule making and enforcing are not to the mother's or the children's liking, "chaos or everyone left out" results. Soon everyone makes rules, no one observes them, and nothing gets done. Stepfamilies that follow this pattern also can anticipate future triangles between parents and children.

Another pattern emerges when one parent makes the rules and the other enforces them. "Anything you say, dear," or "stepparent left out," lets one parent enforce only those rules with which he or she agrees. Worse, this is generally done through subterfuge. For example, a stepfather may decide the children's bedtime is to be 8:00 P.M. The mother says, "Anything you say, dear." But because she does not agree with him, she fails to enforce it and an hour later she says, "Oh my, I forgot to tell the children to go to bed." This traditional family pattern, with the father distinctly in charge, seems harmless. But it keeps stepfamilies from integrating.

Sometimes a mother says to the new stepfather, "Take over," and she means it. Maybe her son has brewed trouble before and she hopes the new stepfather will straighten him out. Dr. Stern found that the child in this pattern is almost always under six years old. When the stepfather takes over, the child fights back and becomes resentful; the stepfather counters with harsher discipline; and the child then withdraws or becomes a worse behavior problem.

"The children in this pattern are in jeopardy because they have no champion," says Dr. Stern. "They lost the biological parent's presence, and now the other parent turns against them, telling them to obey a stranger's orders." If the stepfather in this "child-left-out" pattern becomes a disciplinarian, suggests Dr. Stern, but at the same time acts as the child's friend, whether helping him pass math or building a winning Soap Box Derby car, a stepfamily can integrate. It can happen because the stepfather and child directly interact. But the child must be convinced that the stepfather's presence holds something valuable for him or her.

Finally, in the "integrated, or no-one-left-out" pattern, everyone interacts and shares in rule making. As in all democratic families, children take a more active part in decisions and have as much right to vote against going to the museum as the parents do about voting against going to a baseball game. With this kind of approach to discipline, the stepfamily has a good survival chance.

ROMANCE IN THE MIDST OF CHAOS As leaders of the troop, the adults set the tone for the new family. But if they cannot keep their relationship intact, the rest of the relationships in the family will fall apart or never get off the ground. Few relationships can withstand the bombardment that the adults in a stepfamily are subjected to unless there is also constant nurturance. As a reminder of what can happen, the newlyweds ought to post the remarriage divorce statistic on the refrigerator door. Happy relationships should depend on how people deal with each other, but in stepfamilies, which are often large, sheer numbers can overwhelm.

Most couples interviewed understood that the stability of their relationship is pivotal to their family unity. Yet even though they emphasized communication and the need to parent together, most said they did little to keep their romance alive. A few, whose children were nearly out of the nest, admitted feeling nervous twinges when they sat together in the same room but could find little to say to each other. "We've spent so many years quarreling and handling kid problems," one New York man said, "I wonder if there's really anything else between us anymore."

Another couple shared their concern about their relationship. "All we've talked about for nine years is how to get through the next crisis with the kids," lamented the wife. "Now our teenagers are about to leave, and frankly, I'm nervous." Her husband echoed her concern. "Love her?" he replied to my question, as she went for coffee. "Who's had time to think about love? All we've done is managed to get from one day to the next without killing each other."

When these couples were asked why they were not working at keeping the romance alive, they put the blame on time, or kids, or money. I recognized these as excuses because Walter and I have used them all. Many stepfamilies I spoke with said that at one time or another they poured money into counseling when problems hit the crisis level, yet they were unable to justify devoting time and money to keeping romance in their relationship.

A correlation exists between the energy invested in a relationship and the need for professional counseling. In my family, when Walter and I took time away together to talk and play, we lowered the stress levels and again developed good feelings about each other; when we postponed this alone time because of school, work, or money, the stress built and we were back at the counselor's doorstep. It took us a long while to see the connection. Deep-seated differences or personality problems need to be worked out through counseling, but minor communication problems can be handled by couples who take the time to keep their relationships in tune.

Keeping romance aglow in the midst of stepfamily living requires fierce commitment. Before Walter and I were married, we agreed to give ourselves some time away from the children every six weeks and considered the money as an investment in our relationship. Our favorite getaway was to weekend at a country inn whose intimate nature promoted our effort. A pleasant drive on country lanes, a quiet dinner, a late sleep-in the next day, and walks in the woods with a picnic lunch gave us time to talk about more than children; and in this relaxed atmosphere, our sex life came alive again. Our absences were good for the children also. When we drove home, often they greeted us with a labor of love—a massive, colorful welcome-home banner they had spent hours to produce.

Many remarrieds do something about nurturing their relationship. One couple declared every third weekend as theirs—in their own house. Everyone else had to leave. While they arranged for care of the younger children, the teenagers were responsible for finding a friend, grandparent, or other parent with whom to spend the weekend. Their fundamental reason for staying at home was money; but they also enjoyed skittering about in the nude, listening to records, or eating a peaceful meal they had prepared together.

Creativity such as theirs can overcome a lack of money for trips and dinners out. Wine, cheese, and fruit, tucked into a basket with a book of poems, provide the makings for a special afternoon. Depending on the availability of sitters, the picnic spot can be a corner of the backyard or a secluded mountain stream. A simple bicycle picnic can provide the two- or three-hour breather that a remarried couple with children needs. Many hotels offer inexpensive overnight champagne-breakfast package deals. Exchange weekends with other stepfamilies cost only the time and energy it takes to arrange them. House trades provide new arenas in which to maintain relationships; a city couple can trade with a country couple. The possibilities for romantic reprieves that don't dent the budget are as unbounded as the couple's imagination and determination to make the relationship survive.

THE DAY-TO-DAY STUFF

In tandem with building and maintaining relationships, diverse family histories require adjusting for day-to-day living. To establish a new family unity over events that once were taken for granted, matters such as living space, personal habits, mealtimes, and household chores, must evolve from two different ways into one common routine.

Ways of going about daily tasks are established in first families out of patterns modified from those the couple learned as youngsters. People perform such tasks the way they have always done so, based on habit and tradition. Stepfamilies come together with vastly different ideas about what is right or normal. These issues, which researcher Phyllis N. Stern calls *sentimental order things*, need negotiating. Family rules, she explains, stem from an emotional rather than a logical base. While studying the difficulty that stepfamilies have in integrating, she found that the problems of sentimental order are multiplied because parent, stepparent, and children all have definite, but diverse ideas of how things should go.[9] Neither way should be labeled right or wrong; each should be viewed as simply different. Everyone needs a chance to explain why things are done in a particular way. This is when habitual ways of doing things can be exchanged for sensible and efficient ways. But because habits are tied to identity, the exchange is not without defensiveness. The older the children are, the more difficult it is for them to change; but through give-and-take, satisfactory solutions can be arrived at.

Diverse eating habits are a source of friction in most new stepfamilies. By dinnertime, hunger has everyone edgy. Children come in from play dirty, cranky, and ravenous; parents are exhausted from the workday. Demands are made at the table, and what is acceptable to one family may be intolerable to the other. Dirty T-shirts and uncombed hair may be acceptable to one part of the crew; the rest think a fresh shirt or blouse is suitable mealtime attire. One stepfather complained of the picky eating habits that his wife permitted her children. A youngster griped about his new stepmother's gourmet cooking; he was used to meat and potatoes. As new stepchildren make comparisons between the food they are now expected to eat and their mother's cooking, food that should offer pleasure as well as nourishment can become a weapon to release hostility and anger. Or it can create a win. One plus I had going for me was that I cooked liver better than their mother—a minor achievement, but a victory nevertheless.

Our early mealtime scraps centered on table manners. My children edged their elbows on the table and his held their forks European style. He whacked my kids' elbows with a knife handle; I fussed at his for eating like Bohemians. My new husband used dinnertime as lecture time, so that a review of the day's events led from schoolwork discussions, to criticism about grades, to a monologue about the pursuit of excellence.

When the children got that look on their faces, whatever favorite dish I had prepared could not offset the tension. The dinner table turned into a battleground.

In an attempt to bring order to the dinner table he shared with his wife and nine children, one stepfather organized mealtime with rules and regulations that every child dreaded but adhered to. All were required to wait at their chairs for the father to enter. A parent presided at each of two tables, and little talk was permitted between the children. "It was awful," recalled one of them. "Just waiting at the chair, my stomach started to ache." The stepfather says he now realizes that such regimentation was not the answer. "But as an only child I was used to order, and with my former wife mealtimes were quiet. When food and conversation should have offered a reprieve from a hectic day, dinner in our suddenly large family meant chaos and confusion. I was desperate."

Living space is another thing that requires adjusting. Some stepchildren resent having to move into "the other house" or to share rooms with new brothers and sisters. Some feel infringed upon; the rest feel like intruders. Nor is it easy for the new spouse to move in where ghosts of the earlier marriage linger. Moving to a different house establishes a neutral base for the new family and makes adjustments easier. As family members make a fresh start, putting together new rooms, organizing belongings, and making new friends, a new house can provide a sense of unity.

Household tasks and hygienic habits need consideration. Who folds the clothes, does the dishes, mows the lawn? Are bathroom doors left closed? What time is mealtime? Is the cap of the toothpaste tube replaced? Who picks up dirty socks that are thrown on the floor?

How long original families lived together before the stepfamily merger has a lot to do with these patterns. Yet other patterns are developed during single-parent living. Besides mothering and housekeeping, many women with custody become breadwinners to supplement child support; men tend to hire someone to fill the housekeeping role of their former wives. While money makes possible these contrasting solutions to housework, their diversity can create more adjustments between his and her kids in the stepfamily.

How our single-parent coping styles affected our children showed up when Walter and I began to divvy up jobs around our new house. As a single parent, he had tried balancing parenting, housekeeping, and breadwinning, but soon he hired a housekeeper. Because I could not afford this, my young sons took on responsibilities at an early age. Making beds and tidying their rooms, dusting, folding clothes, and unpacking groceries were tasks they took for granted. Such was not the case with my new stepchildren, and that I expected them to do housework was an unwelcome surprise.

At first my salary paid a housekeeper. But within the year, when I stopped working to start college, this luxury stopped and I assigned more tasks to the children. That my four-year-old son did fewer jobs than my twelve-year-old stepdaughter created feelings of injustice. Because of the age difference, I thought it fair; but to my stepdaughter it reflected her step status. When not discussed openly, changes in the division of labor can breed jealousy.

How the work is doled out can matter. My husband tended to assign tasks to the children; I preferred to post a list of the tasks that had to be done, letting the children divvy up the work. Kids are remarkably fair with each other and tend to squabble and complain less when they have a choice in the work they do. Children are as a rule more efficient, interested, or uninterested in some jobs than in others. The stepfamily's start could be a time for a child to dump a job and take on a new preferred one. Maybe one child had been stuck with emptying the trash for years and hated it. A younger stepbrother might pick that job and the older child might choose to mow the lawn. Regardless of the outcomes, deciding who does what, and when, needs attention right away. For some children who have never had to do much of anything, taking on tasks in the stepfamily teaches them responsibility. With everyone pitching in and adjusting to household tasks, a sense of working together as a new family builds unity and reduces the pandemonium.

Some stepfamilies look back and laugh at the mistakes they made. But during the settling in, adjusting was no laughing matter. The stepfather who demanded order at mealtime also constructed elaborate charts for the children, outlining duties to be completed before his Saturday-morning inspection. At the appointed hour, the children stood outside their bedrooms hoping they had accumulated enough points to be permitted their planned weekend activities. "When he came near with his clipboard, and he was mad about something else, I knew that no matter how hard I tried all week, I'd be short on points," his stepdaughter recalled.

WHAT'S IN A NAME?

As stepfamily life develops, family members must decide what to call one another. Very young children often are eager to call stepparents by parental names; older children do not see it that way.

The terms *Mom* and *Dad* are rooted in biology and are ascribed to parents who carry out that role. Emotional bonding cannot erase biology, but it can become so strong that children may decide to award these names to stepparents. Because the emotional connotations attached to these words are so powerful, stepparents must prove they deserve them. Such a test that reflects the strength of the bond takes trust and time.

An adult stepchild in Manlius, New York, lived with her stepmother for years before calling her anything. "I couldn't name her, not because I disliked her, but because it felt strange. My father never pushed me, but one day suggested, 'Her name is Mom, not her.' Eventually, after I'd grown closer to my stepmother, I could say it and mean it."

A sixteen-year-old stepson from Ohio says he could never call his stepfather Dad. "I feel this man has some responsibility for me, but that's as far as it goes." Yet when someone inquires, "Is that your mother?" he answers yes, not clarifying that his biological father's new wife is really his stepmother. "I let people think she's my mother because it would be great with me if she were. She's neat."

Stepchildren resent being forced to call new stepparents *Mom* or *Dad*, and the pressure makes the relationship more tense. Most experts agree that naming decisions should be left to the children. "If it starts out as Jen, and warms up to Mom," suggests counselor Frank Halse, Jr., "it's more natural and permits the children to make their own choice."

The final word about naming and introductions rests with each individual and will mesh with the experience and emotion that has touched that person's life. Much of the negative feeling associated with being introduced as *step* is rooted in the meanings that society has attached to the word and in the stereotypes surrounding it. When a word that prefaces an introduction is loaded with negative feelings and images, it is understandable why some stepparents are inclined to avoid mentioning the relationship or why others are wounded by it.

Choices about introductions are rooted in reality, denial, convenience, or some combination of the trio. In her refusal to call her stepdaughter something she is not, Marcia Wrytzen faces it head on. As for me, in an effort to maintain my illusion, I needed to introduce the girls as my daughters. Some stepparents find it more convenient to say, "This is my daughter," rather than explain the relationship. Others clarify it by introducing the child as "John's daughter."

The emotions surrounding the choices are important. Even after sorting reality from fantasy and better understanding my relationship with the girls, I could never call Brenda anything but my daughter. It is an emotional response, a gut feeling. What I call her is so entwined with my feeling about her that all the connotations that *daughter* conjure up for me feel right. With Bev, with whom I had established a mother-daughter relationship that was later shattered, the outcome is yet to be written. I have never stopped referring to her as my daughter, but since the sad day at our doorstep she calls me Elizabeth. For now, that works for both of us.

FRIENDSHIP AND PATIENCE

Building relationships. Changing daily patterns. Who calls whom what? These adjustments are not made overnight. Few are quick and clean, and all require time and flexibility. Too many stepfamilies get jittery when all these sortings out and adaptation attempts fail to produce one big happy family.

"The blending of a stepfamily is an ongoing process, not an end to itself," reminds Irene Goldenberg, a psychologist and stepmother. "What happens is that a family system exists and new people enter this system, which then needs adjusting. This may involve changes—different table manners, different responsibilities—which take time. The extent of the adult relationship in the beginning determines the strength and endurance of the system." Given an understanding of what to expect and a dollop of patience, the setting-the-stage phase of stepfamily living can launch good, solid relationships.

As these relationships are built, interwoven with discipline should be a determined effort at befriending the new stepchildren. A parent may choose to enforce discipline by threatening to withdraw love. But in a new stepfamily, such a threat means nothing. Those who take the time to become friends with the children first are more likely to find their discipline attempts successful.

Friendship can be developed in many ways: by teaching stepchildren a new skill, by providing a wanted pet, by guiding them over an emotional hurdle. During the first year of our stepfamily, Walter became Jeff's buddy by building an elaborate HO trainboard setup and supplying him with an engineer's cap and license. He developed a friendship with Hopper during drives to a reading clinic and a sculpture class on Saturday mornings. As I helped Brenda decorate her room and taught her to sew, our friendship grew. No one reached out to Kurt, and the effect began to show in his behavior as he tried to gain the attention he needed.

Those children who were able to build family friendships began to flourish in our new family. Shortly after we married, Sacramento's Albert Einstein Junior High School was to be dedicated. As the high point of the festivities, Dr. Hans Einstein would judge and award the prize for the best ecology speech. Bev said she wanted to try for it, but was afraid. Although my anxiety about public speaking made me appreciate her fear, I couldn't teach her courage by letting her not enter. After encouraging her to research and write about air pollution, we practiced her speech nightly from her notecards. When she became one of the finalists, her self-confidence grew; but because the three finalists had to deliver their speeches to Dr. Einstein, so did her nervousness.

A bit of drama was in order, I thought, and asked her father to bring home a gas mask from the air base. She balked at wearing it, thinking her friends would laugh. Again I encouraged her, and on contest day she walked onstage wearing the gas mask and waited for the snickering audience to quiet. Then she dramatically removed the headgear and suggested they not laugh, for if we failed to clean up our air, we might one day have to resort to such equipment for our survival.

My new daughter cinched the contest. After Dr. Einstein presented her with the trophy, "from one Einstein to another," she looked toward me and our smiles of pride met. A good first step, I thought. I'll need these points.

5   Settling In

As I reared my sons, the bedtime ritual included lots of hugging and closeness. But after I remarried, this became uncomfortable because I felt distant from my new stepson. I believed I should try to love all the children in the same way, but I soon found that I did not feel the same. So the bedtime custom degenerated into quick kisses on the boys' heads so I could get out of the room fast.

Soon my seven-year-old confronted me in tears. "You don't love us anymore," he wailed. Shocked, I asked what he meant. "You don't tuck us in like you used to." As Hopper explained, I knew what he meant, but not what to do. In trying to equalize attention, I had been cheating my sons and myself. Such uncertainty typifies how stepparents and stepchildren feel and act during the early days of stepfamily living.

The celebration ends, the newness dims. The stage is set, roles are cast, and everyone begins to understand the rules. Adjusting and compromising have begun to strengthen the stepfamily's internal relationships. Does all this mean smooth sailing ahead? Not always. As myths that remarrieds believe in are exposed, and as unrealistic expectations go unmet, this period yields disappointment and disruption. Settling-in time becomes a time for testing roles, bonds, boundaries. Kids test each other and their parents. Parents test each other. Outsiders test the family. Power and loyalty struggles reign. Making order from the confusion is a healthy and normal process.

There is a point to all this conflict: Stepfamily members need to check the security and trust levels in the new relationships. After a serious family loss, few are willing to trust without a test. And as the stepfamily settles in, tests run the gamut from defiance of new stepparents, to manipulation, to outright rejection. This fighting-it-through stage proves there is enough care and concern for each other with which to build commitments and love. This important proving time, which may take two to five years, is when the remarriage strains to the splitting point, or it strengthens.

After living together awhile, the new stepfamily begins to fine-tune adjustments that will affect it in long-term ways. New bonds are formed as old ones are maintained. Redefined boundaries between the old and new families are tried and tested. If plans to rear the children are not working, changes are required and roles are clarified. Values and traditions need sorting and melding. What is and what cannot be are accepted. The family's size is determined. How swiftly these adjustments are made influences how soon the stepfamily stabilizes and forms its own identity.

Above all, whether family relationships develop a firm base hinges on whether the couple's relationship develops a firm base. In confronting children's manipulations and tests, a couple must make swift decisions that will help conflict to evolve into commitment. When both partners bring children to the merger, the process of becoming a family often is easier for adults and children. Both sets of children are biological children and stepchildren, and each child has been separated from a parent and must now learn to share the other parent. There is more understanding and more give-and-take between the adults, too; you help me rear mine, and I'll help rear yours becomes an unspoken parenting pact. This contract existed between Walter and me, too, but our differences remained so great that our settling-in time stretched to nearly seven years—and before it ended it had brought our marriage to its definitive crisis.

Our immaturity and ignorance about stepfamily living were compounded by other stresses that threatened our marriage. Sending a child out of the family caused familywide guilt and threat. A vast social change that altered roles and rules caught us unaware. My husband's time in Vietnam made me feel abandoned and burdened with extra children, and we all feared for his life. My return to college resulted in personal growth and change that produced both positive and negative effects on our couple relationship. Other midlife tensions that wreak havoc in any marriage were often mixed up with stepfamily problems.

But Gail Sheehy had not yet written *Passages* to tell us that these stages were normal, and there were no guides for our new family. In an attempt to be what we had hoped our first families would be, and what we thought society expected us to be, we masked as a nuclear family. Trying to be what we were before, only better, got us in over our heads fast, because although we looked like the nuclear family, we were different.

Many of the differences are obvious, but others are ambiguous. Much of the struggle of stabilizing as a family unit stems from the diverse histories of values and patterns that family members bring to the union.

Some must be changed, some accepted; but until these differences are melded, settling-in time can be reminiscent of a three-ring circus.

CHANGING OR ACCEPTING VALUES

Values, the deep beliefs that guide behavior, are learned in first families. They make people different and determine what ways of doing things are acceptable to the members of our original family. The first time people marry, they try to adapt their values to those of the new partners, establishing guidelines for the new family. This is difficult for most young marrieds, and their first year together is likely to be unstable as they forge a new set of values and patterns.

With remarriage comes yet another shift. Value differences may create shock waves throughout the new stepfamily, and working out ways to blend or accept them is a serious challenge. Altering values may entail giving up attitudes or behaviors that people identify as part of themselves and that have guided their lives. Such changing should not be approached lightly. But when vast value differences yield unacceptable behavior within the stepfamily, it cannot be avoided.

Shortly after her remarriage, one California stepmother discovered that her new stepchildren were stealing from stores, from her handbag, even from each other. When she confronted them with it, they lied. "Their values were so different from mine, I didn't know what to do," she said. "But I couldn't tolerate it, lest my own younger children learn from their example." Her new husband's solution was to punish them severely. The stepmother was trapped into being an informant, and the children's lying worsened.

Since fear failed to influence their behavior in a positive way, she tried reason. Rather than tell her husband, she explained to her stepchildren why their behavior upset her. Could they help her? They responded that they needed *her* help because already this pattern had gotten them into trouble at school and with friends. Because the deal included a bonus, the stepmother's task was lightened. "It was not easy," she says. "Helping them to change deeply ingrained values took patience I often ran short of. Now that they're away from home, I know they sometimes resort to deceit, but they think twice about it now."

Her stepdaughter, now twenty, reminisced about the time when she was eleven. "No one had taught us about right and wrong," she said. "Then along came my stepmother, who expected us to know the difference. We clashed a lot, but when she showed us what we could get out of it, we tried to change. I still fall into old habits because I have a strong relationship with my mother, who gets a kick out of shady deals and putting things over on people. But honesty has become important, and when I slip into my old ways I somehow think I have disappointed my stepmother." Not long ago the young woman slipped a chamois shirt into a bag at the store where she worked. Stealing the shirt bothered her so much that she could not wear it until she returned it and then arranged to buy it and pay for it.

Stepparents need not feel helpless about changing their stepchild's behavior or values because childhood patterns do not carry lifelong imprints. Psychiatrist John Visher, who works with many stepfamilies, discounts the concept that a child's values are firmly implanted by age five or six. "Research has proved this untrue," he says. "Stepparents can influence a child's values. But trying to make changes right away only results in rejected efforts, and sometimes creates other problems. Children are influenced most by example and by the kind of person the stepparent is."

That children learn by what they observe is a fundamental theory of learning.[1] Changing themselves on the basis of what they see as example in their new family takes time—not only to learn new values and habits and try them out, but to decide which ones work best. The real problems arise when a stepparent judges one value as right and another as wrong. Values are not absolute. Different families do things differently, and all family members have their own concept of what is right.

Choosing which changes are necessary, and bringing them about, requires careful consideration by the couple responsible for rearing the child. When stepparents discover undesirable habits in their stepchildren, attempting a near total change is asking for trouble—and unfair to the children. But once a few serious problems are selected to be worked on, new stepparents should accept the other traits. This is especially true of adolescent children. Not only have they been doing things a certain way for a long time, but this period of their development offers many other challenges. Insisting that they bend values or change habits may stir up rebellion and resentment.

Once a value is targeted for change, stepchildren need to be told why the trait is undesirable. Talking with children to uncover the reasons behind the behavior sets the stage for change. They may have no reason for their way of doing things and may be quite receptive to trying another approach. Some may actually be relieved to find a different way. The stepchildren who stole, for example, had done so because they had not been taught differently. Then, for a cover-up, they resorted to lying—until their new stepmother showed them a better way to cope with life.

Showing a child what is to be gained by change raises the chances of its happening. And when a child is willing to work on the change, the problem is on its way to solution. Above all, the stepchildren must be made to realize it is the *trait* that is unacceptable, not the children. This can be accomplished by explaining, "I like you, but not some of the things you do." Deciding what is intolerable and what can be acceptable is important, because in the long run, the more acceptance there is in the stepfamily, the more successful it can be. Changes will take time and energy, so they had better be worth the effort. Otherwise, develop a sense of humor and a measure of tolerance. My stepdaughter Bev's earliest resentment toward me developed as she began to feel I was trying to change too many things about her. By selecting too many targets, I began to make Bev feel devalued. And I wasted energy by trying to change my tomboy stepdaughters into frilly little girls.

"Some of the ways Brenda and I did things served a purpose," Bev says today. "We had to wear dresses to school then, but with cutoff pants underneath we could play kickball during recess. When you made us wear fancy panties and tried to change us from tomboys, that was hard for me to accept. About many of the other hassles we had, I knew you were right, but I resented your pointing out so many things wrong with me, and I *had* to fight you. Now I appreciate those changes, but I learned from Dad never to admit I was wrong, and when you pointed out my faults I denied them. You had to be the enemy."

In trying to effect change quickly instead of slowly and consistently, I overlooked a lesson my stepfather had taught me. He raised another man's children with near total acceptance. Since his moral and religious background meshed closely with ours, some of his ease in accepting us centered on common values. Likewise, as a part-time stepmother to Bill's daughters, I accepted them more easily because our values were similar. I realized also that because they only summered with us, attempts at change would have been futile.

But when I took on stepmothering full time, the underlying need for change lay partly in my decision to replace the girls' mother. To be my daughters, they must reflect my values. That mistake was the beginning of many problems, a major one centering on acceptance. But also, I had to decide which of my own values I could not compromise.

ACCEPTANCE—A BASIS FOR LOVING

The long-term consequences of my decision to become the girls' mother are familiar to stepparents who attempt to replace the biological parent. When the girls lived up to my values, our relationships blossomed;

when they resorted to habits and values they grew up with, I withdrew. At the time I could not identify my reaction as conditional.

After a year or two I began to acknowledge to myself that I did not feel the same about these daughters as I did about my own sons. That awareness bred uncertainty. These were good and intelligent children. Why the different feelings? Regardless of what the boys said or did, I loved them. Erich Fromm calls this *motherly love*. A mother gives it to her children simply because they are her children, and not because the children have fulfilled specific conditions or lived up to any expectations.[2]

Carl Rogers calls this tendency to love children regardless of their behavior *unconditional positive regard*. This means having respect for them as equals, without placing conditions on your feelings. You respect their ability to conduct their lives, their ability to make decisions, and their own ultimate responsibility for themselves. Unconditional positive regard flows from your own values and beliefs about people in general. It is hard to fake for long, and both possessiveness and condescension reveal where this respect is lacking.[3]

Since I felt no such unqualified love for my stepchildren, I reasoned that I would be more accepting if they would measure up to my expectations; and like the ones I held for myself, they were high. When they rebelled and rejected me, I began to feel guilty about my uncertain feelings. What is more, I began to lay the blame elsewhere. But it is hard to dispel the anxiety that accompanies such behavior.

In an essay in *Understanding Children*, Dr. Jerome Kagan explains that a primary human motive is to resolve the uncertainty that occurs when one's conception of truth is threatened. He cites three sources of uncertainty: the unfamiliar, an inconsistency between two ideas or between an idea and a behavior, and the inability to predict the future.[4] Because of diverse histories and especially differences in values, each of these agitates most stepfamily members as they attempt to adjust. Stepparents who try to be something they are not in an attempt to meet some need are especially likely to experience uncertainty.

According to Dr. Kagan's work on motives, my anxiety was coming from my inability to resolve these uncertainties. I was trying to behave as the girls' mother when I knew I was not. I was coping with values foreign to my own. And I had no way of predicting whether in the future they would reject me, or whether I would fail at mothering them. Of course my fear and anxiety mounted. When people cannot interpret or cope with uncertainties, explains Dr. Kagan, fear, anxiety, and guilt are natural reactions.[5]

My continued belief in the myth of instant love also created unrealistic expectations. Because I loved my husband, I would love his children, too. And when I claimed his daughters as mine, I *had* to love them because parents love their children. All these elements that seduce stepparents to hold such expectations are complicated and generally subconscious. But when the love doesn't come, they look to themselves as the problem. Yet it is not that the stepparents are lacking but that their decisions or expectations are inappropriate.

BONDING AND BIOLOGY

Many stepparents expect the impossible about instantly loving their new stepchildren—especially if they began to form a good relationship before the marriage. Various reasons make instant love next to impossible. First of all, after losing a parent many children remain angry at the missing parent and direct their anger at the stepparent. Second, remarriage is a phase in a process that began with loss, and as with any grieving process, mourning takes time. Third, children worry about where they will fit into new relationships and are cautious of building new trusts. Each of these may create defensive behavior in new stepchildren that make it quite impossible for new stepparents to like them, let alone love them.

Stepparents need the tolerance and understanding of the angels during the first year or so, as children work out their pain and test new relationships. "I wish you were my mother that would move away, and my real mother would come back and live with my father," a five-year-old told his new stepmother in upstate New York as he sat on her lap waiting for her to read him a bedtime story.

At the start of our marriage my sons were affectionate toward Walter —touching, sharing, loving. His daughters, in contrast, seemed downright cold and rejecting. I took it personally and wondered why my undemonstrative husband got the warm attention and I did not. Years later, one of my stepdaughters explained. "We didn't know about loving, and you came on with hugs and affection. We just didn't know what to do." Both sets of children reacted to each of us just as they had toward their biological parents.

Children can react to new stepparents in ways that hurt deeply, and all the adults can do is be supportive. When stepchildren seem to dislike them, or are unappreciative of their efforts, stepparents may feel hurt; yet comparable behavior in their own children does not bruise them. When my sons said they didn't love me, I heard the voice of their anger; but when my stepdaughters said they hated me, I cringed.

Still another reason prevents identical love feelings toward natural children and stepchildren: biology. Some psychiatrists say it is impossible to love your own child and a child who is not your own in exactly the same way because a step relationship lacks the biological bond that is critical to acceptance. Many adoptive parents struggle with developing feelings for the child they longed for so desperately. Some who adopt older children never can overcome the problem, and many of these children are returned to agencies.[6] Even in biological relationships, many a mother with a newborn feels guilty when she does not experience an instant rush of love toward her own child.

The importance of early parent-child bonding has become recognized in the medical world. It began with classes in natural childbirth and has extended into the delivery room as father and mother stroke their helpless newborn to create strong emotional bonds. Pediatrician T. Berry Brazelton at the Harvard Medical School in Boston prepares couples to establish intimate bonds with their infants.[7]

This secondary bonding takes place soon after birth. But even before that, a primitive bonding takes place during pregnancy as a mother feels attachment to the fetus. This tie between mother and child is the beginning of acceptance and love. Bonding is a psychobiological process different from loving. Some mothers reject their infants during pregnancy, and some adoptive mothers feel something closely akin to a biological bond. But because this strong natural bonding happens with biological children, yet cannot occur between stepparents and stepchildren, it is normal to love them differently.

Bonding works both ways. Stepchildren never feel quite the same toward their stepparents because this process never occurred between them. And stepparents often feel guilty over the discrepancy between what they think they should feel and what they actually feel. This is not to say that love between stepchildren and stepparents does not occur. It does, and deeply so. But it takes time, acceptance, and patience to develop.

Patience was hardly one of my virtues. I expected to love my stepdaughters as I did my sons, and I expected the love to be returned. Instead, all I succeeded in doing was to create a severe conflict in my head and heart.

With no understanding of bonding or the instant-love myth, my difficulty with accepting my stepdaughters continued on an unconscious level. Years later in a psychology class I read Carl Rogers's theory about acceptance and how positive regard affects a person's self-image. "A threat exists when a person perceives there is an incongruity between some experience and his self-concept," my textbook stated.[8] This explanation accounted for my anxiety and that of the girls. Still, events had to get worse before the incongruity was identified.

Severe anxiety attacks finally forced me to acknowledge that something was awry. What I thought ought to be, what Rogers calls an *ideal self*, did not measure up to what I thought I was. I said I loved the girls, because if I was to be their mother, I ought to. But I was unable to feel the way I knew a mother did, the way I did about my biological sons. Because I thought something was wrong with me, I became defensive. My behavior affected my stepdaughters' actions and they reacted to me with their own defenses: lying, sneaking, denying.

The grave mistake of trying to replace their biological mother had revealed its destructiveness. But after I worked with a counselor, an awareness began to end my anxiety—at least with one of the girls. And as Rogers explains, positive regard is a reciprocal process. When I stopped putting conditions on caring about Brenda and began accepting her for the fine person she was, she began to drop her defensive ways. In turn, I began to feel more positive toward her, and she toward me, until eventually our relationship grew into a loving one.

Neither biology nor bonding dictated it. It was special because we worked hard at it. And working at it taught us a great lesson: that all other things in this world can be bought, bartered, or stolen; but love has to be earned.

Stepparents must not feel guilty if love for their stepchildren does not develop. Or vice versa. Even in a nuclear family, children are not all loved the same, psychologist Irene Goldenberg explains. "These stepfamily loving problems are similar to those in a large family where one child is given more attention because of illness, or looks, or intelligence," she says. "Neither parents nor stepparents apportion their time and emotions equally. Not everybody needs the same amount of love and care at the same time. But it is important that nobody just drops through the cracks."

CHANGING THE STEPFAMILY'S SIZE

During the settling-in period, decisions about what stays and what goes may range from getting rid of a family dog that provokes allergies in a stepchild to choosing where to hang the paintings by the former spouse. Some decisions are more critical. A child may have to be shifted to the other parent, or the couple may decide to have a baby of their own.

As we tried to launch our new family, our most difficult decision centered on what to do with my stepson, who was not faring well in school or in the family. My inability to grow close to him heightened my tension and guilt, but problems with Kurt also meant learning blocks at school and sibling spats at home for him.

Some of our turmoil reflected a shift common in stepfamilies: the displacing of sibling position. Birth order is a salient psychological force in a child's development. It determines factors that range from guilt to achievement levels to occupational choices.[9] In his former family, Kurt was the youngest; when Walter and I married, Kurt became a middle child. Similarly my older son, Hopper, became a middle child in the new family. Research shows that parents award firstborn children a position of privilege, and Hopper had to yield it to his stepsister. No research has been done to explore the result of this sudden shifting of family position when stepfamilies form. But my own observations lead me to believe the effect is immense.

Kurt's adjustment troubles increased. He tried constantly to gain attention, by negative means if necessary. Frustrated by the disruptions he caused, and in an attempt to make him conform, his father punished him severely. This made him rebel even more. And the more he threatened our family stability, the more trouble he had in relating with any of us. Even his sisters withdrew. Kurt became the family scapegoat, and finally we realized that this eight-year-old could not survive in such a situation.

Until our family routine calmed, we found a foster family from our church to care for him. With two sons of their own and plenty of affection to go around, this fine family seemed like a positive temporary solution. But in a few weeks they called to say our son was too disruptive and we had to come and get him immediately. More disruption. Kurt was crying for help. Caught in the fallout of his parents' divorce, then submerged in the new family, he was lonely and lost. As for Walter and me, we were trapped in our own fears that the chaos meant our marriage was failing, and we were unable to help him.

Finally, in desperation, we asked his mother to take him. Sending him to his mother reflected our feelings of failure; it also meant our family shape would change and we would become a part-time stepfamily. When my first part-time stepparenting relationships ended, I promised myself I would never do it again. The movement of children back and forth between two families can be disruptive and difficult; having Walter's children and mine living with us eliminated that conflict. In asking Kurt's mother to take him, I broke my vow and again became a part-time stepparent.

But most threatening to me was that the children's mother was back in our lives. Soon telephone calls and child-support checks confirmed it. There was no denying her existence now; and, as the girls whom I had claimed as my daughters entered adolescence, my anxiety about my part in their lives increased.

Although shifting a child to the parent without custody is not uncommon, it is rarely done without pain and guilt. Chaotic relationships between stepsiblings, between stepparents, or between biological parents can produce unbearable tensions, explains Dr. John Visher. Many times painful choices are made by adults as they try to preserve their relationship. "Occasionally, children are shifted back and forth between the parents a number of times, either at the insistence of the children or the wish of the parents," he cautions. "These youngsters usually become disenfranchised children needing professional help to gain a sense of self-esteem and an ability to have a close relationship with other people."

What is often overlooked in these shifts and can be damaging to the stepfamily is what the rejection of a child can do to the couple's own relationship. "It does something to how you feel about yourselves," Dr. Goldenberg says. "And that's expensive, especially for a woman who has been taught that nurturing children is part of her role. Few can do it without paying a great price."

I was one who could not. Even though I was unable to help Kurt, my guilt over his leaving grew deeper as the years passed. The decision to remove him from the confusion of our family was right; I know that today. But how poorly the transfer was managed was another matter. Only recently, as I began to rebuild my relationship with my stepson, did I learn its details, or at least how he perceived it. Years ago, because I felt ashamed of Kurt's leaving us, I asked my husband to handle it alone. And he simply didn't know how.

"I got separated, sent away," Kurt said, years later. "And Dad never explained it to me, none of it, ever. What I remember was the first night when we visited that foster family's house and Dad asked if I would like to spend the night. I did, and it was fun. I liked them and they liked me. The next day, when Dad came by for what I thought was to pick me up, he asked how I would like to stay there a while. I don't know why, but I said yes, but we'd have to go get my clothes. Then he said, and this is the part I'll never forget, 'I have them in the trunk.' My heart sank to my feet. The decision was already made and I never had a choice. I couldn't understand why he did it, and I never asked him. I just stayed."

"Did you get along there?" I asked, recalling his stay to be less than six weeks.

"Mostly I was upset because when you would visit me, or take me places, I felt left out of the things you did as a family. I didn't have a family," he said.

"When you came back home, what happened?" I asked, recollecting the full-scale chaos as he returned to our confused family.

"I got sent to Mom," he said. "I'm glad it happened now. But I still remember feeling nervous about going there, and Dad didn't explain that move either. I felt kicked out of the family again. I got shuffled around so much that for a while I didn't believe my mother was my real mother. Getting adjusted was tough, but things got better."

As Kurt clarified what happened, I grew angry at his father. But how does a guilt-ridden parent who must let go of a child explain it well or kindly? How many parents could reject their children in anything like a proper way?

In *Your Child? I Thought It Was My Child* Nancie Spann shares the pain of letting her son go back to his father.

I, too, had a painful decision to make when I sent my Chris to live with his father several months after our divorce. Chris' behavior, in his confusion and frustration over the family's breakup, was taking its toll on the two younger siblings. Peter emulated his brother's negativism. They fought constantly. Even Ashley, as small as she was, was developing cranky habits. I was working long hours, running a household, trying to be a mother to a zoo act. Something had to change. So I sacrificed one child to save two.[10]

The scars of such trade-offs run deep. When I was a youngster, a similar shift happened to my teenage brother. Faced with the option of summering him on a farm or sending him to a detention camp, my parents opted for the farm. As he recalls it, he did not see the farm experience as an opportunity for a fresh start. Instead, he felt rejected and kicked out of the family. My parents probably had little choice but to remove him from our home; but as with Walter and me, I suspect that guilt affected their way of handling the shift. My brother still copes with his anger; and, although he has long since understood the necessity of such a move and forgiven my parents, he cannot forget it.

Simply removing a child from the family is not destructive, explains Dr. Goldenberg. "Returning a child to the other parent is not the problem; sending him there if the parent really doesn't want him or is not equipped to handle him creates the problems."

When a shift must be made, the way it is handled is as critical as the decision itself. Presenting the move in a positive way can lower a child's feeling of rejection and offer a fresh start. Examine the problems of the present situation with the child. Without making promises that cannot be met, talk about what opportunities may be gained in the new family. Above all, a child must not be made to feel as though the shift is just because of his behavior. A careful detailing of what is happening, and of when and why changes must be made, can reduce both the fears of the new situation and the feelings of rejection.

After the stepfamily repairs such ruptures, it begins to regain its balance. But after a brother or sister leaves the family, the remaining children need a secure emotional arena in which to develop without the fear that they will be the next to go.

TO HAVE OR NOT TO HAVE A NEW BABY

As some couples make custody changes to give children a chance at thriving in a different environment, other couples decide about a baby of their own—to have or not to have.

When a new love is shared, it is natural to want to express that love through a child. Many stepfamilies believe a new baby will strengthen the bond between them. In one aspect of sociologist Lucile Duberman's study, this belief was revealed as reality for the stepfamilies she interviewed. In remarriages in which couples chose not to have more children, 53 percent of the family members rated the stepparent-stepchild relationship as excellent; 19 percent rated the relationship between the two sets of children by former marriages as excellent. But in stepfamilies in which a baby was born, 78 percent rated the stepparent-stepchild relationship excellent and 44 percent said the same about the relationship between stepsiblings.[11]

This news should not serve as an edict for those on the fence to have another child. The Duberman study, undertaken in Cleveland, is the only extensive analysis of the relationships among remarrieds with children; but its random sample (eighty-eight couples) is small and the findings are out of date. More current family studies reveal that it is not marriage but parenthood that places severe stress on a relationship.[12] As women move into the professional world, the decision to have a child is weighed more carefully. Many young marrieds are asking, When baby makes three, can a marriage survive the raised stress level? Having a child may balance emotions and power within a stepfamily, but a baby will not necessarily make a shaky remarriage any better.

Still, for many remarrieds the answer is yes—especially for families in which the stepmothers have no children of their own. Their stepparenting task is difficult, because caring for other people's children generates few thanks and many negative feelings about themselves. With no children of her own, a stepmother has no parenting experiences on which to gauge failure or success. Young stepmothers begin by feeling incompetent; when they have difficulty in relating with their stepchildren, they wonder whether they *are* incompetent as parents and should never have children of their own.

I was a stepmother before I was a mother. At only twenty years of age I married Bill, who was fifteen years older, and became stepmother to his two daughters, who were so close in age as to make it difficult for me to gain their respect as a parental authority. But since I wanted children of my own, I practiced mothering eagerly, bumbling along, doing the best I could, often feeling misunderstood, unloved, even hated. Only when I began to rear my own sons did my self-esteem about parenting change. With my stepchildren, instinct had failed; but with my sons, it worked. At last I felt I was a good parent. And people said I was. Finally, my confidence in being a stepparent began to rise. This is not unusual: Success enhances self-esteem.

Until they had a child of their own, many stepmothers say their marriages seemed lacking. "When we had our baby, I eased up on my stepdaughter and stopped picking on her," admits a stepmother in New Jersey. "Maybe it was because I was busy with our new son, but I began to be more concerned with her feelings, too. That made her respond to me, and I felt better about myself."

The longing for another child in a stepfamily too often may be a one-sided matter. A husband who is already responsible for one set of children may not want another. My former husband would have been content to do without a second family, but he felt it was unfair to me. Even though our pair of sons thrilled him, the responsibility for two sets of children weighed heavily on him; and for years he worked at a job he hated because that was the only way he could manage to support two families.

Having another child is an important before-the-marriage discussion. If having a baby is part of one partner's hidden agenda at the time of marriage, there may be a child unwanted by one partner, or there may be a broken marriage because the other's needs cannot be met.

As reminders of past love bonds, stepchildren may speed up parental urges for the childless stepmother. As much as stepparents might enjoy their stepchildren, there is no forgetting that they represent an intimate union predating the present one. Competition emerges, if not to outdo the first wife's feat, at least to repeat it.

The cost of starting another family is heavy—not only economically but emotionally as well. Money and feelings entwine, and when child-support checks dent the family budget, many remarrieds are forced to put money before desires. But seldom without problems. A young black step-mother in Washington, D.C., got on fairly well with her stepson. As he summered with his father and stepmother, their relationship warmed—until the couple could not justify having their own child because of money. "Each check we sent his mother made me angrier at my stepson. I worked and still we could not afford our baby. I began to take it out on him when he visited. Then he withdrew from me." Finally, after the couple had a child, the stepmother's resentment dissolved. Her stepson lives with them now, and the smiles this teenager brings to his half-brother's face spread throughout the family.

Walter and I could have managed the economics of another baby. But the emotional strain of starting over was more than we could face. Diapers, playpens, and baby-sitters belonged to our past. I had gone back to school and my husband was considering a career change. We could not forfeit our future for another child. I had had a hand in rearing three sets of children, and enough was enough.

More important, since we still disagreed on how to rear those for whom we were responsible, how would a new addition fare? Our children had faced enough insecurities; a new baby might have height-ened their fears of being replaced. With only "mine" and "his," the bal-ance of power between the children remained equal. And for me, while coping with the guilt of my stepson's leaving our house, a new baby could never have been justified. My longing for a daughter continued. But had I borne a son, I would have been disappointed and my husband would have faced more guilt—rejecting one son for another. So although our children urged us to have a child, we agreed five was enough.

BUILDING STEPFAMILY TRADITIONS

Holidays should be joyful times, but as families come together they produce stress. Few married couples have escaped the argument as to with which parents they will celebrate the festivities. The stepfamily's widened sphere of relationships creates an even greater chance for stress because children may be expected to spend holidays with both families.

Moving between families means that youngsters can continue the tra-ditions of the old family at the same time that they discover new ones within the stepfamily. The two sets of traditions that are common to most stepfamilies can become the source of an exciting learning experience for both adults and children. But melding the two requires careful negotia-tion. In multicultural families, is Christmas or Hanukkah celebrated? Or both? I thought everyone expected that stockings would be hung on

Christmas Eve and gifts would be opened on Christmas morning, and that coloring Easter eggs was a family affair. But my new stepchildren expected to open gifts on Christmas Eve and assumed that a rabbit decorated the eggs.

The time when a stepfamily identity is being built offers a perfect time to establish new traditions. Often during the breakdown of former families, few joint activities continue. Creating new traditions provides good chances for the new stepfamily to gain a hold on intimacy.

At our house we made birthdays special. Besides the usual presents and privileges, the dining area was festooned, best dishes and linens came out, and the birthday person chose the menu. In contrast to Jeff's annual request for pizza, Bev's birthday dinner choice was prime ribs, artichokes, and angel food cake.

We made Halloween into a big event too. After a long drive to the pumpkin farm with an autumn picnic, each of us selected the perfect pumpkin. These were then carved during a family affair complete with popcorn and cider. When they were adorned with flash-bulb noses, yarn hair, and a potpourri of hats, the finished jack-o'-lanterns reflected our personalities as well as the fun we'd had.

As stepfamily traditions are being built, dilemmas can produce resentment. A tradition on my sons' birthdays had been to unpack their baby books filled with hanks of hair from their first haircuts, hospital ID bands, and snapshots of toddler birthday parties; and we reminisced about their earlier years. Because I had had no part in the childhood history of my stepchildren, nor did I have such a collection for them, I felt this display unfair and soon stopped it. But giving up a nice tradition hurt me.

Roots and memories are important, and sharing histories brings the stepfamily closer together. If baby books and mementos remain with the biological mother, a stepmother can reconstruct a history by gathering clips of achievements or snapshots from the father or from grandparents. Using this collection as a focus on a stepchild's birthday eliminates guilt and resentment, and a nice tradition is continued.

ALWAYS ANOTHER TEST

Settling in provides many tests. Meeting them depends on patience, tolerance, and honesty as bonds and boundaries inside and outside the stepfamily are tested time and time again. Finally family life begins to feel comfortable, good feelings abound, and survival seems certain.

But just as it seems as though the challenges are being squarely met, another test looms. When Brenda was fifteen, she came to me accusingly. "You don't love me the same way you do the boys." I held my breath. This was a turning point and I dared not deceive her or myself. My struggle with acceptance had been grave.

While I reexamined my feelings, I held her close. Because she fulfilled so many of the dreams of the daughter I never had, I had grown to love her deeply. Many of her traits reflected those I admired. She was an achiever; whether playing her trumpet or winning a tennis match, she did her best. She was assertive; even when risks made her unpopular, she spoke up for her beliefs. As for her sexuality, whether in jeans or in a dress her confidence as a person did not waver. She was responsible; after school and on weekends she baby-sat, cleaned house, or worked as a waitress, yet she managed relationships with friends and family. And she was independent; when her bike needed repair or a skirt had to be hemmed, she did it herself.

Could I have taken my pick for a daughter, this young woman would have fit the bill. And because I hadn't heaped my expectations on her as a toddler, she lacked my hang-ups. As she tested me, our relationship had had its ups and downs; but I knew that I loved her. Yet my emotional struggle with acceptance reminded me that this love was somehow different—not more or less, just different.

That is what I decided to tell her. "You're right, Brenda. I don't love you exactly as I do the boys. How could I? From the moment I first felt them move in me, I began to grow close to them. Nursing them drew the bond tighter. While I was caring for them as sick babies, patching their scratched knees, and watching them start school, we grew closer. They learned my values and ideas so I knew how to predict them. I am linked to them by a force stronger than I can explain. I cannot deny it. You did not come to me wrapped in a soft blanket, and I didn't get to enjoy your innocence as a baby. When we hooked up, you were already ten and pretty angry at people for messing up your life. It would be dishonest to say I love you exactly the same. But let me tell you this."

Then I recounted the traits about her that I had examined and admired, and I also explained why and how I loved her. "If I could ever have had a daughter of my own, I would have wanted her to be just like you. I love the boys because they are my sons. I love you because you are you."

What if a stepchild asks such a question of a stepparent who does not feel the way I did about Brenda? Whatever you say, above all, be truthful. Children see through adult insincerity in a hurry, and failing such a test can leave a permanent chasm in the trust relationship. All people, even those we dislike the most, have good qualities. Sometimes our own biases make them hard to discover, but delve. Hasty or insincere answers that cannot satisfy children only raise deeper doubts. Explain the bonding process that takes place in biological relationships, that took place with their own parent. Without jargon, it is so logical that children can grasp its meaning. Then elaborate on two or three positive traits in the child, building self-esteem.

Telling a lie about loving a stepchild is foolish and destructive. On the other hand, itemizing their good qualities can help children see themselves as likable. Because the test has been met with honesty, such an exchange can be the beginning of a sound relationship.

6 The Other Parent:
Friend or Foe

After years of hostile feelings, it was time to confront my husband's former wife.

But as I drove there, I thought maybe this meeting with her was going too far. For a week my stomach had ached. My nails were chewed. The night before I left, I dreamed the mother of the girls I had reared had carved me into little bits, both figuratively and literally. I awakened uncertain from a fitful sleep, and, driving the turnpike, I considered turning back. Was a visit with his former wife really necessary to the writing of my book?

For ten years, Laura (not her real name) and I had had what amounted to a nonrelationship. Other than a couple of brief meetings and politely aloof telephone conversations, we rarely acknowledged each other; yet the negative impact of this relationship on the children's lives was undeniable. At their urging, we decided to get together; and it was their letter-writing campaign that finally gave me the courage to make the visit.

One winter's day, Laura phoned. "You know, the more I've talked with the girls about all that has happened, the more I think you must be a decent person, not nearly as bad as I've made you out to be," she said. "Why don't you come and visit me sometime and we'll talk?"

To lighten our conversation and minimize the risk involved in such a potentially volatile visit, we joked about how nervous "our husband" would be. Beyond the uneasiness and the jokes, we agreed that the long overdue meeting was a good idea. Each of us had developed attitudes about the other that were based on secondary sources, and such a meeting would provide a way to get beyond the speculation about unanswered questions. Why did she hate me? Did she still love my husband? Why their inability to talk calmly with one another without belittling and name calling? What was the real reason behind her staying out of touch with the children? The more intrigued I became, the more apprehensive I felt. I decided to go.

Upon hearing of the meeting, the girls sent notes. "I wish you two had done something like this years ago," wrote Brenda.

"Mom's as nervous as you are," wrote Bev. "But it's important to all of us."

But as I drove along the turnpike, I questioned my decision. En route I stopped to have lunch with a friend who seemed amused and astonished at such a get-together. He asked me who I was going as.

"What do you mean?" I asked, thinking the visit sounded like a masquerade.

"I mean, what role are you going to play? The present wife? Her daughters' mother? A writer with notepad in hand? How about interested observer?"

This confusion already was one of my problems, and I had no idea where she stood about all this. I decided to go as only I could—as me. But I was nervous because the meeting was to be more than a coffee-klatch; I was to spend three days with this woman whose existence I had tried to deny, this woman with whom I had developed a competition that left me threatened.

By the time I drove toward her street, butterflies danced in my stomach. I would also encounter Kurt, the stepson I had rejected when he was a youngster. To have to face either the former wife or the young man would have been enough. But both of them would be there.

When the tall, svelte redhead opened the door and welcomed me into her handsome apartment, my intuition told me everything would be fine. But why couldn't she be sloppy and unkempt? I searched for a tangible reason to go on disliking her.

PARENTS DON'T DIVORCE CHILDREN

Beyond the new husband-and-wife relationship, the stability of the stepfamily hinges on how well the parent without custody accepts and is accepted by it. Since people divorce each other but not their children, this symbol of the former marriage remains a part of the stepfamily's relationship network. The former mate, in the case of divorce, is a living person with whom the spouse and the children will continue to interact.

Depending upon the quality of the relationship, this link between two families can pose a threat to the stepparent of the same sex, set up a competition, or create jealousy. Or, when the relationship with the other parent is friendly, the link can become a building block to the new step-family by extending a supportive web of love and opportunities for the children. As they go back and forth between the two families, the children can draw strength from both without loyalty conflicts that diminish their sense of worth. And, at ease in two homes, children can learn extra skills, values, and attitudes to help them become better-adjusted adults.

The way children see the adults in their complex family treat each other establishes patterns they will carry into their own lives. When the adults in both families treat each other with respect, they too can direct their energy toward strengthening the stepfamily.

Both interviews with stepfamilies and research with children of divorce shows the relationship with the other parent to be a critical one that determines how well children adjust to the loss of one family and to the building of the stepfamily. The attitudes of both former spouses were found to affect the stepfamily in the Cleveland study on reconstituted families by sociologist Lucile Duberman. Ex-wives may directly influence the children to reject their father and new stepmother; and, indirectly, a former wife may cause the second wife to be jealous. Former husbands who resent losing control of rearing their children may fail to maintain strong relationships with them or may mail late child-support checks.[1] Money is often used as a control device between the two families. One stepmother told me her new husband made her write the support checks each month "because it janged up his former wife" to see the new wife's signature where hers used to be.

Negative feelings toward former spouses actually increase once women remarry, discovered sociologist William J. Goode in his study of divorced women. He suggests that this happens because the women compare their ex-spouses to their new husbands, and the ex comes up short. Goode also found that the remarried women felt themselves in a better position to deal with their former husbands' power plays with the children.[2]

Both the Goode and Duberman studies reveal that the former husband's influence is minor. More than half of Duberman's subjects felt indifferent toward the former husband, and only 29 percent said he had a negative effect on their stepfamilies. But husbands feel differently. A total of 41 percent reported negative feelings about the ex-wife and her influence on the man's relationship with the children.[3]

In our stepfamily, the relationships with former spouses were both ways: one friend and one foe. Our interactions with them reflected research findings and greatly affected our children's lives. After my former husband, Bill, and I altered our relationship with each other, he became a positive influence in our family. But that never happened with Laura and Walter, and their unresolved hostility affected both the children and the way she and I felt about each other.

The negative feelings that Laura and I held toward one another were rooted in the relationship with the children's father, but we reacted somewhat differently. I kept her at an emotional distance by pretending that she was not a part of our lives, that she did not exist, that she was unimportant once she left. Her reaction toward me was best described as hostile. Part of her dislike for me I accepted as being the way society expects ex-wives to act—and, as compared to my former husband's first wife, Laura was downright friendly. From what Bill had said, his ex-wife refused to utter my name and referred to me as "The B." Still, in contrast to some remarrieds I interviewed, both my relationships with former wives have been neutral. Some people told tales of former wives ranting, screaming obscenities, depriving the children of visits at whim, making demands, and manipulating the stepfamily until fathers could visit their children only in the ex-wives' homes.

It never came to this extreme with Laura and me. Most of the anger that she unloaded on the children was over Walter, and although she occasionally called me names or put me down, usually that happened only when she drank. But why, after I had spent ten years rearing her children, was she hostile toward me at all?

My pretense about her existence was both emotionally tricky and costly to maintain. Keeping the former wife at a distance was possible because of geography; it became necessary because of my illusions about her daughters. Before Walter and I were married she had moved across country, and for nearly three years Laura remained out of touch with our new family. That suited me fine because, with her physically out of the picture, denying her existence became easier.

However, keeping Laura at a distance emotionally was far more difficult. First of all, two of the children looked like her, and pretending this pair belonged to me was absurd. In other subtle ways, her absence strengthened her presence. She had left two of her paintings, and many of our merged household furnishings reflected her taste. The children carried her picture, and on birthdays and holidays when the phone rang and it was not she, their bitter disappointment was often displaced toward me.

I blocked this other woman from my mind and avoided talking about her, thus making it difficult for the children to resolve their own feelings about her. Soon we all avoided talking about her, and none of us dealt with our suppressed feelings. Although her absence satisfied Walter and me because it simplified our lives, it was not good for the children.

Denial messages are easily deciphered by stepchildren. When body language or tight facial expressions fail to mesh with what the stepparent says about the missing parent, children interpret this accurately. Saying nothing at all also says a great deal. Or stepparents may say nothing to the children, but may be overheard making cutting remarks about the absent parent. Soon the children also learn not to speak of that parent. As a first-time, part-time stepparent I was mindful of this problem. During summer visits, I made certain Bill's girls wrote weekly letters to their mother. See what a fine, secure stepmother I am to handle this so well, I thought then.

But the second time around, things were different. Maybe the change resulted from the hypocrisy I felt when I cajoled Bill's daughters into writing duty letters. But the real reason was that I never tried to be the mother of my first stepchildren, only their stepmother or friend. There was no need to deny their mother because she clearly remained in the picture and wrote and called them.

BUILDING AN ILLUSION

Such contact was not the case with the girls of my remarriage. When Laura chose not to remain in touch with her children, I read that as a signal for me to take over. Her absence—which we translated as indifference—coupled with my desire for daughters provided the sanction for my approach to my role as a stepmother the second time around. And it was the difference in approach that prompted my denial of this "other woman."

My competition with Laura stemmed from the conflict of knowing these girls were her daughters and wishing they were mine. Although I adored my sons, I was disappointed at not having a daughter. So marriage to a man who had two daughters seemed a dream come true. I decided to become their mother, introducing the girls as my daughters and treating them as such. If it is a joint decision, there is little harm in this and it provides a comfortable bond between stepparents and stepchildren. The trouble comes when stepparents try, as I did, to replace the biological parent.

Denial that we were a different kind of family also prompted this decision. It seemed logical to return to square one—to replace our broken families with a new one. And we shared the mistake of so many other stepfamilies when we tried to function like the nuclear family, which means *one* mother, *one* father, and children. That structural necessity provided yet another reason to look on these girls as my daughters.

But they belonged to another woman. As much as I tried to deny that reality, facts were facts, and eventually my self-deception created anxiety that pushed me toward confrontation. But by then, a pattern women learn as children repeated itself. It is at Mother's knee that we learn to compete with the other woman. It was Nancy Friday's chapter on competition in *My Mother, My Self* that encouraged me to confront issues that I had discounted as absurd.

Women compete poorly with other women because they have not learned how. While men learned to compete with other men in social situations from Little League to campus debating teams, women were taught to stifle it. Today we are learning its rudiments as a survival tool, but the lessons we learned as children remain poignant reminders that we are not number one. In spite of all we tell ourselves about our skills and strengths, competitive urges are frightening because we are reminded that we could be left for another woman.[4]

Discounting or outdoing the other woman reflects the subversive lesson we learn young. My mother rarely spoke of Lucy, my stepfather's former wife. But she might as well have, for when the subject came up, Mother's lips tightened and she quickly changed the subject. We are not told to hate, fear, or compete with the other woman, writes Friday. We are shown.

I learned the lesson well and did the same thing for my stepdaughters. My silence about their mother created a taboo subject, providing them with no outlet for talking about their feelings. My denial of her was heightened by her absence and by Walter's attitude toward her. Our uneasiness taught the girls to avoid talking about her, too. But their hearts were not silent.

In both marriages I competed with the former wife, as I believe many second wives do. When either husband spoke of his former wife in a negative way, I glowed, stored the data, and—no matter what—refused to repeat that trait. What they did well, I tried to do better. One sewed; I took tailoring lessons. One graduated from college as an adult; I repeated the feat, but all the while played Supermom and maintained a high grade-point average.

To top off my insecurities, the other woman in my life was a redhead. For many men, redheads are a favorite fantasy, as I was reminded not long ago when a male friend nearly drove into another car as he checked out a redhead who had caught his eye. "I can't resist them," he said, grinning.

In contrast to my short, stubby frame, Laura is tall. Like their mother, both Brenda and Bev are also tall, and one has magnificent red hair—constant reminders of my competition.

When stepchildren are the image of their missing parent, there is no denying that one's spouse had an earlier relationship with someone else and that their life together was not altogether miserable. A simple acceptance of that truth can reduce competitive urges, and much jealousy can be avoided by talking about these feelings. "I'm jealous of your ex-wife" was never a conversation opener I chose, but it should have been.

Competition between the stepparent and the biological parent of the same sex is active in the stepfamily. The prize is the love of the children. When such competition exists, sociologist Jessie Bernard suggests in her remarriage study, it is likely to be far more intense between a stepmother and a biological mother than between their male counterparts. This is because traditionally, for most women, motherhood has been a more vital experience than fatherhood has been for men. When a mother loses or yields custody of her children, her pride is damaged. The loss is equated with a slur on her character.[5]

In competing with the stepparent, the biological parent without custody is at a disadvantage. It is difficult to spend quality time with the children as a part-time parent, and once the child acquires a new stepparent, the biological parent's impact diminishes. To measure up to this threat, some feel compelled to fill visits with trips and treats so their children can view them as number one.

Competition for the girls' affections was at the core of my relationship with Laura. In other remarriages, the competition may be for the husband, especially when a divorce resulted from a triangle. The new wife may worry that she cannot keep the prize and the former wife may actually try to break up the remarriage. One former spouse said it was one thing to lose her husband to another woman, but to have her children like the competitor was an outrage.

Sometimes a stepmother's success with her stepchildren heightens the competition between the two women. It is difficult for a mother to accept that another woman is filling the role she considered hers alone—even when she was the one who chose to end her marriage.

When competition gets in the way, it is also difficult for stepparents to avoid being judgmental. Most stepmothers admitted they knew the former wife little if at all. One said she remained judgmental about any woman who could leave her children. "As I became a mother to her children, I wondered what kind of mother could settle for such minimal contact with her children. Later I understood. Here was a woman using all her resources and energy just to keep herself pulled together so she could work. There just wasn't anything left for the kids."

When her own marriage broke up over another woman, this once judging stepmother repeated the pattern and left two of her children with their stepfather, knowing full well the other woman might become her children's stepmother. Unlike Medea of Greek mythology, who killed her children rather than face that option, she said, "I have no reason to believe she won't do as good a job of raising them as I might. In fact, since she's younger, maybe she'll do better."

Those few stepmothers I interviewed who were able to talk with the ex-wife and deal with their competitive feelings said they had healthier relationships with their husbands and with their stepchildren. As more and more fathers take custody of their children, too few stepmothers have positive words about the mothers of the children they rear. Although they insist that they merely echo the words of their husbands, those words are not uncommonly embellished with the competitiveness that eats at the stepmothers.

The responsibility for reducing competition lies with both remarriage partners. Just as hiding one's feelings can damage a relationship, unaltered former relationships can fuel one's insecurity. Unchecked competition can foster jealousy, an emotion that most people experience at one time or another.

An attractive Sacramento stepmother recalls the first time she met her new husband's ex-wife. "I was sweating down to the waist and she looked as cool as could be, wearing shorts and throwing her gorgeous legs around. I was sick. The only thing I could find wrong with her was that she wore too much eyeliner." Jealousy of the former wife never stopped, she admitted, until the day she made *longevity*. "When I had been married to my husband for eight years—as long as she had—somehow it all became different. At last I felt secure and unthreatened."

Most theorists agree that jealousy has two basic components: a feeling of battered pride and a sense that one's rights have been violated. Margaret Mead observed that the shakier a person's self-esteem, the more vulnerable one is to jealousy.[6] Battered pride, shaky self-esteem, and loss of rights are the fallout of hostile divorces. When the hostility filters into the stepfamily, competition and jealousy can reach all-time highs.

Jealousy is a human frailty we prefer to think of as beneath us. Who, me? Jealous? Ridiculous. Yet in the wake of jealousy, competitive urges rise full throttle; so do insecurities that provoke destructive questions. Was she more desirable? A better wife? A better mother? Such questions are rooted in competition. Jealousy wears many masks, but all forms conceal the same poison: Seeking to preserve love, it destroys trust and creates hatred and ugliness.

EMOTIONAL HANGING ON

The problems that affect children's relationships with their biological parents belong to the adults. Had my husband resolved his relationship with Laura, he would have been more comfortable in their later dealings; and had he and I talked of her, I would have felt less threatened.

The relationship between Laura and me remained cool because I was insecure and she was angry at Walter because she believed he had not dealt with her fairly during their divorce. She reflected her anger in putdowns to the children.

One of the cruelest ways for former spouses to get back at each other is through their children. Not only are the children used as camp spies, bargaining tools, or victims, but they are also compelled to listen to harangues and putdowns about the missing parent.

Throughout my growing years my mother reminded us that my father drank, beat her, ran with other women. I never could understand her need to rehash these unpleasant truths. To justify the divorce? To make my stepfather look better? This tearing down of my father made me obsessed with finding him. When at eighteen I finally did, I learned that much of what my mother had said was true. But for years later I felt resentful and angry at my mother because there was another side to my father that she had not told us about.

The children are not the only losers in these squabbles. Parents who use their children as a means of hurting their former mates hurt themselves as they distress the children they love. Not only did I resent my mother's reports about my father, no matter how truthful, but I also developed a negative feeling about myself. As children will do, when she recited chapter and verse about my father's badness, I interpreted that as meaning I must be bad, too. After all, I was part of him. Maybe if I had been better, he would not have left, I reasoned, as my guilt over the divorce grew deeper.

One painful profit of being a child of divorce is learning lessons to carry to adulthood—more and more often to stepparenthood. Because I remembered how it hurt me to hear my father torn apart, I tried not to malign my former husband, or our daughters' mother.

But when anger surfaces, silence is difficult, and sometimes I failed. For a time, Bill salved his ego by dating women the age of his daughters and then boasting of his prowess in bed with them. After he decided not to work again, which meant no more child support, neither Walter nor I appreciated his reports of trips and good times. I felt guilty that my new husband was compelled to support my sons. Frankly, I also felt jealous and angry; both the other parents were footloose and free, whereas I was rearing four children—two of them angry because their father was gone, and the other two angry because their mother was gone.

But airing unpleasantnesses about Bill to appease my anger could only harm our sons and ultimately damage my relationship with them. My silence paid off. And later, as our relationship improved, our behavior demonstrated to our children that divorced people do not have to hate each other.

Restraint provides another reward: It permits parents to retain their dignity. When parents defame their former mates, they actually erode the respect they command from their children. Oddly enough, children tend to idealize the absent parent, and putdowns simply double the pain.

Even when the other parent seems removed from their lives, many children daydream that their parents will one day reunite. Our girls recall the battle ending their parents' marriage, the telling-the-kids scene, and their mother's leaving the house with her belongings. But they always expected that she might return—perhaps because of what their parents implied as they tried to lighten the shock of the divorce, or because of what the parents failed to tell them, or because of their own fantasies about reuniting their parents.

Some youngsters go to great lengths to try to pull off reunions. Witness one eight-year-old boy who lived with his father. The man lived with a woman in a situation that provided far more stability for the boy than he could have had if he had stayed with his mother, an alcoholic who had a hard time keeping a job. When the couple married, the boy and his new stepmother got along well. But whenever the boy visited his mother, she put down the new wife and told her son that were it not for the stepmother, his father and mother would be together again.

Because of his intense desire to have his biological parents together, this youngster set about trying to reunite them. He antagonized his stepmother. He rebelled. He made the situation so impossible that to save her marriage, his stepmother insisted that he be moved out of the family. This manipulated child lost twice.

One former wife whose fantasies centered on reunion admitted that even after ten years she still loved her ex-husband, long since remarried. While she waited out the time until his return she developed only superficial relationships, mostly with married men. Her lingering hostility toward her husband for remarrying made life difficult for the children and the new stepmother, whom this woman could only see as an intruder. As for her former husband, he has made it plain that he would never return to her, not even if his present marriage were to fail. Yet this woman clings to her fantasies and shuts out the possibility of happiness.

My husband and his former wife never dealt with the anger and resentment that led them to court. Their hostility surfaced whenever they had to communicate about money and the children, and rarely could they talk without yelling. Even after twelve years they remained emotionally entangled.

I'm well aware that feelings are not dissolved by a court decree, because for nearly three years after I married Walter, I remained emotionally attached to my sons' father. Although we had agreed to maintain friendly relations for the sake of the children, we were edgy in our dealings with each other. Time helped, but we could have speeded up the process by talking about his anger at me for hurting him and my anger at him for neither understanding nor forgiving.

Fear finally prompted our emotional divorce. When I was informed that Bill was to undergo heart surgery, I recalled the many differences we had left unresolved. He had survived a similar operation during our marriage; would he survive this one? Or would I be left with an enduring sense of guilt? I explained to my husband that I had to go to Bill, to talk.

Bill survived the surgery, and we got our chance to talk. Only then did we come to understand that, just as it takes two people to make a marriage work, it also takes two to break it apart, and there was no single guilty party. Reducing our guilt made it easier to step back and survey what we retained in common that was important—our sons and our respect for each other.

Although I still cared for this man, I began to understand the nature of that feeling and to rid myself of my guilt over being married to one man while caring for another.

Once I was free from this emotional entanglement, the competition between Bill and Walter diminished, and their relationship took on a new warmth. The real winners were our sons.

Summer visits now took on a new pattern. Instead of flying the children to the West Coast and rushing with them from Disneyland to Marineland to the San Diego Zoo, Bill began to summer with us in upstate New York. Our more traditional neighbors raised their eyebrows, but the results of this arrangement made it all seem worthwhile. On their own turf, the boys now were able to share their day-to-day life with their father.

I recall the summers when Bill's daughters used to visit us. While he worked, it was my duty to entertain them. We tramped from the swimming pool to the shopping center to the movies, until by the end of the summer we were all exhausted and resentful, waiting out the last few days until each of us could return to normal living. But when Bill came to New York, that fatigue merry-go-round was stopped. He and the boys fished, biked, hiked, raked the lawn, worked in the garden, and got to know one another. Such an arrangement also meant yet another bonus: Walter and I could take a holiday.

Was Walter more mature, less jealous than I, to handle the other man in the house? Not until it was obvious that my emotional ties to Bill had ended did Walter cease to feel jealous. Before that, our defensive behavior toward one another fueled the competition, and Walter insisted that mementos of the past—from inscribed Christmas tree ornaments to the blue Mustang that Bill gave me—had to go. After he felt less threatened, it was he who suggested that Bill stay with us, he who drank cocktails with him. And when Bill brought several of his newest paintings for our family, it was Walter who suggested that one was perfect for our bedroom and mounted it on our wall. But none of this could have happened until Bill and I had severed our emotional ties.

Although having two husbands in the house created some tension, more often it was a source of amusement. When the boys would preface a comment with "Dad," and both stepfather and father would answer, we all laughed. But oh how lucky we were that we could laugh, for in their comfort with both men who cared about them, our sons could be free of loyalty conflicts.

Admittedly, such a relationship is unusual. For some it may sound radical, indeed impossible. For others, this civilized arrangement may be appealing. But in order for such a situation to be feasible, the former relationship must be altered. And this, as was said earlier, is most effective before the remarriage.

The real winners are the children who can see their parents acting as mature adults. A black teenager in Washington, D.C., told me that when his mother comes to visit from the Midwest, she and his stepmother greet each other with hugs. He feels good about this, he says, because he loves them both and doesn't feel caught in the middle the way he once did. And the stepmother says that since she's gotten to know the boy's mother, she feels less jealous and better about herself.

For my stepdaughters, unfortunately, such a warm relationship never came to be between their father, their mother, and me. My insecurities caused me to feel jealous; but as every phone call between Walter and

Laura degenerated into another argument, I knew the blame belonged to all of us.

Their battles continued. So did the conflict in my stepdaughters' feelings toward their mother: loyalty and abandonment, love and rejection. The dichotomy confused the youngsters. My sons had few doubts that their father loved them, because although he lived a continent away, his presence affected them in a positive way. He refused to lavish gifts on them to buy their love, but he called and he wrote, often embellishing his notes with his drawings.

In contrast, the girls had little contact with their mother, and when she did get in touch they were left with explanations that failed to satisfy them. Our daughters could not understand why, if our family could have such a warm relationship with Bill, we could not have an equally warm relationship with Laura. Her presence was as strong as Bill's, but in a dissimilar way.

COMFORTING STEPPARENTS

It is difficult for stepparents to tell their stepchildren that a parent who does not come around or even keep in touch still loves them. According to psychologist Irene Goldenberg, stepparents must avoid concocting dishonest stories about the parent who has dropped out of a child's life just to ease a child's pain. She suggests explaining that the parent's absence probably has little to do with the child. A missing mother may think she was not a good parent or may think she made a bad decision, from which she is now hiding with her guilt. The only person who can satisfy a child of divorce that the missing parent still loves him or her is that parent—by reestablishing some sort of relationship with that child.

Understanding stepparents can provide an arena in which stepchildren can vent their feelings about their missing parent, freely and without threat. That missing parent still plays an important role in the stepchild's life, and whether the parent died or lost custody in a divorce action or walked out of the child's life, the child needs to deal with the feelings that surround the situation. A mature tolerance on the stepparent's part can help a new stepchild to deal with these feelings, and such an understanding can help cement the bonds of the new step relationship.

When parents and stepparents avoid talking about the parent without custody or skirt questions about that parent, children may conjure up their own ideas of what happened. As a youngster, I did. If children are allowed to develop invalid ideas about their other parent, they will later have to unravel these misperceptions. The child who has experienced a broken family has two options: to work it out in bits and pieces in the environment of the new stepfamily, or, as I did, to work it out years later with a variety of counselors.

When Laura stayed out of touch with the children during those early years, I was grateful. At that time my gratitude was rooted in my own insecurity and immaturity. But as I matured, acknowledging her existence and importance became critical to the well-being of the children I had grown to love. Continuing to keep her out of our lives would have been easier—many stepparents agree on that. But I began to recall the gnawing ache of wondering about my own father when I was a young stepchild.

Throughout my adolescence, questions about his exodus from my life fueled my desire to find him. Why did he leave me? What was he like today? Did he care for me at all? My longing to know my father led me to encourage my teenage stepdaughters to get in touch with their mother so they could avoid the confusing emotions I have endured.

REOPENING DORMANT RELATIONSHIPS

Eventually, each of the girls established a relationship with her mother. One summer Bev lived with Laura, and when Brenda was fifteen, she got in touch with Laura. Because they feared rejection, the visits were tense times that often started with hostility toward me. As they packed their bags, they seemed to need to start an argument with me so as to leave bad feelings behind. But the visits ended with their sharing the fun they had had in rebuilding their relationships with their mother.

At times I felt more jealous than ever. As Bill had done with our sons, Laura shopped with the girls and played with them; but the responsibility of parenthood ultimately was mine. Even though I understood her need to compensate during the visits, I felt cheated and shortchanged. The other woman was definitely back in our lives—in conversation, communication, and contact. During insecure times I'm inclined to wish it had never happened; but as I suspected then, and I know now, that is the way it must be.

Sometimes stepfamily configurations change. Custody may be altered, or as children grow and develop they may want to live with the biological parent of their own sex. While changes may or may not be welcomed by the stepparent, most of them create apprehension because for the stepfamily they mean a good deal of shifting and adjusting to accommodate the new person.

A stepmother in Vermont had been married to her husband fourteen years when his seventeen-year-old daughter phoned him in the hospital after his heart attack. After this first contact with her father since the divorce, the stepmother invited the girl to visit. "I was anxious to find out what kind of a little gal she was and I knew it was important to her father. During that call she was so scared and crying, but she said yes and came. A couple of times later she returned and we have had fun. But now I am terrified she wants to come and live with us, and I don't want her to. Our lives are very different from that of the mother who raised her, and having her live with us would make things difficult for our marriage relationship. None of us gets along with her mother. I don't know what to do. I feel selfish for not wanting her, but I'm too ashamed to tell my husband."

Reopening dormant relationships with the other parent takes courage on everybody's part. Basically, it involves the management of fears: Children who have felt abandoned may fear more rejection; parents who have avoided dealing with their children may feel guilty; and stepparents may feel threatened by the introduction of the other parent into their family system. Such feelings are valid and very real to the person experiencing them, but once examined they can be overcome.

As stepchildren learn to cope with two sets of family relationships, manipulating the two can become a favorite ploy. When conflicts arise at one house, they call the other to repeat the stories, embellishing them through tears. As our daughters rebuilt a relationship with their mother, this was not uncommon, and Laura began to view us as ogres. Sometimes I wished she had not come back into our lives.

In her writing about the stepchild, Anne Simon quoted a psychiatrist who said, "Stepmother-love is tested by its capacity to recognize the importance of mother-love and the ability to let mother-love flourish unimpaired by rivalrous action. However delightful the scene the stepmother paints, it is . . . constructed not by the child's need, but by the woman who wished to replace the husband's first wife in the ultimate act of becoming her children's mother. It is for herself that she loves the child . . . and this is not true caring."[7] The words are blunt, the impact painful. But if stepparents would accept that truth, unnecessary competition and guilt would cease. When Walter and I were married I read Simon's book, and although many sections bear penciled notes and marginal comments, the page with this quote appears as clean as it was when the book was taken from the vendor's shelf. Maybe I missed it. More likely, I was not ready to hear its truth.

Recapturing the entire three days of my visit with my husband's former wife is unnecessary. After a few hours with Laura, I realized that I could in no way intrude my professional tools into this intimate time. During the sharing of anger, guilt, fear, and resentment, I could not have taken out my notebook or used my tape recorder.

We talked as friends rather than foes and got to know each other somewhat. Brenda and Bev often said we were vastly different; my husband agreed. But as the visit progressed and our defenses were lowered, I noted many similarities. Both of us came from low-income, broken families, and neither of us had had a secure childhood. Both of us were led to believe that marriage and motherhood would fulfill us; when they did not, both of us chose to go to college.

Today it is Laura I have to thank for keeping me from repeating a pattern she and many other women chose in the late sixties during a time of rapid social change. Laura broke from her domestic role, finished college, and left her children with their father so that she could pursue her career goals and search for her identity. The closer I came toward my degree, and the more I talked with other women who had shed their mates in search of themselves, the more I was convinced that leaving my family was part of the process.

That I did not leave cannot all be chalked up to wisdom. Some of my reluctance was grounded in fear, guilt, and the horror of another failed marriage. And by then I had emotional investments in two sets of children, both of whom had been through divorce. To add yet another divorce to their lives meant more guilt. My second thoughts about the decision centered on Laura. After the girls reestablished a relationship with their mother, they shared with me how she was handling her decision over yielding custody of her children. I knew that I could never survive the guilt either.

Laura's guilt showed up in nail biting, heavy drinking, and overwork. Research has revealed that even mothers who voluntarily give up their children because of economics or the knowledge that they disliked motherhood, and can justify to themselves the wisdom of their decisions, are unprepared emotionally for the guilt that often consumes them. After careful consideration, a Rochester, New York, mother decided to relinquish her eight-year-old daughter to her husband. Now this mother says, "My guilt was not centered on giving up my daughter as much as on my failure to be the kind of mother I should be. And my family and friends and others compounded my guilt when they showed their disapproval and blamed me for what I did."

Society's disapproval forces some women to hide, discovered a University of Southern California graduate student who tracked down more than a hundred mothers who had given up custody of their children. Most kept the decisions secret; one never told her parents. Most of them had married young and had been unprepared for motherhood, but as they coped with their guilt, rationalization was their common refuge.[8] Like many of the women in the study, Laura maintains that Walter took the children because he was angry over the divorce. But she also says she left the marriage in the hope that she would find an identity of her own beyond that of Walter's wife or the children's mother. She says she would probably do the same thing over again. "But this time, I'd leave from a position of strength and not burn all the bridges behind me."

Laura and I were alike in other ways. Both of us were late bloomers professionally. We both had problems in dealing with people that stemmed from our having felt rejected as children, but we handled these problems differently. I was eager for reassurance and approval, so I surrounded myself with people. She sought to avoid being hurt again, so she built a defensive wall around herself to keep people out. Although we differed vastly in our way of dealing with people, values, and beliefs, enough of us was mirrored in the other to form the basis for a rapport.

I liked the woman I was supposed to hate.

LOWERING GUILT AND RESENTMENT

The poignant visit was the beginning of important resolutions in our family relationships. When I discovered she was not angry at me, but at Walter, my defenses lowered and we talked about common feelings and how they had affected us. Two significant issues Laura and I dealt with reflected a common theme in stepfamilies. If stored in the human heart, guilt and resentment can do more damage to the vessel in which they are contained than toward the person for whom they are intended.

Guilt had nibbled at both of us until our feelings of self-worth were low. Until we began to talk, she had no idea that I shared a sense of guilt over her girls. Not only had I tried to deny her and claim them as my daughters, but I had failed to be the perfect parent I thought I could be. Now, as we talked, the source of that guilt seemed so funny that it made us laugh. What parent does not yearn for a chance to do it over? But I shared more with her—how it hurt to have the girls leave home in such a disruptive state, and how ashamed I felt at being unable to accept her daughters without trying to change them. Neither cause deserved the amount of guilt I had allowed to consume me, we agreed. Her eyes moistened and she said, "I'm sorry you had to raise my children. I had no idea it would be so hard, and I could have made it easier for you."

Cooperation between the stepfamily and the other parent is critical to relationships within both sides of the family. It also affects how the individuals feel about themselves.

Cooperation is linked to control. This issue affects both sides of the stepfamily and centers mostly on the children. Often when Bill saw how Walter disciplined our sons, he left the house and went for a walk because the solutions were so foreign to his notion of how his sons should be reared. Yet because he had yielded control he refused to intervene and cause more trouble. But not all parents without custody see it that way. Laura did not.

Some of Laura's resentment resulted from major decisions we had made about the children without consulting her. We had decided, for example, to have Bev attend boarding school to eliminate a triangle between us during her adolescence. Another decision was to put Kurt on tranquilizers. "His learning problem was dyslexia," she cried. "But the psychologist told us he was hyperactive," I said defensively. Although I know now that too many children with emotional problems are dosed with tranquilizers, in the chaos of establishing our new family we failed to question the expert's advice. When Kurt went to live with his mother carrying with him a bottle of pills and a prescription for more, she was furious.

At the time, there seemed little question about control and decision making. She had moved, so why consult her? But she felt differently, and looking back with a new awareness of what is best for these complicated relationships, so do I.

The more space, emotionally and geographically, that parents without custody create between themselves and their children, the less control they can expect to have over their children's lives. On the other hand, those who refuse to let the stepparent become a significant part of their child's life must analyze their desire for control in the stepfamily. Is such holding on reflecting a sincere concern for their children, or an unresolved relationship?

Sometimes a new husband justifies his excessive concern over his former wife's emotional and financial affairs as necessary for the children's well-being. When pressed, one former husband admitted, "I probably do too much for my kids and ex-wife, but I feel so guilty about leaving them. Yet I was so unhappy, I could stay no longer." Attempts to assert control over the stepfamily for reasons beyond the children's interests exert great pressures on it.

One control link is the check for child support. For some fathers without custody, money is the only way they retain a relationship with the children. Echoing the feelings of many, one father has repeatedly asked his children to write or even call collect, but unless he mails the check late or the kids need something, he hears nothing from them. "I feel like a forgotten uncle waiting for Christmas to roll around so I can send presents," he laments. "I feel lonely and left out, and I miss raising my kids." His resentment over losing control of his children's lives continues, and if his ex-wife remarries before he resolves his feelings, the relationship between father and stepfather probably will be tense.

Other attempts at control between the stepfamily and the other parent can include presents, telephone calls, and letters. Overindulgent gift giving can create hard feelings and competition, and the two families need agreed-upon limits on gifts. If a child's bike is stolen because he left it carelessly on the sidewalk, his stepfather may refuse to replace it and insist that the child earn most of the money to buy a new one. During a weekend visit, the child laments his loss to his biological father, who delivers him home with a new bicycle. In his eagerness to meet his son's need and appease his own guilt, the father undermines the stepfamily's efforts to teach the boy responsibility.

One stepmother and her husband agreed that their Christmas present to his young sons who lived with them would be a trip to Disneyland. Only a few small gifts would be under the tree. "Wow, Disneyland," exclaimed the excited children. "The best present ever." Not quite. Just before they left, the express truck delivered their mother's gifts: an expensive minibike for the seven-year-old and another costly toy for the two-year-old. After the trip, the boys declared they liked their mother's present best. This is the way that resentment toward the other parent builds, along with a strong competitive urge.

Many former spouses control by telephone, calling in the middle of the night over incidents that could wait—report cards, invitations to school plays, decisions about camp. Then there are letters. When Laura once interfered where I felt she should not have done so, I wrote her. Many stepmothers who have difficult relationships with former wives said that out of sheer frustration over roles and decisions having to do with control, they had mailed similar letters. Each got the same response as I—more hostility and resentment.

When the urge arises to compose brilliant edicts to former spouses, don't yield. While wearing the guise of being written for the sake of the children, most such letters take a holier-than-thou attitude. Tainted with proselytizing and power plays, they serve only as a nettle in an already tender relationship. Except to start a war-by-mail, such monologues may actually thwart all efforts at a beneficial dialogue with the other parent.

The issue of control is complex. No clear-cut answers exist about how much control the other parent should have in the stepfamily's decision making. One thing has become clear. The psychological implications of being out of touch with a biological parent are long term, and researchers are only beginning to study the consequences. From my experiences as a stepchild and as a stepparent, I have little doubt that to keep their identity intact, children need a healthy contact with both biological parents. When this is maintained, the children can accept authority in both homes, be defensive about neither, and grow up feeling like more than mere survivors. But in order for them to absorb the best of both worlds, the two families must cooperate.

Concerned parents who want to remain a part of their children's lives are turning to alternative custody arrangements—split custody or joint custody, for example. And today, attorneys and the courts have become sensitized to the emotional complexities surrounding these needs. In the conciliation court in Los Angeles in 1980, one in every five custody cases ended in a plan for joint custody, a pioneer plan to keep both parents active in a child's life.[9] If a divorced couple can be united enough in expectations and requirements about the children to write such an agreement at the time of their divorce, fewer conflicts will be left for the stepfamilies to face. And when both sets of parents can agree upon and define issues, children are less able to manipulate either family.

But if parents could not get along before the divorce, ask the foes of such an arrangement, what will make a difference afterward? Some suggest that agreement is all but impossible. The authors of *Beyond the Best Interests of the Child* believe that control needs to be in the hands of one parent with custody, even to the extent of that parent's deciding whether the other is to be allowed to have visiting rights.[10] This position is somewhat softened in a later book, this one entitled *Before the Best Interests of the Child*. But one of the authors, Dr. Albert J. Solnit, a child psychiatrist and psychoanalyst, argues that by definition joint custody cannot be the best arrangement for the child. It is important for children to know there is one adult who will be responsible for them—an anchor. Joint custody, he believes, provides only two half anchors.[11]

Those who support joint custody as a stabilizing influence on a child's life ask whether any single parent with custody can be relied on to make all the right decisions for the child. Melvin Roman, a professor of psychiatry at the Albert Einstein College of Medicine of Yeshiva University, says he believes that half of all divorced couples could work out such an arrangement if they had the proper counseling.

The benefits of joint custody for the new stepfamily become obvious. When parents have worked out the detailed arrangements and agreements about their children that complicated joint custody plans require, the usual hostility that sets up competition, guilt, and resentment is diminished, if not resolved.

Along with our guilt, Laura and I shared resentments. She resented me for rearing her daughters; I resented her freedom to pursue her new career while I reared them. As far as I could see, she had the better deal and I resented her status—until once when I remarked about this to my former husband. I told Bill I coveted his freedom and Laura's as the parents without custody to play and escape from childrearing duties. His sad blue eyes pierced me before he said quietly, "You have no idea what you are talking about. I would have given anything to raise my sons and daughters, and I'll bet she feels the same way. If I could ever have done one thing differently in my life, it would have been that."

But as one stepmother in downstate New York said, "There's no justice. She left her kids, is off traveling and working, and I get the day-to-day drudgery of raising them. Then she shows up for visits, crams them full of treats and presents, and collects the mommy goodies. After she disappears again, I get to hear how successful and wonderful she is, as well as having to live with the grief her visits stir up. I feel terribly resentful, but there's nothing I can do. There are few rewards to this job."

NEW BEGINNINGS

Harbored guilt and resentment toward the other parent are unproductive feelings—the product of bad decisions and judgment errors. But all they represent is human failing, and people do not have to nurture or live out mistakes. These can be identified as such and corrected. After Laura and I talked about these feelings, we felt better; but how sad that we permitted them to fester for ten years.

From a need to protect our bruised selves, our honesty with each other had its limits. Laura declared that she had avoided contact with the girls so as to give us a better chance to establish our family. But what I saw and heard led me to believe that her hiatus reflected guilt rather than generosity. As for the limits on my own honesty, when Laura asked me whether it bothered me that Bev's red hair was a constant reminder of her, I laughed flippantly, pooh-poohed the idea, and said, "How silly."

Our sharing helped each of us to understand where we had been before we came to this point in our lives. Our anger at Walter for being more concerned over his own needs than the children's or ours, the resentment and jealousy we felt toward each other, the private guilt we suffered alone—all were shared. Had anyone told me that my husband's former wife, the other woman whom I had feared and who was supposed to have hated me so, would end up holding and comforting me, I would have howled with laughter and denial.

But once our need to dislike each other was removed, we were simply two women who, through unresolved conflict and a lack of communication, had lived out years of guilt and resentment over a set of children who were part of both our lives. In harboring hostile feelings about each other, we had hindered the children we both loved as well as ourselves. Now we were simply two human beings beginning to free ourselves so we could each move ahead—a long overdue task.

7 Invisible Enemies

When our marriage was at its rockiest, my eleven-year-old son became upset. Always a good student and a happy child, Jeff regressed, began doing poorly in school, became sassy, then depressed. He gave up his favorite pastime—riding at the ranch—to curl up in front of the television set. Once independent, he began to cling. He denied anything was wrong until one day I pressed for an explanation and he broke into tears. "You're getting a divorce, aren't you?" he sobbed. "And I'll lose this dad, too." His stepfather had reared him for twice as long as his biological father had done; on this second relationship hinged his identity and security. Without a doubt we were having bad times, I explained, but a counselor was helping us work things out.

Fear is only one of many invisible enemies chipping away at the stepfamily. Because most family members have lost a family once before, the fear of it lingers, intensifies daily stresses, and intrudes on relationships. Anger, jealousy, guilt, resentment, and shame are also part of the stepfamily's emotional heritage.

Feelings influence all human relationships, and every family must deal with a multitude of them. But the stepfamily's extra ties to the past confuse or heighten feelings. When feelings from past relationships remain unresolved, their effects spill over onto the new stepfamily.

When writing the first draft of this chapter, I categorized all these feelings as enemies, negative and destructive. But feelings are vital to our existence, and even those we think of as negative provide important cues to our relationships. In his book *Feelings*, New York psychologist Willard Gaylin lumped the emotions of anxiety, guilt, and shame together. As signals directing us toward goodness, safety, pleasure, and group survival, he writes, these feelings serve as a testament to our capacity for choice and learning.[1]

Denial of feelings is a common way of dealing with tension and anger. But denial merely dulls the pain; it cannot erase feelings.

To avoid this danger, an analysis of the diverse and often denied feelings within the stepfamily is needed. Unexplored, these emotions create problems for two reasons: First, because some of them seem to represent our darker side, we are quick to deny them even to ourselves. Jealous of the former wife? Never. Competitive with his teenage daughter? Not me. Resentful of child support? No, I knew from the beginning that he had to pay. Interviews ring with such answers, which were my answers, too.

Second, once in touch with these feelings, they must be talked about. Too often, when the feelings have been identified, steppeople feel reluctant about discussing them for fear of unleashing greater problems. The idea that another family could fail is too painful to consider, and some people are afraid to reveal their feelings lest they stimulate that failure. Yet in fact just the opposite is true: Feelings that go unrecognized or denied may topple the structure of the stepfamily like dominoes and turn the threat into reality. On the other hand, dealing with these feelings can help bring the family closer, building a stronger family unit.

FEAR—THE BREEDER OF UNCERTAINTIES

Fear wears many masks. Only after peeling away the layers of rebellion, hatred, jealousy, and other emotions is fear revealed to be at their root.

Fear is powerful. It is also useful. As part of the biological response system, fear supports our behavior in emergencies. It stirs the survival instinct and, like anger, is a servant of security. Heroes are well aware that fear can serve as a motivator, but blind fear of the unknown is something else. When we try to control our misplaced or unexamined fears by avoiding them, reason is put aside and we misdirect our judgment into destructive behavior. The most violent form of fighting behavior is motivated by fear, writes scientist Konrad Lorenz in *On Aggression.*[2]

As long as stepfamily members privately retain fears, allowing them to dictate behavior, fear may become a weapon to harm innocent victims—part of the new clan. Fear is a signal that all is not well.

Unexamined fears can produce useless worry. Fears of inadequacy as a stepparent led me to play what-if games. What if they hated me? What if the energy I devoted to rearing these stepchildren should better have been directed toward my own? What if I didn't do a good job? If used as a springboard for problem solving, examined fear can be constructive as it relieves stress and tension and progresses toward a solution; but like guilt, it can become a cycle feeding back on itself—focusing on a problem while avoiding a solution.

Most stepparents take their roles seriously, and most do a better job than they think. One example of fear as an intruder was revealed in a study by anthropologist Paul Bohannan at the Western Behavioral Institute, as he compared children with biological fathers to children with stepfathers. The stepchildren generally were just as happy and successful —socially and academically—as the children in nuclear families. Youngsters got along as well with stepfathers as with biological fathers. The stepchildren and their mothers said so.

But worrywart stepfathers thought otherwise. When Dr. Bohannan asked the stepfathers how they thought they were doing, they rated their youngsters as less happy than biological fathers rated their children. Stepfathers also judged themselves less effective at parenting than biological fathers.[3] "Because they take on an awesome task and want to do a good job, stepfathers spend a lot more time than natural fathers in thinking about their roles and responsibilities," says Dr. Bohannan. "While natural fathers go on instinct, stepfathers are more self-conscious about their effectiveness and more critical of themselves." This is also true of stepmothers.

Fearing they are failing their stepchildren is only one side of the coin for stepfathers. These men also worry about whether they are handling the relationship with their own children well, and such unresolved fears may evolve into guilt feelings. Among the other fears common to stepfathers are money, adoption, inheritance, and understanding their wives' problems. Many men fear the sexual feelings they experience toward a seductive teenage stepdaughter. With no biological ties to this young woman, the cultural incest taboo is weakened, creating a climate where incest—or, more properly, secondary incest—is likely to occur. A middle-aged New York state doctor admitted he felt terribly guilty over his thoughts when he admired his wife's trio of scantily clad nymphets running about the house. The fantasies can so easily become realities that in a California clinic specializing in treating incestuous relationships, half the family cases dealt with stepfathers and stepdaughters.[4]

In their effort to protect their families and to control their own fearful feelings, many stepfathers retreat from their teenage stepdaughters. A Maryland technician says, "I really liked it when she crawled all over me, hugging me, calling me Daddy. But as she grew, it scared the hell out of me because she was such a vivacious little thing and I'd have sexual thoughts about her. She was A-one material, gorgeous, incredibly gorgeous. I didn't feel dirty or guilty, but I was scared." His decision? He distanced himself from her, and throughout her adolescence their relationship became one long battle as she tried to gain his attention.

As stepdaughters may, this teenager felt rejected. Not understanding the reason behind this withdrawal, young adolescent women may look on themselves as unlovable or undesirable. At this critical time of identity formation youngsters need affirmative signs they are okay people. Should they decide to demand attention from their stepfathers, adolescent daughters may compete with their mothers. With competition between the two women thus heightened, more problems may arise out of the mothers' jealousy of the relationship between their daughters and their new husbands.[5]

When secondary incest occurs in the stepfamily it violates trust and affection. To lower the stepparent's fears, the stepchild's feelings of rejection, and the competition between stepmother and stepdaughter—or between stepfather and stepson—the matter of incest must be addressed within the stepfamily. One way to deal with this is to have family discussions of questions having to do with incest and competition. What is the meaning of a family? Its purpose? Its moral obligation to its members? Its boundaries? Getting family members thinking about the purpose and commitment behind their stepfamily may diminish any lingering threats. Family members who harbor such fantasies or fears may feel relieved to air the issue and reduce their preoccupation with the idea.

Some professionals think that talking openly about incest may be too bold, that it may convert a dormant problem into an active one. Others agree with me. "Feelings should be expressed in words and dealt with," says Dr. Goldenberg. "And if they involve thoughts about incest, then those fears and fantasies need discussing."

At some level all mothers feel jealous of their daughters and compete with them. But when this rivalry becomes upsetting, Dr. Goldenberg explains, women need to say to their husbands, "It bothers me when she's in bed with you. You belong in bed with me, and I would like that playfulness stopped." But if it becomes more serious, as it frequently does within stepfamilies, Dr. Goldenberg suggests that the wife bring her fears about incest out into the open. "I'm concerned that you may begin to have sexual feelings about her." Maybe, she suggests, this bold statement of fear must even be said in front of the two of them.

"What is critical is knowing the difference between actions and feelings," she says. "Fantasies are healthy and shouldn't be interfered with too much. But actions must be confronted as directly and openly as possible."

Another thing that most stepfamily members are afraid of but don't talk about is the loss of another family. When this fear gets out of hand, or the couple feels the marriage coming apart, many remarrieds panic. As it did at our house, overreaction can worsen matters. Feelings are contagious.

Meeting a friend who is emotional about some event may heighten our own feelings.[6] The adults' uncertainty about their relationship spills over into the children's lives and affects them the way it affected my son Jeff.

Children of divorce rarely forget the breakup of their family, and they worry about new relationships. Will these last? Should they trust this new person in their lives? Children respond to threats to their security with poor sleeping habits, whining, and bedwetting in youngsters; a drop in school grades and changes in habits during early puberty; and outright resistance and rebellion during the adolescent years.

"Children live by feelings, not words, and are sensitive to subtle expressions and feelings to which grown-ups, dependent on words, have become dulled," writes child psychiatrist J. Louise Despert in *Children of Divorce*. One mistake parents and professionals frequently make, she says, is to date children's maladjustments from the point of the marriage break. The drama starts long before a separation, and children recall the fights and lack of affection between their parents. Divorce is not the beginning of a child's troubles, but the end result of the breakdown. Some parents attempt to shield their youngsters from the conflict, but children's sensors are acute.[7]

In our stepfamily, the growing conflict between Walter and me was not private. Disagreements became frequent and loud, sometimes shocking me because in my first marriage Bill and I had rarely raised our voices to each other. But holding my feelings in had brought on migraine headaches and depression. Although bringing everything out into the open as I did with Walter made me feel better, the children suffered from the conflict as their fears of another family failure grew.

When conflict breeds fear that makes remarrieds jumpy, couples can unite in dysfunctional ways. Sometimes they use one of the children as a scapegoat. In what Harris S. Goldstein calls *pseudomutuality*,[8] the child willingly becomes the center of the tension by acting out in school or in the family. After all, even negative attention seems to be better than no attention. While the conflict usually is between the parents, the resulting havoc sets the child up for the scapegoat role.

Hearing quarrels between Walter and me made our children fearful that our family might break up. Aware that their biological father was ill, my sons were doubly fearful over the possibility that they might lose both fathers. In response to our conflict, each of the children rebelled in some way or withdrew. So did we. As I neared the end of my college work, my husband felt threatened because within six months of collecting her college diploma, his first wife had left. From my experience of losing my father and my first husband to divorce, I, too, feared yet another family loss. None of us shared our fears with each other and, as we denied them, they were magnified and became our enemies.

Children can share the responsibility of keeping communication channels clear to lower conflict levels. This can be done by helping to create an atmosphere in which both children and adults feel free to talk about their fears without feeling silly or threatened. Answering children's questions also helps to manage their fears. Admit that troubles exist, but make it plain that they are being worked out.

STEPMOTHER STRESS

When everyone hurts, who is first to admit feeling afraid or resentful or jealous? Frequently, the severe psychological stress impels the stepmother to seek help. In the traditional nurturing role a stepmother can help the children with their insecurities and fears and help her husband with his guilt over his former wife and children. But what happens when the stepmother feels ashamed because she dislikes one of her stepchildren? What happens when she is forced by a stepdaughter into competitive triangles over her husband? When her own stress is high, a stepmother is unable to help her family.

In the first formal study of its kind, psychologist Janice H. Nadler documented the stress that stepmothers encounter. According to Dr. Nadler's findings, many stepmothers think that emotions such as jealousy, depression, anger, and resentment are uniquely theirs and that somehow they are the source of the problems.

Dr. Nadler compared the stress levels of full-time stepmothers, part-time stepmothers, and biological mothers. The age of the children and whether the stepmother cared for them full time or part time created variations in the stress patterns.[9] But beyond these differences, *all* the stepmothers experience more anxiety, anger, and depression than biological mothers. Part-time stepmothers were the least involved in family life and had the most conflict—with their husbands as well as their stepchildren.

Stepmother stress centers on four issues: too little support from her husband; too little support from her community; too little support for her personal needs; and too little support for her self-esteem. Explains Dr. Nadler, "If she has another role—a job, career, children of her own—where she gains good feelings about herself, her self-esteem base is less threatened."

Several women psychologists who are stepmothers acknowledged that even their professional skills and their ability to tune in on human relationships did not prepare them for the stress of the stepmother role—especially where teenage stepdaughters heighten competitive urges.

Stress creates troubled relationships in both the full-time and the part-time stepfamilies. The full-time stepmother conflict centers on diverse values and backgrounds; just getting the aliens in one house together is enough to overwhelm her. The part-time stepmother resents the disruption of her family life; the children's arrival takes away from the time she ordinarily shares with her husband. Since the visits are short, discipline is an added problem. She feels torn between making the children's brief stay as enjoyable as she can, often at her expense and in spite of her resentment, and expecting them to pitch in and be part of this family's life.

Dr. Nadler believes the situation can be turned around. In spite of rejection and resentment, she suggests that stepparents try to leave the door open to their stepchildren, who may very well take advantage of this opportunity to build a better relationship.

In stepfamily workshops, Dr. Nadler provides stepfamilies with awareness and communication skills that can help to make their families work better. If personality problems or other psychological issues are severe enough to demand attention, she directs steppeople toward counseling. But for most participants, simply identifying the feelings and dealing with them provide the basis for a positive change. These stepfamily workshops are but one example of groups that are burgeoning throughout the country, many under the auspices of the Stepfamily Association of America, Inc., in Palo Alto, California.

Altering old relationships does not necessarily require therapy. But elusive feelings must be dealt with by the people involved. "You've got to hang in there and finish relationships," says Dr. Irene Goldenberg. "A man cannot get along with his wife well if he has not worked through his relationships with his parents, and an unresolved relationship with a former wife is worse. When people learn to avoid issues, the knack carries over into the new relationship, making it more complicated than ever. But when you work through a relationship with someone, it lays the groundwork for your relationships with others. One of the biggest problems in the stepfamily involves all the unresolved relationships filtering into the new ones."

So much denial exists in the stepfamily because people hurt. They've been burned or wounded, Dr. Goldenberg explains. "These distressed people move into a family system much more complex than that of first families. Family members can resolve these feelings by talking about them, sharing. Since everyone hurts, a bond exists. But when emotions are denied, relationships reach a crisis, everything blows apart, and it takes therapy to put things together again."

COMPETITION—THE CREATOR OF CONFLICT

Making a stepfamily is like trying to grow two separate cultures within one petri dish—a survival match. Competition is part of the struggle, and it is heightened as more people vie for the family's limited resources. One dictionary definition of competition is "the act of endeavoring to gain what another endeavors to gain at the same time; the striving of two or more for the same object." The ecological definition of competition is "the struggle among organisms, both of the same and of different species, for food, space, and other existence factors."[10]

Competition is common to all families. Little boys compete for the attention of their mothers, and little girls compete for the attention of their fathers. In the nuclear family, ultimately these conflicts permit each child to identify with the parent of the same sex. Depending upon the age of the children, the formation of a new stepfamily again may trigger children's needs to defend their rights against any threatening person. The stepparent may be seen as the intruder, the competition.

As they defend personal rights, rivalry among biological brothers and sisters also is common. A new sibling is a threat to a child's place and role in the family. The older child may therefore display hostility at having to share the attentions of the parents and yield the limelight. Given the number of children in many stepfamilies, sibling rivalry can be raised to epidemic proportions as each child fights for an identity within the new family.

When competition gets out of hand, jealousy in the stepfamily can create combat situations. Sociologist Jessie Bernard outlined six relationships that fuel competitive fires within the remarried family with children. They are (1) between the child's biological parents; (2) between the new parent and the biological parent of the same sex; (3) between the old in-laws and the new spouse; (4) between the new father and the children; (5) between the new mother and the children; (6) and among the children.[11] The common denominator is the children's affections.

Conflict wears two faces. It can disrupt or destroy; or it can force changes in relationships, helping people to grow. All family life is filled with coalitions resulting from conflicting emotions and searches for power. But diverse perceptions and values, together with extra people in the stepfamily, make the higher conflict level inevitable.

Triangles provide a way to resolve conflict. In *Two Against One*, Theodore Caplow explains that a triad is the only social group having an equal number of members and relationships. The triad has a tendency to divide into coalitions, two members against the third.[12]

Stepfamily triads remain unresearched, but obvious differences from traditional family triads make them far more complex and volatile. In the nuclear family, love and hate are acted out in triangles; but beneath the conflict is likely to be a base of affection and loyalty. The nuclear family works as an organization, and, according to Caplow, it possesses a collective identity.

Becoming a stepfamily is a process that takes time. The longer the settling-in period, the greater the delay in working as an organization.

Until common bonds form a family identity, stepfamily triads are destructive. Extra relationships provide more possibilities for triad conflicts—the new couple against the former spouse, one child and the biological parent against the new stepparent, two children against the stepparent or against another child.

The stake in a triad is power. In stepfamily triads the power is unequal because blood ties and emotional ties, common to nuclear family members, are missing. In a daughter-father-stepmother triad, for example, emotional and kinship ties exist between father and daughter, and legal and emotional commitments exist between father and wife. But between the stepmother and stepdaughter, no tie exists. The emotional bond may bloom later; it may not. With this uneven balance, who wins depends on the coalition's strength.

Competition occurs within stepsibling relationships, too, although little research documents it. Whether stepchildren are visitors or permanent members of the household, upon remarriage they are suddenly thrust into new relationships with each other and expected to get along. Sibling rivalry can become serious in stepfamilies because diverse personalities and histories, coupled with rivalry for the parents' attention, make compatibility difficult. But research shows that the better the relationship between stepbrothers and stepsisters, the stronger the family.

How well stepsibling relationships fare is determined by a variety of social factors, as one study reveals. When both sets of children live in the same house, they get along better. When the oldest child is not yet thirteen, and especially if this is the father's child, the siblings remain happier together. Unlike what happens in the nuclear family, stepsiblings of the opposite sex tend to develop stronger relationships than same-sex siblings. This could be because of an initial sexual interest that evolves into long-term friendships. And when a new baby is born to the remarried couple, the children seem likely to have more harmonious relationships with each other.[13]

"Mine against yours" was never a problem in either of my stepparenting experiences. Rivalry existed only between one son and one stepdaughter when they vied for my attention. From the time that Brenda taught Jeff to play catch, these two were devoted to each other—until I walked into the room. Then they fought and poked at each other. Recognizing what was going on, I hugged them both openly and laughed about the situation to let them know there was enough love to go around. Although the rivalry took time and patience to identify and resolve, their special closeness remains one of the joys of our merger.

My son Chris and my stepson Kurt, who are the same age, have developed a warm relationship. Kurt admits he resented the time and concern that Walter focused on my sons. But Chris and Kurt never fought over it. If anything, whenever they're together these teenagers team up against Walter.

Manipulation or peacemaking attempts may be the catalyst that triggers conflict. When a third person intervenes to settle a problem that should be worked out between a pair of family members, the intervention may serve as the trigger. Once, when Bev refused to clean the room she shared with Brenda, they came to me for a solution. I gave Bev the option of cleaning the room or moving to the basement to live as she chose. When I returned from work, she had moved her bed and belongings to the basement, and although I was uncomfortable with her decision, I let her stay.

Until the novelty eroded, Bev enjoyed the attention and took pains to show everyone where she lived. And Brenda got a tidy room of her own. But the conflict yielded frustration for me as I was impelled into the wicked stepmother role, and it brought anger and resentment for Bev. Although she won the power struggle, in the long run she lost and displaced her anger onto me. Soon I heard a rumor that I had forced my stepdaughter to live in the basement. Later I learned that Bev wrote this version to Walter, who was in Southeast Asia at the time. This drove a rift between him and me that was not soon healed. What is more, the incident set up future conflicts among the three of us. Sometimes she lost, sometimes I did. But each conflict heightened the competition between us and intensified the war.

This experience illustrates how the Cinderella myth can continue. Jessie Bernard suggests that the cruel-stepmother syndrome can be approached from two points of view: It can be seen as a persistent myth serving some symbolic function; or it can be accepted as true with an explanation for its occurrence.[14]

Being maneuvered into triangles illustrates the kernel of truth inherent in the characterization. A stepmother might use an identical parenting method with her own daughter, letting her decide between two options. When the child found that her own decision had put her in an untenable position—such as living in a basement—she would have to take responsibility for the decision. But the stepchild can try to avoid that responsibility by resorting to the crutch of the wicked stepmother. "See what my stepmother did?" And caught between myth on the one hand and frustration on the other, the stepmother, dumbfounded, can only nod in agreement. "Yes, I guess the stereotype really does fit me." And the guilt lies heavy on the stepmother's head—even though she is not the one who made the decision. On the other hand, the biological mother is not intimidated by any such stereotype and would assume little or no guilt in this scenario.

"No one could have told me I'd become a cruel stepmother because I was a good Christian," a Maryland stepmother says. "And because I had a hard life as a stepchild, I bent over backward to be kind to my stepson. But the bitterness and resentment were there, although he didn't always know it. No one could have told me I'd be ugly toward him, but sometimes it's hard not to be. It takes a superhuman effort."

While I was having an especially difficult time with my stepdaughter, I was relieved to hear that a friend had a relationship with her teenage daughter that rivaled ours in difficulty. We joked that their temperaments must reside in their red hair, but I was relieved to learn that the problem was not mine alone, nor was it confined to step relationships.

As every parent is aware, adolescence is a time filled with rage, disappointment, and uncertainty. It is in teenagers that suppressed anger and anxiety come to full flower. And, having lost parents and the security of their first families, stepchildren have a deeper reservoir of such feelings than most teenagers.

Bev unleashed all her rage at me. At that time I did not understand the source of her fury, but it equaled the fury I had felt as a teenage stepchild. Had I been able to work out my own feelings by then, I might have been able to identify the source of her anger and help her. Because I could not, our conflict grew. Bev also was close to her father. She was his first child, and he lavished attention on her. As she grew, their private time in car rides evolved from spouting childhood nursery rhymes and solving simple number games to working out sophisticated algebra problems. Just as I followed my father from bar to bar to gain his approval, my stepdaughter spouted mathematical answers like a computer to gain Walter's approval.

After the divorce, when they lived as a single-parent family, Bev became his confidante, his helper. She had to make her own adjustment to the loss of her mother, then adjust to several housekeepers, then adjust to me. When I became part of the family, the attention she got so easily from her father shifted to me. Her anger over this lost attention remained suppressed, making our adjustment time fairly calm—until her adolescence. Our relationship worsened when her father flew bombing missions during the Vietnam War and she began to fear the loss of yet another parent.

JEALOUSY—THE DESTROYER OF RELATIONSHIPS

I understood none of this, nor did the counselors we asked to help us. As most stepmothers tend to do, I assumed that her anger was personal, and our conflict and jealousy continued until our relationship threatened the rest of the family. Competition with my stepdaughter was rooted partially in remnants from my life as a stepchild—my need for love and my fear of rejection and abandonment. As a stepchild she responded to me from the same basis, yet I bore the guilt. Triangling was one way she vented her jealousy and delivered her anger. I did, too, but even now those words make me shudder. Who, me? Jealous of my stepdaughter? Never! Yet because our feelings remained unexplored, we were left with no other option but to go on being jealous of each other.

Jealousy is closely associated with competition. When a person feels left behind in a competitive race, the fear or insecurity may take the form of jealousy. Competition between a mother and her own daughter involves highly complex psychological processes; and, as Nancy Friday discusses in *My Mother, My Self*, these powerful love-hate competitive relationships breed conflict—especially during adolescence.

If a teenager's mother is fifty years old and spreading at the hips, it's easier to deal with rivalry. But if her stepmother is close in age and attractive, it's far more difficult not to feel jealous. "The stepmother may feel a special guilt for actually coming and acting out the fantasy of taking the father away," explains Dr. Irene Goldenberg. "And these two sets of feelings play on each other, raising the competitive urges. How intense it becomes has a lot to do with how secure the marriage relationship is."

Research has shown that in a first family children are likely to think of their parents as asexual beings. But remarriage forces teenagers to face their parents' sexuality, and it disturbs them, explains Dr. Emily Visher. At a home for unwed mothers the psychologist learned that many teenage girls get pregnant at the same time as their remarried mothers or stepmothers.

Research that reveals that problems between stepmothers and stepdaughters are difficult is hardly surprising. If the age difference between the two women is slight, the rivalry heightens. This was the case the first time I was a stepmother,[15] when only ten years separated my oldest stepdaughter and myself.

"Competition increases between the young stepmother and adolescent stepdaughter because peers are competing," says Dr. Goldenberg. The relationship must be worked out between the women, and how they do it must hinge on what is right and comfortable for them. Although the pivotal point can be a number of things, it is wise for them to understand what it cannot be. The stepmother is not the mother and that is not her task, especially if the adolescent only visits. Trying to be the stepdaughter's pal may not work because the stepmother may not be the kind of peer the girl would have chosen herself, Dr. Goldenberg explains.

The relationship needs to be the kind that develops between related people, yet without forgetting that it is not a biological relationship. It must be forged with a closeness in mind, says Dr. Goldenberg, but with new rules. Maybe it can only be a minimal relationship. But if the two recognize the reality and deal with it, that is all right.

Neither Bev nor I liked our tense relationship, but each of us reacted differently. After conflicts, I couldn't wait to make up because our tension spilled over into the family. But Bev had a reserved personality, which, coupled with her fears, made it difficult to resolve such conflicts. As she waited for my move, often for days, we cringed from each other. Tension headaches plagued me. My stomach churned. Only gradually did she learn to apologize and take part of the responsibility for our conflict.

After one battle we held each other and cried. "You make friends easily and so many people like you," she said. "I feel jealous." And to her I admitted, "I feel jealous of your tremendous brain, your analytic skills and comprehension. You have so many more opportunities than I had." And again the relationship lurched forward.

Unresolved competition kept us in a continued state of tension. As Nancy Friday illustrates in dealing with normal mother-daughter jealousies, Bev and I were actually fashioning our own relationship. But without the kinship tie as a mooring, the step relationship magnified this conflict. And in my case, my own unresolved childhood feelings and my approach to the role of stepmother fueled the problems.

Without a blood tie, a stepmother may view her stepdaughter as the other woman, competing for her husband's affections. And as the stepdaughter blossoms into adolescence her physical presence provides a daily reminder of the former wife. The more she looks like her mother, the more difficult it is to forget that this child is the product of another love relationship.

RESENTMENT—ANGER FROM UNRESOLVABLE SITUATIONS

Resentment nibbles at stepfamily relationships. It represents emotions aroused from being able to identify and understand certain situations as reality, even rational, but wishing they did not exist. Indicative of the behavior that resentment yields are some of the words that Roget's thesaurus lists as reflecting this emotion: *sullen, grouchy, moody, irritated, jealous, envy, retaliate, revenge.*

Some of these behaviors result from a shortage of resources. Most comfort and happiness levels of family life can be influenced by the availability of two assets: time and money. In the stepfamily, both resources must be shared with another family. A woman may be aware of her future husband's financial obligations to his other family. She may understand that child support and alimony will dent their family budget just as clearly as her husband realizes that her devotion to her children will deprive him of time with her. Because many stepfamilies suffer a shortage of time and money, accepting such realities without resentment is difficult.

Money is power. And, evidenced by monthly checks to the other family, that power reminds remarrieds of the first family's influence on their lives. Often, in their eagerness to escape unhappy marriages, men agree to anything, at any price. The accounting comes later. In the meantime, generous financial support to his first family helps lower the guilt he bears for leaving. At the time of their divorce many men and women swear they will never marry again. But within three years, four out of ten men and slightly fewer women remarry; and the new family feels the pocketbook pinch.[16] This financial link to the past can lower the stepfamily's standard of living. If the new wife has child support coming in, the two may balance. If not, resentment festers.

No matter how much he pays, money can become a weapon between a man and his ex-wife. During my first marriage, Bill paid a generous child support, in addition to medical, dental, and travel expenses for his daughters. After taxes, we retained less than half his salary for rearing our sons.

But each time his children came to summer with us in last year's clothes, we took them shopping. "Mom just didn't have time to buy us new clothes," they reported. Twice we had to borrow money for their plane tickets. That they would skip a summer because we lacked the money was out of the question, and the one time I suggested it, I felt guilty for months. Because they spent every summer with us, in the seven years of our marriage Bill and I had but one vacation together alone. Resentment became my companion as a part-time stepmother because no matter how little we had, the children from his first marriage seemed to come first. I knew it; I understood it. But I resented it.

As my own stepfather did, some men stop supporting their own children so as to make financial ends meet. Others try to support both families. But stretching money between two sets of children creates tugs-of-war not only on the purse strings and the emotions, but between the women in the man's life. Many second wives must return to work. When the money they earn is used for a new car or a family vacation, they do so willingly; but when it is used to meet financial obligations to the former family, resentment builds. And, just as a second wife resents it when money is diverted to her husband's children and ex-wife, the ex-wife resents it when her former husband spends money on his stepchildren.

"I never hated the ex-wife," explains a Washington, D.C., stepmother. "But I resented her because of those monthly checks, which reminded me of all the things we could not have. The real problem came when I directed that resentment toward my stepson."

Often fathers use money to assuage their guilt, overindulging their children when they are together. This stirs up resentment in the new wife as well as in the former wife, who cannot measure up to his Santa Claus visits. It was no wonder that my sons loved weekends with their father. Just as we did for his daughters during those summers twenty years ago, to make up for not being with the children he loved, Bill provided a three-ring circus when they visited. But back at home, their stepfather did not.

Money can also be used as a weapon, and children can get pulled into fights. In a money tangle with her ex-husband, one woman turned the phone over to their son, who demanded of his father, "When are you going to meet your financial obligation to me?" He parroted his mother's words, but he was missing data. For ten years the child-support check was regular, and the withholding of money centered on a power struggle with his ex-wife, not a lack of concern for the child. Some parents with custody put off spending money on movies, records, or a new shirt, telling their children, "Have your father take you shopping this weekend."

The end of child-support checks is not the end of money problems in stepfamilies. Inheritance matters can become an emotional arena, too. Dispersing heirlooms requires decision making, sometimes bordering on the absurd, when trying to make things equal or keep them in the "right family." Unless youngsters have been formally adopted, or unless a stepparent has clearly spelled out what is to be done in a will, stepchildren have no legal inheritance rights.

Mistrust can develop from legal incidents. When my former husband died, in addition to small loans from me, he owed over $10,000 in child support. Since we needed the money less than he, we never pressed him. The year before he died, Bill confided that he had left his insurance policy in my name and, although he had borrowed heavily against it, the remainder was ours. His savings were to be divided among the children of his two families. As it turned out, the insurance balance provided less than half his child-support debt.

Shortly after the insurance check arrived, my former stepdaughter called. "Why have you done this?" she asked. Although she accepted my explanation, the tone of her voice led me to believe she doubted my word. Because we had made so many sacrifices for his daughters as we reared our sons, I felt hurt that she might think I would deceive her. I felt our verbal agreement was as fair as we had been to her father. But to leave the inheritance situation ambiguous was unfair on Bill's part because it developed mistrust between his daughter and me.

The drain of money from one family to the other is one taxing challenge; finding the right balance of time to meet everyone's needs is another. Trying to meet the diverse needs in a stepfamily is like running and standing still at the same time. Exhaustion and a sense of martyrdom are by-products, and both fuel resentment.

One of the saddest laments of stepmothers who have children of their own is about sharing the energy and time they once devoted to their own children. They feel torn; and, in trying to be good stepmothers, many discover they slight their own children. "For five years I've bent over backward to give them more than my own, so they could in no way feel deprived," says one stepmother. "If I couldn't buy shirts for everyone, then no one got shirts. But now I feel I've shortchanged my own children, and I feel resentful."

Stepchildren also take away time from adult relationships—a problem for the part-time stepmother whose stepchildren seem to descend only on weekends, holidays, or summer vacations. She may work all week and look forward to a quiet weekend of shopping, dinner, and a drive in the country with her husband. But the shopping may include holding the hand of a stepchild, dinner conversation may center on the Muppets rather than on the Mets' new star, and the drive in the country may include an unhappy and whiny child whose real needs are not being attended to.

Again, resentment. With my first stepchildren, the money division bothered me less than the time; never having a summer alone with my husband cut deeper than the cost of plane tickets. While I understood the girls' right and need to be with their father, I resented their failure to appreciate what I did for them. The second time as a stepparent, my stepchildren entered adolescence first, and much of my time and energy went into coping with their problems. Again I was resentful, and my resentment nurtured guilt.

GUILT—THE GUARDIAN OF GOODNESS

"It's hard not to act guilty when you feel guilty," a Santa Ana stepfather told me. I circled the word *guilt* or identified that feeling in interview transcripts many times. I had once believed that only stepmothers felt guilty, but this emotion is the common denominator among stepfamily members.

As Dr. Nadler has documented, stepmothers suffer the greatest guilt. In their desire to make up for past family losses, stepmothers often serve as the emotional sponges of the family. Many charge in as saviors to reestablish a family. They will love their stepchildren as their own, and family life will be better than ever, they tell themselves. As these unrealistic expectations are not fulfilled, the women feel responsible—and guilty. Guilt feelings also arise from disliking the other woman, although most admit they don't know her, and from feeling resentful over situations they understand intellectually but cannot accept emotionally.

Guilt, then, is self-disappointment. It is anguish that we have failed our own ideals.[17]

Guilt becomes predominant in stepfamilies when people feel they cannot meet the challenges this complex family presents. In reality, they cannot meet their own unrealistic expectations and feel they have fallen short. I was disappointed in myself because I had failed to be the kind of mother to Bev that I had hoped I could be. Not only had I made the mistake of trying to replace Bev's biological mother, but I had charged in to soothe troubled feelings and had instead seemed to make everything worse. This was imagined guilt at its peak; but it felt very real.

As they cope with guilt, sometimes stepmothers overcompensate. One upstate New Yorker said she sends her four-year-old stepson to nursery school only one morning a week because if he went every day, people might think she was trying to get rid of him. "We both need time away from each other—he for learning to play with other children, and me just to unwind without a toddler underfoot," she said as he crawled on her lap. "If he were my own, I'd send him every day, but with him I'd feel guilty."

I, too, overcompensated to reduce guilt. One of the sources of my deepest guilt—my stepson—visited us occasionally. Had it not been for me, he might still be with his father and sisters, I'd think, overlooking the fact that he lived with his mother, not in an orphanage. To compensate for our lack of year-round attention, we set the household in a whirl during his visits. Although the party atmosphere delighted him, it must also have reminded him that he was a guest, set apart from us. I did all I could to make him comfortable, but I was relieved to see him leave. He was living proof of one of my failures as a stepmother.

Stepfathers also harbor guilt—for leaving their own children, or for being unable to support them, or for rearing someone else's children. They may react by resenting their stepchildren, or by overindulging their own children when they visit, or by dropping out of their children's lives.

In a Syracuse stepfamily, a woman asked her husband to shop with her for his stepdaughter's birthday gift. He declined. Too tired, he said, as he answered the phone. The caller was his son, who lived with his former wife. This time his response was different. When the boy had taken a paper route, his father had ordered a wagon for him (right after a budget lecture to his wife). Now the store had called to report that it was in. "Don't worry, I'll go right over and get it," the father told his son. Likewise, when his former wife calls to say the boy should visit his grandmother, the father writes a check for the plane ticket; yet if his stepchildren telephone their father, they must pay for the call or call collect. Money satisfies this man's unresolved guilt over his son, but his unequal treatment of his stepchildren builds resentment.

In appeasing his guilt over his own children, another Syracuse stepfather avoids intimate relationships with his stepchildren. "I could do things with her kids, but I squelch the impulse because I can't do it with mine. When my kids skin their knees, I can't comfort them, so with my stepchildren I let their mother take care of them. I know it's guilt over leaving my kids, but I just cannot bring myself to be affectionate with hers."

Many a man admits feeling guilty for not having been more sensitive to his wife's problems as she cared for his children. "I used to wonder what was wrong with her for not being able to love my children," one stepfather said. "Now I marvel at all she did for them with no thanks from any of us." Turned inward, such guilt can provoke destructive behavior. When problems in one New York state stepfamily reached crisis proportions over a teenager's lying and stealing and destroying himself with drugs, his father began to drink heavily. Once he beat his wife, who finally insisted on counseling. "He carried around feelings from his first marriage—guilt and mistrust, besides disappointment over his son," she said. "And he brought all those emotions into our marriage. He needed to take out his frustration on someone and I was there, but he feels terribly guilty about having put me through all this."

To lighten their emotional overload, stepparents need to distinguish between real and imagined guilt. Even when the guilt is real, not imagined, its basis may be faulty judgment. "Imagined guilt occurs when people believe themselves responsible for other people and their behavior," explains counselor Frank Halse Jr. "They judge themselves by the behavior of others. If your stepchild lies or steals, you feel guilty because you must have done something to cause the child to act that way." In stepfamilies, such behavior may result from different values and from a child's upbringing in the first family. But many stepparents think it reflects on them.

"Real guilt occurs when a person does not fulfill his or her commitment to other people," says Halse. "Unlike imagined guilt, it is not manipulative and allows others to be responsible for their own decisions and actions." Understanding this difference can help stepparents recognize where they can be effective and where their guilt is wasted energy.

Although stepchildren rarely identify the feeling by name, they feel guilty, too. "I used to hear my father say he would have split long ago if it weren't for me," a California teenager said. Many children of divorce feel responsible for their parents' breakup. Or they feel guilty about their stepfathers who cannot see their own children except during contrived visits. Because of bonds to their missing biological parents, children often feel guilty if they even *like* their stepparents. And stepchildren who direct hate and rejection toward stepparents rarely do so without guilt.

Guilt can lower our self-esteem. When unresolved, it feeds upon itself, damaging the guilt-ridden person's relationships with others. But as a signal of transgression in a relationship, guilt serves as a guardian for goodness. The only way to find relief is to confront the individual involved with the feeling. In this capacity, as guilt helps us to recognize mistakes and avoid them, it represents the most noble and painful of struggles.

Sometimes, unexplored feelings burst the boundaries of rational behavior, leading us to act in ways we never thought ourselves capable of. Perhaps such shock is necessary to jolt change. As a case in point, I once acted like the cruel stepmother of fairy tales. Angry and disappointed because Walter was on military alert Christmas Day and could not be with us, I directed my frustrations at Bev, then sixteen. By then, such displacement had become a reciprocal ritual.

After Christmas dinner we all decided to go to a movie—a depressing way to spend Christmas Day. Bev was on restriction for something or other, and I told her she could stay home or come along and sit in the car, but her restriction meant no movie. No one believed I would follow through on such a threat, and I don't think I believed it either. But she was rebellious and antagonistic in the car, and I actually carried out the threat. The combination of conflict and our depressing Christmas Day had turned my heart to ice.

In lowering myself to the level of a hurting child, which I was also, I debased myself. My insensitivity to her needs, on a day I once celebrated in the name of love, filled me with self-hate, guilt, and shame. These feelings interfered with my relationship with others, as well as with my studies. But because I felt so ashamed of what I had become, that day was a turning point.

Looking back on that event, that time, and that stage in my relationship with Bev, I wonder why it was only her scream I heard, and not her pain. Her lashing out was the cry of a youngster begging for love and acceptance. Why could I not acknowledge it earlier or understand the anger, competition, and fear? My inability to detect the early signs and real implications of her behavior widened the chasm between us—and within myself. Our severed relationship led to the day when her father kicked her out.

SHAME—SISTER OF GUILT, SAVIOR OF THE SELF

For nearly two years after Bev left home I was beyond anger and filled with rage. Rage is different from anger. Rage protects the self from further exposure and further experiences of shame by insulating the self and actively keeping others away.[18] Sometimes I directed that rage toward those I loved the most, indulging in uncontrollable behavior that took a lot of sorting out to begin to understand. Then I called it guilt, but it was rage rooted in shame.

Is any feeling more humiliating than shame? Mine became more destructive than guilt, for shame pervaded my sense of who I was. To be ashamed was to be alone, naked, and vulnerable.

Shame is rage turned against the self, says Erik Erikson in *Childhood and Society*. "He who is ashamed would like to force the world not to look at him, not to notice his exposure. He would like to destroy the eyes of the world. Instead, he must wish for his own invisibility." Shame supposes we are exposed and conscious of being looked at: self-conscious. It is expressed in the impulse to bury one's face or sink to the ground.[19]

Erikson's description reminded me of a luncheon interview in New York City as a stepmother struggled to describe her feelings about her twelve-year-old stepdaughter. Our eye contact had been strong. But as she talked about her jealousy of the girl, her head lowered, her hand went to her forehead, and her eyes turned away. When finally she identified her feeling as shame, tears streamed down her cheeks. Although she was the only one I interviewed who spoke the word aloud, I think I saw shame often as stepparents talked about feeling they had failed.

The shame I felt as I perceived myself to be a bad stepmother was matched when, as a child, I was asked by friends about my father and I could not explain why he had left or why I lived in a stepfamily. And now, as a stepmother, what I had tried to do in the name of love—rearing these girls as my own—had soured. Since I carried most of the family's emotional responsibility, like most stepmothers I assumed the blame. During one of the darkest times of my life, I directed the guilt and shame inward.

Shame is the sister of guilt and often is confused with it, explains Dr. Willard Gaylin. They serve similar purposes: Both emotions deal with violating our codes of conduct, and both are supporting pillars of the social structure. But they work differently. Guilt is an inner-directed emotion, a feeling we have when we've done something wrong. It often drives us to seek exposure. In contrast, shame incorporates the community, the family, the other person; it is the experience of being bad as a person and begs for privacy. Guilt serves as an individual conscience, shame as a community conscience. Guilt needs communication to be alleviated; shame retreats into privacy for repair.[20]

When emotional ties are established between people, a bond of trust is formed. That bond is an interpersonal bridge, making it possible to be vulnerable and open with another person, to understand, grow, and change within the relationship. When that bond is broken, trust ends and shame takes over.[21] Inevitably, shame becomes bound up with identity formation. To experience shame is to feel fundamentally defective as a person, so shame is accompanied by a self-protective rage.

Five years into our marriage Walter and I had made all the classic mistakes of stepparenting. Neither of us had explored past feelings and relationships before we remarried. We did not understand that we were a different kind of family unit and pretended to be like the families we had just left. I claimed the girls as my own, discouraging a relationship with their own mother; and then later, when my own self was crying out for survival, I could not meet their needs. During our family life, none of us dealt with the feelings that gnawed at us, denying their existence until these emotions became our enemies.

That disavowal led me to fulfill the Cinderella myth and led others in the family to indulge in equally destructive behavior. Our denial nearly cost us our family. Too many stepfamilies pay that price.

I have survived guilt and shame by stripping away the layers to make some sense of what happened. My willingness to share may not help others avoid similar incidents, because each of us must learn what no one else can teach us. And we cannot learn it until we are ready. But it might alleviate the self-hate, guilt, and shame that many steppeople turn inward.

In order to share publicly my descent into guilt and shame I had to learn to distinguish between feeling ashamed and a sense of shame. A sense of shame arises out of the belief that certain things are private, and it guards these things from public view. We must be primary guardians of our private self, writes Dr. Gaylin. But in feeling ashamed it is our misdeed or wrongdoing that is exposed. In either case, we are aware of that something is being exposed that ought not to be, and its exposure reflects badly on us.

Stepparents and stepchildren must get past this fear. The shame that often accompanies damaged step relationships is magnified by stereotypes and society's unenlightened attitude. Had I done the same thing with my own sons that I did with Bev, I would have been disappointed in my parenting skills, but the deficiency would not have been so devastating.

My stepparenting mistakes were not so much misdeeds as misinformation. I was reacting to problems that originated in my childhood, and nobody helped me understand them until much later in my life. I was functioning with too little knowledge and I did not think to look to society as being partially at fault.

No longer do guilt and shame pervade my life, because as I began to understand the purpose behind these feelings, I was forced to confront and deal with them. As painful as the confrontation was, it helped me in my relationships with my stepchildren, my stepfather, and my biological parents. Only when I hid from my emotions did they become enemies. But when I stopped seeing them as useless and destructive, they began guiding me to rebuild family relationships.

8 Shadows from Stepchild Land

"After the first crash, I ran into the room to find my father swearing and pitching dishes at my stepmother sitting on the hearth," a young New Hampshire woman recalls. "As he aimed the plates above her head, she never flinched. Had he not been drinking again, he wouldn't have acted like this. I knew better than to interfere. But with each broken dish I felt a deeper fear than for her safety.

"That night I dreamed that I lost this mother, too. She did not die, but like my first mother, finally she had enough of my father and left us. Broken dishes, broken marriage—who knows what the dream meant," she said. "All I know is that every time they fought, I was afraid they would break up."

The fear of losing another family lingers in the mind of the stepchild like a nightmare that only daylight can dispel. Many youngsters interpret the loss as rejection, some as abandonment. Few forget it. Children from broken families need little stress to trigger off fears that again their lives may be disrupted. Such feelings may keep them from building trusting relationships within the stepfamily. Others don the stereotyped label of stepchild, translate their status to second-rate or make-do, and live out their lives feeling in a one-down position.

Labels become tidy catchalls. They identify attitudes, beliefs, behaviors; and the world reacts accordingly. Accepting these labels and living the behavior associated with them is even more dangerous. A person who accepts the manic-depressive label has little incentive to control moods; a man who accepts a male chauvinist label expends little energy on understanding or changing his behavior toward women.

STEPCHILD AS SCAPEGOAT

A time comes when we outgrow labels or are forced to give them up. But labels serve as crutches, and giving them up can be far more difficult than adopting them. Perhaps filling these pages with the remnants and scars from my childhood years would expose the insecurity and unhappiness of being a stepchild.

Shadows from the past, however, do not always reflect reality, as perception distorts memory and feelings. In tandem with images—mental pictures held about something—perception can form strong subconscious bases from which decisions are made and behaviors carried out. Awareness is one step toward directing the future; giving up a label and the perceptions surrounding it is quite another. But once I had decided to share my experiences, I was forced to unravel these experiences to confront truths I had never understood.

My coat of armor was crested by my stepchild label and all the misperceptions I had attributed to it. Society's myths, fairy tales, and lack of empathy have stamped all things "step" as negative. I accepted this as truth. The Cinderella story, which has survived for centuries, affected my thoughts of myself. If stepchild was equated with being poor and pathetic, then stepfather and stepmother were associated with wickedness, cruelty, and neglect.

Having accepted the stereotype as my heritage, my status, second rate was all I could expect of myself. I became a wife and stepmother, then a wife and stepmother for the second time. On good days I could talk myself out of second-class citizenship, but my feelings about myself were rooted in the Cinderella image.

As I attempted to pin my shortcomings and fears on being a stepchild, writing this chapter made my head ache and discomfort gnaw at my gut. One day, as I explained these reactions to a friend, he asked, "Are you lying in your book?" No, certainly not.

What I did not know then was that I was deceiving myself. Through my stepchild's eyes, I could displace my troubles on stepparents because I had struggled with anger at having grown up feeling so insecure. I could also identify the emotional games that hurt and angry children play on stepparents, making the role even more difficult. Yet I could not help my stepchildren avoid similar feelings and behaviors. I had experienced step relationships from both sides, but still I could make no sense of this situation.

In trying to understand my life, I was not evading the truth consciously. But my notion that step was bad, negative, second best let me wear the mantle of victim and yield responsibility for the direction of my life. This kind of subconscious protection from what is too painful to confront is called a *defense mechanism*. It comes in diverse forms: rationalizing, intellectualizing, projecting our problems onto someone else— devices to avoid facing reality. To nurture my illusion, I leaned on several.

While interviewing others, and while writing, I experienced a metamorphosis in my own attitudes. My research began as I scribbled notecards of recollected injustices of my childhood; all of us have such storehouses. In Nancy Friday's book, I marked passages that validated my perceptions of how life as a youngster had been. Only later did I come to realize these had been in relationship to my own mother. If a daughter's identity is tied to her mother, what then of the double whammy of having two mothers? A blessing or a curse? I began to rehash my own experiences and those of my stepdaughters. Despite the problems, I felt I had had a positive effect on their lives. Why the internal confusion, the continuing need to view being a stepchild as negative?

In Washington, D.C., I began interviewing people, expecting to find vast support for my premise that stepchildren are innocent victims. Several adult stepchildren acknowledged that they harbored feelings of hurt and insecurity, recalling the anguish of never feeling adequate, never feeling as if they belonged to anyone. Some had suffered emotional or physical abuse. A forty-year-old printer delved only slightly into his past before clamming up. "The damage is done," he said angrily. "Emotional abuse is lifelong." He avoids talking about the past with his stepmother, saying he prefers to work it out in his head. His wife, also a stepchild and now a stepmother, vented her anger about what her stepfather had done to her. Her reactionary parenting efforts with her stepson are based on her determination not to repeat the pattern, she says.

A thirty-four-year-old Baltimore woman shared her frustration at failing to overcome the insecure feelings she developed as a stepchild. Her stepmother praised her prettier and more talented cousins, but there was no affection or praise for her. Or at least not in the doses she needed after her mother died. In a choked voice, she said, "I developed no sense of myself, no sense that I was good enough to accomplish anything. I grew up feeling that I was a failure, that something was wrong with me. No one ever said this directly, it was just a feeling." Now, as stepmother to a teenage boy, she understands better her stepmother's point of view.

Other stepchildren held similar feelings. When I asked one set of children what the term "stepfamily" meant to them, a twelve-year-old boy shouted, "It's not like the real thing." I winced. He described how he felt growing up, and the words fit me. Interviews with stepchildren often validated my notion that being a stepchild is a terrible thing and we live with the scars forever.

During a month spent alone, I began to face reality. Fooling others can be easy, but deceiving oneself is difficult. Just as we can manipulate statistics to prove a point, we can also shore up our convictions by hearing what we want to hear. Now, in this month of introspection, I began to question my own convictions.

Then I read an article by Harvard developmental psychologist Jerome Kagan. The gist of his article was that, just as beauty is in the eye of the beholder, parental love or rejection is a belief held by the child, not a set of actions by the parent.[1] The article lowered my stepmother guilt, but conflicted with my belief about being a deprived stepchild. Dr. Kagan had to be wrong, I decided.

UNLOCKING THE PAST

Seeking answers to questions his article provoked, I went to Harvard. My expectations were high. Why would I *choose* to believe that my father did not love me? Or my mother? Or my stepfather? Why would *any* child perceive a situation to be other than it really is? Did my stepchildren cling to such beliefs, too? If such delusions are self-destructive, why do we carry them into adulthood?

I explained to Dr. Kagan the effect his article was having on me. As both a stepchild and a stepparent, I found its implications confusing. He had hinted that my beliefs about my life as a stepchild might not be what really happened at all. What is more, his suggestions were defeating to me as a stepparent; no matter what I did, my stepchildren might see the situation differently. I might have no effect on them at all; or they might blame me for their lives.

As we talked about my becoming a stepchild, what was dramatically clear was the loss I felt over my father's departure. As the eldest of five children, I spent a good deal of time with him on the farm, and whether riding atop a ten-foot-high wagonload of peas, or washing the cows' udders, or learning to mix the chickens' feed, I felt useful and loved. Often he took me to bars and introduced me as his favorite girl. I sang songs for his buddies and danced on the bartops, collecting coins for my bank—and beers for him. Usually he was drunk we came home, and mother was angry. But I had a wonderful time.

Then he was gone. For a while he visited us, but it was never the same. Since he rarely made child-support payments after the divorce, Mother had him thrown in jail. For a short time he worked under the Huber Law in Wisconsin, which allowed him to spend his nights in the county jail and go out by day to work. The money he earned was sent to Mother for our care. This arrangement troubled me. If he didn't have to support me, I reasoned, he could be free.

Finally he left the state. I can't blame him, but as a child I felt abandoned, rejected. Throughout my adolescence, my mother reminded me of my father's cruelty. But since he had done nothing to me directly and I loved him so, I remained obstinately blind to his flaws. Each harangue about him made me fantasize more until I had him on a pedestal; soon Mother and I were no longer talking about the same man. Today I understand that the contrast in his treatment of the two of us was what made the relationship between my mother and me so difficult.

"But then I got a new father," I explained to Dr. Kagan, "and I expected he would take over where Daddy left off." Instead, I was unable to get what I needed or wanted from him emotionally, and I concluded that it was my fault. When I tried harder to be good or affectionate, I created more conflict with my mother—until my stepfather maintained a proper distance from me. Happy times existed between us, but they never offset the rejection I felt or measured up to the times with my father.

"But most of this happened before you became a stepchild," Dr. Kagan said. "You're attributing your anxiety to the wrong thing."

"You mean my feeling of loss and rejection was not from being a stepchild alone? Why would I imagine my stepfather did not think me valuable or love me? And why would I cling to so destructive a belief for so long?"

Dr. Kagan's response was enlightening. "To avoid insecurity and anxiety as an adult, in this society a child has three tasks to work through. One is to gain some of the qualities this society values—physical endurance, language or math skills, learning to solve problems. The second task is to believe you are valued by at least one parent. The third is to feel you are not evil. Failing in any of these tasks can create a sense of inferiority, and failing in all three will make you a very anxious adult. That you are a stepchild is trivia. By the time you were ten, you might already have been anxious about more than one of these tasks."

As he talked, that became clear. How could I feel valued by my father when he left me? Or by my mother when I suspected she was angry at me for going off with my father and leaving her behind with four tots? A child may delight in getting what she wants or needs, yet feel guilty about it. Like so many children of divorce, I assumed the blame for my parents' breakup. Since children can only view life through the eyes of their own self-interests, explanations for things gone awry also must begin with themselves, especially if no one has taken the trouble to tell them otherwise.

With my stepfather I felt valued even less. Sometimes he introduced me as his stepdaughter, a simple, straight fact. But I knew little about steppeople other than Cinderella's stepsisters, who were selfish, mean, and ugly. Being called a stepdaughter reminded me of that stereotype, and I carried it even farther. Since I was those things, how could he love me? Worse, the introduction revealed that I was not his real daughter. And worse yet, I knew that somewhere Ben had two daughters of his own. But because he loved my mother, he was burdened with caring for us and could no longer see them. He never played martyr and never spoke of it. But were it not for me, I imagined, he could still be with them.

Sometimes I feared he, too, would leave us, and I tried extra hard to make him come close and love me. This alienated my mother, and for a long time it seemed as though I had lost her, too. In her rare free time she lavished hugs and kisses on Ben, and I resented the attention he got. Years later, Bev reminded me that I repeated this pattern. "When my mother left, we all got close to Dad; and when you two got serious, I felt left out," she said. "I still remember the first holiday you took and my shock when you left me behind."

The fear of being replaced makes children of loss distort reality. From there, misperceptions can run rampant. And as Dr. Kagan was making clear, inaccurate perceptions make it harder to resolve normal childhood tasks.

"But why?" I asked. "Why did I misperceive and mistranslate events? What purpose did it serve to see my life as a stepchild as a sad thing?"

Dr. Kagan explained patiently. "Anxieties and fears are common human experiences, so why blame it on being a stepchild? Your syndrome is as common as sand on a beach. Seek out people with similar backgrounds who are not stepchildren. They will tell you the same thing. It is not that your stepfather did anything to you. If you thought being a stepchild was a terrible thing, then you made it terrible."

I disliked what I was hearing. This candor left me with a sense of anger (because my lifelong beliefs were toppling) and anxiety (because I was still unable to identify my conflict). But an awareness was surfacing that an explanation other than mine might exist.

I left his office frustrated. If this eminent man lacked the answers, who would have them? Purpose depends upon perspective, Dr. Kagan reminded me. He suggested I read Lagerkvist's *The Eternal Smile*, in which an interrogator asks God, "What purpose did you have in mind when you created men?" To this God replies, "I only intended that man would never be satisfied with nothing."[2]

Maybe I will prove him wrong, I thought. What of all the stepchildren whose experiences were similar to mine? The notion that parental love was in the eye of the child was Dr. Kagan's point of view; I would demonstrate mine.

PARENTING, PERSPECTIVE, AND CULTURE

As I went on with my research, I tried again to tie stepchild living into a bleak, sorrowful package. In many ways, six weeks with my brother, now a stepfather, validated that living as stepchildren had taken its toll on our family. During the years I spent in and out of therapy, two of my brothers wrestled with alcoholism. The night before high school graduation, another brother was killed in an auto accident following a drinking celebration. As unhappy stepchildren, I concluded, we were acting out our negative feelings about ourselves.

But as my brother and I talked, my thinking was exposed as narrow-minded. Never for a moment did he think of himself as a stepchild. He was a toddler when our mother married Ben, knew little of our father, and remembered his growing-up years as happy. We grew up in the same house but viewed life as stepchildren very differently.

Research has shown that developmental stage and age affect children's adaptation to the loss of a parent.[3] The same factors influence their adjustment to life in a stepfamily. Older children have more difficulty because they were more deeply involved in the former family and are experiencing the normal crisis of adolescence. Younger children tend to look to the acquired stepparent as a substitute.[4] Three teenagers I interviewed who had been reared by stepparents since they were tots said they felt their stepparents to be their real parents. Their gripes centered on typical adolescent issues—curfew, car, responsibility—rather than injustices or cruel stepparents.

Ready to arrange these puzzle pieces, one day I sat trembling with fear and reread Dr. Kagan's article, trying to understand the roots of my anxiety.

Western society clings to the idea of a prescription for lifelong emotional security. An infant who is loved will be forever protected from misfortune, we believe. This is based partly on the idea that parenting practices with young children can affect adult personalities. Dr. Kagan suggests that parental love as central to a child's self-image could simply be a culture-bound belief—albeit a powerful one.

Parenting practices in other cultures differ. For example, a Norwegian mother living near the Arctic Circle sees her four-year-old blocking the doorway. Without saying anything she bends down, picks him up, and moves him out of the way. Is this a sign of indifference or dislike? No.

Most mothers in northern Norway act like this, and the children give no evidence of being rejected youngsters.

A parent cannot be evaluated as hostile or accepting by simply observing behavior, according to Dr. Kagan. "Neither love nor rejection is a fixed quality of behavior. Parental love is a belief held by the child, not a set of actions by a parent."

The implications of this jarred me. If parental practices did not dictate my value as a stepchild, I had imposed a meaning on those events. Did my stepfather's distance have other reasons? Did the fear of incest scare him? Did he feel guilty over abandoning his own children? Why did I perceive that he did not love me because I was unworthy?

Dr. Kagan's logical argument prodded me to review my life as a stepchild, this time as objectively as I could. I was not abused like the foster child next door, whose hands were held over a candle flame in front of me at supper one night because he'd lied to his foster father. We were poor and we knew it, but we were always well clothed and well fed. Out of necessity, we all worked—and learned a sense of responsibility. Each of us was involved in school and church activities. At home we played together, consuming great quantites of popcorn over Monopoly and other board games. My parents fought little, but when they did, it was over us. As I looked back on those years without anger, the negative taint began to slip away.

What then of the deeply sad feelings I harbored? My stepfather was good to me, often handling difficult situations with a sense of humor I wish I had adopted into my life. That he cared for the five of us during difficult times should have been enough. But my emotional needs were high. Sometimes I pretended he was my father, and nearly always I avoided telling my friends otherwise. When they found out, I acted as though it was no big deal to have a stepfather. But for me, it was.

When the loving and attention I wanted did not come, I fought about seemingly unimportant issues. Curfew. Rules. Chores. I fought them all, because to accept my stepfather and his rules without a fight would have seemed unfair to my own father. There was no logic to this, just a feeling. My stepfather would have to prove he was good enough to replace my father.

Today, researchers explain my behavior and confusion by saying that what I had blamed on being a stepchild had more to do with being a child in a low-income family. In societies stratified by class, a family's socioeconomic position exerts a great influence on a child's development. One of the family's many functions is as a model of identity for the children.

Even before children start school, they come to learn what society values or does not. Material wealth, certain vocations, and certain cognitive skills are desirable; unskilled jobs, the inability to read and write, and broken homes are undesirable. When low-income children compare themselves to classmates these differences make them feel shame.[5] Long before I became a stepchild I had compared myself to my friends at school and failed to measure up because most of the children I knew lived with both parents and were middle-class.

My mother's remarriage made me feel even more an outsider. I was a stepchild when it was less common than it is today. Like a child looking wide-eyed through Macy's Christmas windows, I looked enviously through the nuclear-family windows of my peers and thought it must be wonderful to live there. With only my fantasies to guide me, I was unaware that even in nuclear families life can be grim.

People put up barriers to cope with hurts. Barriers that are effective become habitual and are maintained even when they become dysfunctional and self-destructive. These coping mechanisms persist simply because they are habits. As Dr. Kagan had said, using labels and blaming parents or stepparents "worked for you because you couldn't think of anything else that would rationalize as well. We're wired to think this way in our society. In the fifteenth century the explanation would have been witchcraft.

"Sorcery and the stars do not provide rational explanations in the modern West, but the past and personal relationships do," Dr. Kagan continued. "Most of us who feel unhappy or inferior turn to our childhoods. We need to shed the blame because the responsibility of unhappiness is too hard to bear, and our culture provides explanations that fit. You are a stepchild, and it was not your fault. That is why you are anxious as an adult, you tell yourself. It satisfies because the burden is off you."

"But why have I clung to a negative perception if nothing bad really happened?" I begged him to explain.

"Something did happen," he said. "As a child, you came to conclusions. Suppose at ten you stole something and decided you were wicked. Children come to conclusions." And on those childhood conclusions, formed in reaction to fear and hurt, we build our lives.

Six months after talking with Dr. Kagan, a year after reading his article for the first time, accepting its implications still troubled me. Giving up the stepchild label was too threatening. But he was right about perspective and perception, and once I became aware of it, I was forced to examine feelings and decisions that have governed my life.

Before I became a stepchild, I made decisions. As a low-income child who could not measure up to the schoolmates I chose as models, I decided something was wrong with me. I had already learned of my father's disappointment at his firstborn's being a girl. And as a firstborn with a tendency toward guilt,[6] I decided that my parents' divorce was my fault, that my mother disliked me because of my father's attention, and that if I had been worthy, my father would not have left. That I was at fault and unlovable was the only explanation I had.

As a stepchild I came to other conclusions, equally unfounded. It was my fault that my father was jailed and that my stepfather could not see his children. And I must be wicked for considering my stepfather an intruder when he really was trying to make our lives better.

PERCEPTIONS AND STEREOTYPES

As I grew up, bit by bit I heard things and experienced others to form these conclusions. My dark portrait of step was gleaned from stories I heard and feelings I developed about not living in families the way my friends did. Today, one-third of the children in school live in a step relationship of some sort. When I was a stepchild we were a much smaller minority and I felt different and alone.

Only recently have researchers begun to study the long-term effects of divorce on children, and at last one critical observation has been made: To develop healthy attitudes about themselves and to avoid feeling rejected and abandoned, children of divorce need the influence of both biological parents in their lives.[7] The issue of children of divorce cannot be approached without looking ahead to the reality that most of these children will become stepchildren and ultimately many of them will be stepparents. When children are left to their own devices to cope with their confused feelings over the loss of a parent, their misperceptions about themselves may generate serious problems that spill over into the stepfamily.

In some way, each of us carries within us the child of the past that affects our adult life. Stepchildren, especially those who like myself are now stepparents or may be, need to work at erasing shadows from the past that might affect their ability to rear someone else's children. If their belief about life as a stepchild remains as askew as mine did, it may affect new relationships at levels impossible to detect or understand.

Getting along with a new stepparent seems to be the most difficult for low-income children, researchers find. In one study, two reasons are cited. First, even before the stepparent comes on the scene, the children already arc disturbed. Their security is threatened, and their parents have few resources to help the children understand what is happening to them. To the parents, feeding them takes priority, and children often are left to deal with their feelings as best they can. When children are afraid, hurt, lost, or confused, they act to gain immediate relief. If the adults around them fail to understand, or if the children's actions are misinterpreted, ignored, or punished, the children react more strongly and the problems snowball. Having little help in gaining relief, as is the case for most low-income children, their fears and insecurities conjure up mighty misperceptions.

Second, after the remarriage, the discipline scene becomes a testing ground for the new stepparent. Middle-income parents are expected to earn and maintain their position through rational behavior and justice toward their children. But in low-income families, parents derive authority merely by being the biological parents. Few children question their parents' authority; they just respond. But such authority is vested only in the biological parent, not in the stepparent, and children do not transfer this without a fight or at least a severe test.[8]

Such tests come in many forms. In their need to measure love, all children keep a tally of gifts from parents—psychological or material. A parent's company and attention get high marks, but the real value of the gift depends upon its scarcity.[9] In my case, I knew better than to expect my stepfather's time. It was focused on working—sometimes at two jobs, to feed us—and on my mother. Although I understood that his welding job could barely keep us going financially, I fantasized that if he would buy me something it would be a sure sign that he loved me.

Downtown one day, I asked Ben to look at clothes with me. I coveted a pleated skirt and modeled it for him, assuring him I had enough baby-sitting money stashed at home to pay for it. Until we got home, would he lend me the money? Of course he did. Later, with excuse after excuse, I avoided paying him back. He rarely mentioned the loan, but Mother did each time I wore the skirt. Finally, to avoid her reminders about the money, I sneaked the skirt out in a paper bag with my gym clothes and put it on at school to collect compliments. "My father bought it for me," I said. My blush was less from pride than from shame over my lie. I despised dishonesty, but thought the deceit had been worth the price. When I was eighteen and moved away, the first check I wrote on my new bank account was to repay Ben.

Many stepparents bear the brunt of their stepchildren's behavior that is rooted in pain and confusion. A Maryland teenager said she moved out after years of fighting her stepfather "to the bitter end, rarely over important things, but more to make life rough for him." Why? She didn't know, but her years as a stepchild had been "bad, miserable times."

Later she leaned back and smiled. "You know, being a stepchild wasn't that bad. I made it that way. My stepfather is really a fine person, a good person. He did far more for me than my father ever did. Oh, Dad sent the checks to support me, but this man worried about me, tried to show me right and wrong, and fathered me." Reflective for a moment, she looked sad. Recalling that I was thirty-eight years old before I told my stepfather I appreciated him, I asked her if she had ever shared these warm feelings with him. "No, not yet," she said. "But someday I will, when I figure out why I saw things the way I did."

Until confronted with the roots of my misperceptions, I never knew the effect of fairy tales and stereotypes in creating images of life as a stepchild. In literature and folklore as well as in fairy tales, the stepfamily has left a bad image, especially for stepmothers. It continues today. In the *Second Treasury of the World's Greatest Fairytales,* up front, in full color, sits Cinderella in her rags, her haughty stepsisters and stepmother in their finery. The *First Treasury* does not carry the tale; it is depicted on the cover.[10] References to cruel stepfathers exist—who can forget Murdstone in *David Copperfield?*—but they appear mostly in adult literature. The stories children read are part of the information that forms their attitudes and perceptions—or misperceptions.

Some experts defend fairy tales because they serve a symbolic function. In *The Uses of Enchantment,* Bruno Bettelheim views fairy tales as important in helping children find meaning in life and come to terms with good and bad feelings about their mothers by splitting them into two images (the stepmother serves as the bad mother). His defense of the *Cinderella* tale centers less on the stepmother image than on the agonies and hopes surrounding sibling rivalry. Bettelheim notes that the degraded Cinderella wins out over the stepsisters who abused her, and through her own efforts she transcends her lowly state. "It can be true then for the child reading the tale, can it not?"[11]

Perhaps, if the child reading the tale hooks into the idea of rivalry. But Bettelheim discounts the many others who focus on the wicked stepmother and the deprived, abused stepdaughter. He ignores the great damage this negative imagery does to those living in stepfamilies. As I asked people what meaning the tale held for them, I found that the wicked stepmother stereotype lives. One librarian said she reads the story often in children's story hour because it represents hope that *even the poor stepchild* could get a Prince Charming.

As I heard the negative interpretations of this fairy tale, especially in low-income families, I realized the impact the story had had on me as a stepchild. When my mother remarried, I became Cinderella, and since her stepparent treated her cruelly, the same would happen to me. From the beginning I felt deprived and feared the worst. I reacted defensively. The element of hope, of which Bettelheim writes, escaped me. Prince Charmings, fairy godmothers, and stately balls were the stuff of fairy tales; stepparents and stepchildren were real.

Bettelheim's intellectual justification keeps alive a negative myth affecting millions of people who do the best they can with the challenge that stepfamily living presents. To start the cycle of changing attitudes, I want to see tales of wicked steppeople ousted from the literature, and at least one researcher agrees with me. By the time children are six, they can distinguish good from bad without polarizing the experience and splitting the two images apart, writes psychiatrist Michel Radomisli, disputing Bettelheim's premise. Dr. Radomisli suggests that by protecting the biological mother's authority, such myths serve the needs of parents better than the needs of today's children, many of whom live in stepfamilies. Splitting images may indirectly benefit the child because it makes the biological mother feel more secure; but now stepmothers play a prominent role in family living, and such tales are unacceptable.[12] What children need instead are empathy and positive models about stepfamily living.

A new children's literature about the stepfamily will provide an arena in which children can ask questions and reveal their feelings. This is beginning to happen as more children's stories examine the guilts and fears that beset youngsters after their parents remarry. A story's line may lead a child into acknowledging that he does not love his stepmother as he loved his mother who died. Or that she is afraid her stepfather will leave as her father did. With guilt and fear now exposed, these feelings become more manageable.

FIGHTING FEARS

The fear of losing another family is a reality to stepchildren. Conflict and crisis are bristly reminders that family loss remains a possibility well into adulthood. I lost a father to divorce, a stepfather to emotional distance, a husband to divorce, and another husband to various lovers; and each time, my insecurities peaked. When I felt rejected, I panicked. Fear caused me to overreact and try to make people love me so they would not want to leave. Sometimes I played the victim game to gain approval. This game involved controlling people, and as I manipulated and stifled people

I also smothered possibilities. It took the loss of two important relation-ships with women to make me identify the damage that living up to a label was doing.

The fear of abandonment and rejection is the legacy of many children of loss. My reluctance to take risks for fear of being rejected reinforced my fears well into adulthood. A while back, to research a magazine article, I attended a seminar on depression. The psychodrama workshop leader asked if any of us had been depressed recently. I laughed aloud.

When he asked what I found so amusing, I explained that I had been feeling depressed for weeks. We discussed my fighting an emotional breakdown years back and my battles with the holiday blues each Christ-mas season, as the house was festooned, the cookie jars were filled—and my spirits sagged.

Seating me in a chair facing the group, the group leader asked me to talk about what was bothering me. I told of the fear that at times crippled me, explaining it as being afraid to complete worthy goals that would force me to grow. Balancing college and family had been a long haul, and the year I graduated my stop-again, start-again pattern was resumed. I described myself as afraid of failure or success.

That popular explanation was comfortable, so I donned the fear-of-success label willingly.[13] How relieved I was to know I was simply a victim.

But the group leader urged me to talk more. To encourage me to confront my depression directly, he invited a woman to sit in the chair across from me and pretend she was my fear. We could deal with each other any way we liked. I told her I was afraid to write my book because I might fail. She nagged and said I was weak. With this nerve hit, I began to fight. We exchanged chairs, and fear yelled at me, goaded me, called me a coward.

Her accusations continued until I wanted to strangle her, to rid myself of this demon once and for all. "I'm not a coward," I screamed at her. "I've helped raise three sets of children, started and completed college as an adult, won writing awards while still in school. . . ." As I reeled off achievements, I realized I was afraid of neither success nor failure.

"Then if that's not what you're afraid of," fear continued, "how can I control or affect your life?" As the shadows of my fear began to envelop me, I felt the way I did as a child.

"You can keep me from having what I want," I sobbed. "If I do this book, I'll lose my family."

Again the gnawing fear that I would be abandoned, rejected. But I could keep people loving me by not writing the book, not leaving my family while I did the research, not exposing what happened in our house. I could settle back into my safe job of writing environmental science news.

By then my identity seemed linked to writing my first book. But it was not worth the loss of my family; nothing was worth the loss of my family. I would give up the writing project.

After the psychodrama workshop made me understand that I could remain in control and that this fear was yet another false perception rooted in childhood fears, I talked with my husband and children about how I felt.

Talking cleared the air for all of us. No one in my family was totally pleased about the book because it interfered with my ability to meet their needs. And as I grew professionally, my husband worried that I might leave; his former wife had. My youngest son missed me while I was gone; his biological father had died the year before and his own fears of loss were high. I explained to them that I, too, had fears and that, as exciting as it was to travel, being away bothered me. Often I worried that they might not be there when I came back. When the fears were exposed they seemed manageable, but until we talked, my family had had little notion of my fears or vulnerabilities. When they understood, they supported my efforts and did not want me to quit.

EXAMINING REALITY

Misperceptions and stereotypes often determined my attitudes and behavior as a stepparent. Sometimes I repeated what I had gotten as a child; sometimes I took the opposite road. Repetition and reaction—each course was followed unknowingly, and both were destructive.

All of us are survivors of our childhood, and all of us use different survival tools. As a stepchild I viewed life through distorted lenses, my misperceptions coming partially from society's attitudes and stereotypes. Just as Norman Rockwell painted the American family as he wished it were, rather than as it really existed, to better cope with my losses I perceived that life as a stepchild was supposed to be negative.

The stepchild label provided an excuse to feel like a victim. And victims are not responsible for their behavior. This worked until I was forced to confront the situation from the perspective of a stepparent. Besides seeing how difficult the role of stepparent was, I began to realize that the second chance I was given at family life made me more than a survivor. As an adult I was changing and growing. There is ample evidence in my own childhood that life in a stepfamily was a positive alternative to the life my mother could have made for us alone and on her limited earnings.

This growing awareness kept my feelings in conflict. Somewhere in reality lay the fact that probably my parents *did* love me, that my step-family *was* a real family. And, in spite of feeling like a wicked witch, I probably *have* had a positive effect on my stepchildren's lives. But as long as I went on believing we were all victims, the anxiety continued.

Fearing rejection and feeling uncertain about their identities, step-children need to deal with a sense of being less than real, less than enough. This task, which is critical to a child's development, can be made easier for stepchildren by altering patterns and stereotypes that under-mine their self-images. Stepparents can help their stepchildren to avoid dragging their emotional baggage into the future, but first they must have their own relationships clear. The journey toward realness need not be as long as mine or filled with such conflict if children are not left to grope for explanations or live with labels on which they pin their hurts.

Like the boy who said his stepfamily was not like the real thing, stepfamily members need to examine what realness is all about. Webster's definitions of "real" include "existing as a fact," "actual, rather than ideal or imaginary," and "true,"[14] all of which apply to the stepfamily state. The stepfamily is no less a real family simply because it is different.

Stepchildren need to distinguish between their real parent and the other parent. But a dual meaning exists behind this delineation. When I asked stepchildren to explain what they meant by real mother or father, two patterns emerged. For most, the real parent was the biological par-ent. But for many, real reflected love and concern, and it referred to the person who reared them—the person who cared, taught, tolerated, and ultimately influenced them to become the kind of people they were.

No one explains realness as well as the Skin Horse who had been around the nursery for a long time, in Margery Williams's *Velveteen Rabbit*.

"Real isn't how you are made," said the Skin Horse. "It's a thing that happens to you."

"Does it hurt?" asked the Rabbit.

"Sometimes," said the Skin Horse, for he was always truthful. "When you are Real, you don't mind being hurt. It doesn't happen all at once. You become. It takes a long time. That's why it doesn't happen to people who break easily, or have sharp edges, or who have to be carefully kept. Generally, by the time you are Real, most of your hair has been loved off, and your eyes drop out and you get loose in the joints and very shabby. But these things don't matter at all, because once you are Real, you can't be ugly, except to those people who don't understand."[15]

The realness problems of which stepchildren speak are linked far more deeply to their being children of divorce than to their later status as stepchildren. But because the stepfamily is part of the reorganization of the family, the two remain entwined. Professionals who work with children of divorce must look ahead to this family structure in which most of them probably will live. Attitudes about stepfamily living will change when divorcing parents and their children learn that it is all right to love both parents. When the children are cut off from one biological parent, they develop misperceptions that follow them into adulthood. Then the patterns are repeated and the destructive cycle continues.

Shown no other way of dealing with my pain, I blamed my problems on my stepfamily. Today I know that many of my troubles stemmed from losing touch with my father. No research has yet compared the children of divorce who kept healthy relationships with both parents and the ones who could not. But my experience certainly is not unique.

While writing this book, I lived some months in an area reminiscent of my Wisconsin childhood. The dairyland country constantly reminded me of my father, and my journal filled with childhood memories and longings to see him. Next year, I told myself. That was what I had been telling myself for years. The truth was that I knew I had to connect with my father again, but I was afraid.

A few years earlier my brother had found our father and stayed in touch with him. Although he felt guilty when he shared the meetings with our mother and stepfather, that guilt was the trade-off for being able to be with him.

Now, one day my brother telephoned to tell me that our father was in a Phoenix hospital about to undergo emergency surgery. The doctors suspected cancer.

I was panic-stricken. Just when I was about to tie up the loose ends from my childhood, would I be denied the chance to work out this critical relationship? What if he died in surgery and I never got the answers I needed? What if he never knew how much I loved him?

Two hours before the surgery, I got through to him at the hospital.

"Daddy? This is Toby."

The line was silent. My parents had had childhood nicknames for each of us: Toby, Skeeter, Buster, Bowser, Binkie. Maybe he had forgotten mine. Maybe he didn't want to be bothered with me when he was afraid and in pain. As I repeated his name my heart pounded.

"Is it really you?" he finally asked. And then, again, a long silence. But this time our hearts touched, and through my mind flashed memories of my childhood on the farm. We talked reassuredly of our love for each other and of the future.

The surgery was successful and no cancer was found. Luck, reprieve. Another chance to do what I had tried to do once before. Not only as a child but well into adulthood I had been unable to love both my father and my stepfather without feeling guilty and torn apart. Finally I stopped keeping in touch with my father. Fifteen years had passed since I had seen him when I dialed the hospital, yet never had I stopped longing to love him freely.

Now, I no longer have to feel guilty about loving both of my fathers. Each man shares a part of my being the person I am today and each deserves my love and concern.

The cry within my heart is quieting.

9   Nobody Understands

On their grandchildren's birthdays, two Maine grand-parents gift-wrap crisp five-dollar bills. As the children tear open the gifts, they fantasize about what they will do with the money—all, that is, except the new stepgrandson. He gets two pairs of socks. This eight-year-old thanks them politely, but last year he came to his mother with tears in his eyes, holding up the socks and asking, "Why?" Perhaps one of the most painful lessons in being a stepchild is learned early: that inequality exists even within the family. This boy thought he was part of the family; his stepfather's parents saw it another way.

The stepfamily does not live in a social vacuum, and the network of external relationships affecting it is vast. How grandparents, aunts, and uncles accept the new family contributes toward its ability to attain harmony. But friends and acquaintances, teachers, lawyers, ministers, even counselors also affect the stepfamily as it struggles to integrate. Negative imagery is not unique to fairy tales; today an equally inaccurate portrayal of stepfamily life is foisted on us by the media. All of society's institutions have an immense effect on the stepfamily, and until recently it has in most cases been a negative influence.

THE EXTENDED FAMILY—SUPPORT OR SABOTAGE?

How family kin mesh into the relationship network is fairly clear in a first marriage, but a stepfamily alters this by shifting pivotal links among kindred, creating an imbalance between the remarrieds and the kin of their former spouses. When marriages dissolve, relatives do not become ex-grandparents or ex-aunts or ex-uncles. Kinship ties to children remain intact; and, when a parent remarries, children gain what anthropologist Paul Bohannan calls *pseudokin*.[1] Although the new relationships lack a biological tie, they extend the kinship network, providing potential extra resources and support for the stepfamily.

144

Because of conflicting feelings and confusing roles, too often these quasi-kin work against the new stepfamily. In-laws can influence any family greatly, and in-law troubles are common in all family styles. Again and again, social workers report that relatives are at the core of clan disputes, and studies cite mother-in-law troubles as a common root of marital disputes.[2]

Remarriage upsets many grandparents psychologically. The older generation is faced with a family tree bearing unfamiliar fruit, and these new stepfamily relationships stir up conflicting feelings that impose difficult choices on this older generation. The decisions they face range from holiday gift giving and inheritance issues to the treatment of a child with whom they have no emotional history. Whether attempting to stretch a fixed income to include presents for five new stepgrandchildren or attempting to keep control from the grave over who retains the family antique brooch, many grandparents are confused.[3] And those who are ambivalent about their own child's second or third spouse certainly will have trouble warming up to their unusual inheritance from their offspring —stepgrandchildren.

Grandparents of divorce and remarriage react negatively for various reasons. Much of their anxiety is linked to their distress over the broken family. Seeing their family systems threatened, most are anxious about where they will fit into these complicated relationships. When marriages end, researchers find that relationships most often change between the spouse without custody and the former in-laws. If the broken family results from divorce, parents may side with their own child and direct their anger at the former in-law. Some dole out this hostility with the milk and cookies. And the grandchildren are caught in the crossfire.

As parents keep in touch with those they speak of as their children's relatives, in-laws can become outlaws, writes Dr. Bohannan.[4] Some in-laws use the children as camp spies, having them for a day or weekend and plying them with questions about the stepfamily or the parent with custody. Such meddling sets up loyalty conflicts, and eventually many children prefer to avoid the visits. Unable to see that their own destructive acts cause the alienation, in-laws may lay the blame elsewhere—often on the stepparent. Others may have grown close to their son- or daughter-in-law and take a stand against their own child. One upstate New York woman maintains a close relationship with her former husband's mother. While the marriage died, the friendship between the two women flourished, providing the children with a closeness to their paternal grandparents. Even now, after her remarriage, the friendship continues.

This situation is unusual, according to one study on kinship and divorce. The divorced women in this study had little contact with their former husbands' families. The remarried women and their children were virtually isolated from their former husbands' kin but were integrated into the kin networks of their new husbands' families.[5] Although studies show that children maintain more contact with maternal grandparents, in today's mobile society not even that is a certainty.

Divorce is but one road toward the making of stepgrandparents. When a remarriage occurs after a son's or daughter's death, parents may be fearful of losing contact with their grandchildren, too. The loss could be compounded by a move separating their grandchildren by distance or by an in-law who refuses to permit visits.

Grandparents need no longer fear that parents without custody can do this. In 1975, Wisconsin became the first state to pass a law permitting grandparents to petition the court for visiting rights. Since that act, more than half the states have enacted similar statutes. While the laws show an awareness that the impact of divorce reaches far beyond parents and children, using the courts is not ideal. Forced visits embellish problems and intensify anger, turning the visits into an empty gesture that makes the children feel guilty.

Sometimes, between death or divorce and remarriage, grandparents may have to care for the children. If a mother had a hard time letting go of her son the first time around, being a surrogate mother to his children may make it even more difficult for her to accept another daughter-in-law. But when grandparents remain hostile toward the new in-law, such feelings filter down to their grandchildren.

Differences between the generations in values and ways of doing things often complicate matters. Older people may be especially hard put to acknowledge such social changes as the reorganization of their family system. Accepting a broken link in their family network is one thing; accepting a new parent for their grandchildren is another. For some, the most difficult challenge is accepting stepgrandchildren to whom they have no biological tie. As a rule, grandparents don't cotton to instant grandchildren. Such radical changes upset them, and their behavior may reflect this.

Inequitable gift giving reflects a common bewilderment about accepting new children into kin networks. For years, two grandparents in Maryland have brought identical gifts to their granddaughter and her stepbrother—$25 checks. But they never could resist bringing something a little extra for the girl—a piece of jewelry or cologne—just to let her know she is more special to them. This teenage girl says it makes her uncomfortable.

At times members of the extended family can seem downright cruel. Some may try to retain power over their grandchildren through manipulation. An aunt may woo her niece at the cost of creating a chasm in the new stepfamily. Choosing between a loving and supportive aunt, and a stepmother who must be dealt with daily, may confuse children. A deep kinship bond between a brother and a sister may threaten a remarried spouse. Erotic and familial love differ vastly; but misunderstood, they can cause a sister and wife to compete, jeopardizing both the brother-sister support system and the husband-wife relationship. If this triad results in competition for the man's time; the children within the stepfamily become the losers.

Relatives who compete with new stepparents can be troublemakers. Children respond to their grandparents with affection and spontaneity that may threaten a new stepparent, stuck with day-to-day childrearing. It can hurt a stepmother to see a grandparent collect affection from the child who rejects her.

While extended family members may seem intruders during the stepfamily's difficult first years, most are simply confused by the complicated relationships. This is especially true of grandmothers, traditionally the nurturers of grandchildren. When their grandchildren's status changes or they become stepgrandparents, what is expected of them? Where do they fit? What are the limits? Must they treat all the children the same?

Attuned to these delicate relationships, enlightened in-laws can help the stepfamily. And many do. No one demands that they love these extra children, but in acknowledging and respecting *all* the children of the stepfamily, in-laws can help it stabilize faster. Recognizing that the new stepparent may do things differently from the former spouse of their child, they consult with the new parent about limits and changes. Because gossip mars trust levels, they avoid bad-mouthing the parent without custody.

One remarried man says his ex-wife's family "was really wonderful to me, and that made a lot of difference during very trying times with the children. Without their understanding, raising 'mine' and 'ours' could have been a real mess, because the kids tried to manipulate all of us." A teenage Syracuse stepchild said, "My stepmother's parents are a regular grandmother and grandfather to us, and it feels good."

As children make the transition from the old family to the new one, rather than erecting barriers, relatives can build bridges. When children are filled with fears and insecurities during the emotional upheaval of death or divorce and remarriage, grandparents can be especially important. Maintaining a closeness with loving grandparents is vital to a child's sense of self. For the child whose family has come apart, this special relationship may be the one stable, steadying influence.

Other extended family members can reach out to the stepfamily and help the children feel a greater sense of self-confidence and happiness. An enlarged kinship network provides a breadth of experiences from which to sample life. But as children lose contact with their kinship network, their roots erode and their feeling of belonging diminishes.

When the kinship system shifts, the debate over where to spend the holidays heightens. Just because everyone has always gone to Auntie Jane's for Christmas, that tradition holds little meaning for a new wife and her children, who have not yet established an emotional tie to the family. On the other hand, new spouses must understand the family kinship ties and traditions of their mates. To avoid such competition, the new stepfamily may want to have the first year's holiday meals alone at their house. This may provide the intimate time needed to establish new traditions and plan future gatherings.

A rather unusual idea that might be just right for some families is suggested by Dr. Irene Goldenberg, who believes that holidays include being in the bosom of one's family "because it feels good to be nurtured there." She recommends that the stepfamily's members celebrate holidays with different families of biological origin. "Rather than bicker over which place means family and tradition to whom, why not let them all be where they really want to be?" she asks. "Why should the stepfamily be forced to select one family or stay home?" Of course this suggestion is not traditional, but neither is the stepfamily. And such a solution will not work for everybody. "If such a plan is rooted in anger, or if someone feels distressed at not being with a spouse at holiday time," she cautions, "then it will fail."

With such crisscrossed kin relationships, stepfamilies might be wise to look toward the strength that the extended family once offered, and that still remains a strength within much of the black community. In a slim volume, *The Strengths of Black Families*, R. B. Hill focuses on five factors, including kinship bonds, that provide such strength.[6] Using the extended family to fill gaps, to step in during crisis, or to take in children, temporarily or permanently, black families have always provided strong support systems through kin ties.

Dr. Alvin Poussaint, professor of psychiatry at the Harvard Medical School, backed up Hill's observations and left me feeling that children reared in black stepfamilies with this advantage may be confronted with far fewer loyalty conflicts and feelings of rejection than white stepchildren. But no comparative studies have been done, and my feeling is strictly speculative.

One example supporting this notion is that black families take in extra family children more readily than whites. And rather than give children up for adoption, blacks tend to keep their own kin within the family. In white families 33 percent of illegitimate children are kept home; 90 percent of black illegitimate children are reared by parents or relatives of the unwed mother.[7]

Some trace this kinship support to the African culture, where everyone took responsibility for the children, Dr. Poussaint explains. Others point out that blacks were not served by adoption agencies and, out of necessity, placed children on their own, often within the extended family. Blacks stress the teaching of bonds and relationships far more than white families, and a large family system can diffuse difficult feelings within a family. "Since black families tend to be more extended, individuals feel less stigma if they are reared by an aunt or grandparent," says Dr. Poussaint.

"Extended-family relationships also tend to soften jealousy, providing a place of warmth and love during the transition to stepfamily living," he suggests. "Say a stepfather has a poor relationship with his stepson initally. Grandmothers, aunts, and uncles can pick up the slack and ease the pressure, giving the relationship a better chance to grow."

Just as families can cushion the settling in for the stepfamily, so can friends. Divorce tends to disrupt friendships, and remarriage tests friendship further when a new person is introduced. A study of divorcées showed that only half the women kept their old friends.[8] Friends and neighbors may not understand that the dynamics of stepfamilies and nuclear families are different. Outsiders tend to be critical of the chaos, often hearing only one side of a story, and children become seduced into conversations over "ain't-it-awfuls." A hurting stepchild or a resentful stepmother can tell a poignant tale.

Without accurate data, outsiders interfere or hurl unkind barbs. At eighteen, one of my stepdaughters and a friend got into a minor scrape with the law. The boy's mother called with her solution—through her friendship with the district attorney, bail them out of a court appearance and launder their record. (Her son was applying to medical schools.) I rejected her plan, saying that the teenagers knew what they were doing and should be responsible for their actions. "If she were your own daughter, you would do it differently," she retorted.

SOCIETY'S INSTITUTIONS—AT THE CROSSROADS OF CONSCIOUSNESS

The lack of understanding of the stepfamily is attributable to our institutions. What is an institution? Social scientists have no end of definitions. The word means something established, formed, set up, and stable. For our purposes, let's use a composite definition: An institution is a social, political, or legal segment of society organized enough and powerful enough and influential enough to subject people to obligations, provide them with formal authority, and apply legal sanctions.

The institutions designed to support American society often drag their feet in their relationship with stepfamilies and, through neglect or misinformation, inflict damage on millions of stepfamily members. Trying to be what society expects them to be—a carbon copy of the nuclear family—many stepfamilies fail, and they blame themselves for their failure.

But the problem lies at society's doorstep. Lawyers, teachers, counselors, ministers, politicians, therapists, the media—all have the potential of helping the stepfamily work from its strengths. But in viewing it as deviant rather than different, most of society's servants indeed have hindered the stepfamily.

The nuclear family has been the norm, with its inherent stability, but now alternative family forms are common. With today's stepfamilies numbering in the millions, society's institutions need to update their approach. The issue of children of divorce cannot be addressed without looking ahead to the stepfamily—the next phase in the reorganization of the family system.

THE SCHOOLS—LEARNING IT RIGHT FROM THE BEGINNING

Reshaping society's attitudes can start in the schools, one of the most stable influences in a child's life. Today, nearly one-third of the children in classrooms are involved in some sort of step relationship.[9] That figure will grow; of the children born during the seventies, 40 to 50 percent will experience divorce,[10] and most of these will become stepchildren.

The school system can respond to the stepfamily in which these children will live when their parents remarry. From a kindergartner's crayoned sketches to a high school senior's thesis, chances to explore the dynamics of stepfamily living abound. The five-year-old can be encouraged to talk about his complex family to schoolmates, or the senior can

research the roots of myths and misconceptions surrounding the stepfamily, thus educating at the grass-roots level.

Such learning may be less traumatic for the students than for some
teachers. Hooked on the notion that the nuclear family is sacred, many
teachers feel anxious when children talk of two households or two mothers or when they ask for three tickets to the school play so that all their
parents can attend. Although divorce is common, many schools still avoid
the emotional situations surrounding it. Now they must deal with new
family forms, of which the stepfamily is one of the most confusing, and
stop keeping their sights set on the ideal of the never-divorced family.
The school is mandated by society as a primary guardian of America's
children for much of the day; its teachers, counselors, and administrators
should no longer find the stepfamily mind-boggling.

Schools cannot hide from the reality of the stepfamily because they
are probably the first segment of society to encounter the child's crisis of
divorce. In the classroom the youngster's response to a broken family may
range from depression and withdrawal, to acting out with sex or drugs, to
academic failure.

Many schoolchildren who reach guidance clinics are associated with
divorce trauma. When their parental support system comes apart, they
are faced with either forced independence or excessive emotional demands. As children in newly formed stepfamilies try to cope with their
original family loss, they may displace their fears onto their stepparents.
During this turbulence the familiar setting of the school with its predictable adults, routines, roles, and rules can offer strong support. Because
home problems spill into the school setting, parents often turn to the
school for help.[11]

Only recently have some schools adopted programs to meet the needs
of children of divorce. One successful program in Hastings, New York,
boasts a support team of counselor, nurse, psychologist, learning specialists, and teachers who work with these children in small groups. To avoid
labeling and isolation, children of divorce are placed with children from
intact families who also have problems.

District learning coordinator and psychologist Audrey J. Clarkin reports that the children's concerns and fears are shaped by their developmental age and social skills at the time of the divorce. In the first four
grades the common themes are fear of abandonment, loss of affection, and
guilt about having caused the divorce. In the middle school, the students
are angry at both parents and uncertain about trusting their parents or
friends. Teenagers in high school are troubled over family loyalty conflicts, sex, drinking and drugs, and dependence on peers.

Dr. Clarkin sees the school as an economic and efficient way to deliver this service to a normal population experiencing this social stress. Within the everyday school environment, children need not be labeled as sick, and this help also reaches low-risk youngsters whose family finances, conflicts, or attitudes might otherwise keep them from finding emotional relief. Such services are exciting; they are also rare.

Although school districts formulate policies on divorced and remarried families, these policies are interpreted and applied by the individual schools. In most schools, the parent with whom the child lives is assumed to be the sole parental authority and is given all the rights and privileges; the rights of the other biological parent and of stepparents are ignored or viewed in diverse ways.

Schools interpret parental authority differently. Some take a hard-line approach: No custody means no report cards and no access. Other schools work with interested parents, custody or no custody. Before giving out information to a noncustodial parent, some schools seek evidence that the parents' relationship is cordial, lest they arouse ill feelings between warring or punitive parents.

The 1974 Family Educational Rights and Privacy Act (the Buckley Amendment) added more confusion. The amendment allows only parents and legal guardians to inspect and review official student records, files, and data. When this law is improperly interpreted, explains Isolina Ricci, a child and family counselor in Palo Alto, California, the parent without custody is no longer considered a parent. In such cases, unless the parents have a joint or shared custody arrangement, or a specific agreement about the child's education, the noncustodial parent cannot even get a copy of the child's report card. But when this law is interpreted correctly, the parent retains rights and privileges with regard to the permanent records.[12]

Other reminders reflect the school-stepfamily gap. Tickets for social events are issued for one family. Presents for Mother's Day and Father's Day are limited to one per parent per holiday. Report cards and notices generally are sent to one home. Textbooks portray the never-divorced family almost exclusively. School forms are designed for one home with two biological parents rather than for two homes, each with a biological parent and perhaps a stepparent. This leaves two options: The biological parent can take care of the formalities, leaving the stepparent out; or the stepparent can sign on the dotted line, but not without being forced into deceit about roles.

School conferences provide another arena for disaster or enlightenment, depending upon the flexibility of school personnel and parents.

Counselors who understand the family configurations in which their students live can offer counsel that is pertinent to the youngsters' needs. But to counsel from ignorance is dangerous. During a crisis at our house, my stepdaughter confided her version of the conflict to a teacher. Unaware of our feelings or the dynamics of the stepfamily, and without conferring with us, this woman advised our confused adolescent to leave home. My stepdaughter took the advice, triggering many more problems, which the uninformed teacher did not have to handle, but we did.

A one-home view of family life can trap a child of divorce in the middle. When told to bring things home, a child must choose which home. Some children feel pushed into divided loyalties or pushed out of step with other families. If these predicaments are accompanied by closed-door or haphazard policies toward noncustodial parents and stepparents, the schools could be viewed as a threat to parent-child relationships or even somehow responsible for family estrangements.

Some educators help mend sad hearts and make the stepparents' tasks easier by letting them know what is happening in school. A Syracuse stepmother told of her gratitude to her eight-year-old stepson's teacher, who helped him when he cried in school, wanting his own mother. The teacher offered warmth and sympathy, told him she understood how sad he must feel, but emphasized how lucky he was to have a new stepmother who also cared about him.

Despite the number of stepchildren sitting in classrooms who will become stepparents, major colleges and universities rarely include the stepfamily in marriage and family study curricula. Because the misperceptions about stepfamily life are not dealt with, these young people may perpetuate the mistakes that others made before them.

THE RELIGIONS—MIRRORS OR WINDOWS?

Religious or not, nearly every American family is affected somehow by the church—an association of people organized to act together.

Marriage is sanctioned in the church, and the church has a continuing influence on the family. Numerous studies have linked marital problems with a lack of religious influence.[13] The church's influence on family values ranges from grace at meals and family prayer, to festivals and celebrations, to sex and fertility, to childrearing. Family members can find solutions to problems in settings from Sunday School to discussion groups to counseling by the clergy.

The church provides status, social fellowship, and solidarity. It acts as a stabilizer and an agent of social control and reform. It helps people define life goals and purposes; and, through its recreational, aesthetic, economic, or ethical functions, it teaches values.

We turn to religion for our rites of passage—the ceremonies and rituals that help cushion shock and carry people from one stage of life to the next. Baptisms, confirmations, *bar* and *bas mitzvahs*, weddings, and funerals are all conducted through a house of worship. In many religions these rituals symbolize a special divine favor.

The marriage ceremony is one such ritual. To Catholics, marriage is a sacrament that confers God's grace; to Protestants it is a holy ordinance; to Jews it is *kodosh*, a sacred consecration. All three religions endow marriage with a sacred element, and all three promote the stability of marriage and the family.[14] But all have failed to help families cope with today's reality. Although divorce and the reorganization of the family have been a fact of life for some time, only recently have religious institutions softened their stance and offered solace to members of broken families.

The church can help to bind wounds instead of creating them, as it does with the one-home view that still pervades clerical counseling; yet the church doesn't hesitate to perform a remarriage ceremony.

The remarriage ceremony gives the church family its first chance to accept the stepfamily. By speaking to guests, the pastor, priest, or rabbi can make friends and family understand how they can be supportive of this new family. And giving a special blessing for the children involved in the remarriage can help these young family members to accept a share of the responsibility for making the stepfamily work. But even before the wedding ceremony, the church should offer premarital counseling to people who have children and are considering remarriage. By teaching them the dynamics of stepfamily living, the clergy can help them to recognize how their new families will be different.

"To keep its commitment to *each* person," says Frank Halse, Jr., a minister of the United Methodist Church, "the church must understand the context within which *each* person lives and must speak to individual needs. That's caring at a truly sensitive and effective level."

The church traditionally has stressed the importance of the commitment between marriage partners, Halse explains. More recently it has begun to stress communication between the marital partners as basic to a working relationship. "It is clear that, however firm that commitment, and however skilled that communication," he continues, "couples will experience severe strains in a stepfamily if they do not understand the mechanics of normal behavior that seems negative."

Those who counsel in the churches can help these families avoid such stress. From local parishes to larger denominational policy-setting boards, stepfamily education should be part of the church's attempt to meet its community's needs.

THE THERAPISTS—WELLSPRING OF HOPE?

Until recently, stepfamilies in crisis have had little help from professional counselors. As long as these professionals viewed the stepfamily as a nuclear unit, they based their treatment on that model. Such attempts generally failed.

Like many stepfamilies, we were disappointed that our new family was not meeting our expectations and we felt ashamed because we thought we should be able to do better. Alone as well as together, Walter and I made the therapy rounds. Then one of the children went. Next the three of us went together. But we gained little help. The Freudian wasted time digging up the past. The transactional analyst offered intellectual bandages that hid the source of our pain and failure. Another therapist administered Rorschach tests, cheerily said, "You and your daughter have so much in common," but kept the secret to herself.

Some counseling has been successful with stepfamilies, but until recently the occasions have been rare. One stepfamily told of a therapist who involved all the children and both mothers. The focus: the children's loyalty conflicts, the new mother's jealousy, and the father's role with both women.

This is the basis of *family therapy*, one of the best options for the stepfamily in trouble. It is preventive and quick, and it transfers the focus from one person to the interrelationships. Having just one family member in therapy may worsen stepfamily problems because it makes that person feel responsible for the family's trouble.

Making haste slowly is paramount. By the time stepfamilies resort to counseling as a last-ditch effort to save the marriage, most are in crisis. During first visits, there is no time to delve into the past or explore deep personality problems. Therapists must offer tourniquets to stop the loss of the family's lifeblood.

The critical first step is to validate the feelings involved in the stepfamily's pain, explains Dr. Emily Visher. "Many stepfamilies come in with a profound sense of helplessness; and, when we can find ways to help them immediately control even one or two of the complicated situations in their lives, a tremendous amount of anxiety can dissolve. Sometimes emergency action is needed to calm an explosive situation so stepfamily members can get some distance, and then we work on the troubled areas."

To get them through until the next session, stepfamilies need something to grasp; homework of a sort encourages them to continue at home what was started in the therapist's office. Next, counselors help them to deal with their unrealistic expectations and to understand the stepfamily's special characteristics and feelings.

Professional therapy is not a cure-all. Ultimately the work must be done among stepfamily members and between families. But sorting out and shoring up sagging relationships may be facilitated by counselors who are aware of the stepfamily's particular pitfalls. Once steppeople learn that they are different, that their difference is normal, and that they are not alone, they can stop blaming themselves and acting defensively.

The greatest promise for the stepfamily's future lies in education. A stepfamily awareness movement began with two statewide foundations, one in New York City, the other in Palo Alto, California; another has since formed in Michigan. As information resource centers, they provide speakers, counseling, educational material, and newsletters. They offer peer counseling in which steppeople can get together to share problems and work out solutions. There is no substitute for talking with someone who has traveled the same rough roads and endured the same gut-churning feelings.

The most effective counseling is premarital, says Jeannette Lofas, executive director of the Step Family Foundation of Manhattan in New York City. Getting people to come in during courtship is difficult, but the wise ones, those who identify potential conflict areas, do seek advice. "Some people believe crisis must occur before progress begins," she says. "Premarital counseling teaches what stepfamily living is like so people can prepare for the storm. The trouble is that most people don't know when they remarry that there are storms ahead."

Lofas is tough with clients. During the education sessions, she runs a tape the family takes home to review. She gives homework—structuring family responsibilities or making agreements. If she thinks clients are not working, she fires them. "I walk out and leave the tape running," Lofas says.

The counseling emphasis centers on specifics. A living-together couple came to Lofas because the man believed the woman he was about to marry did not interact well with his children. She insisted that when the children came, he paid no attention to her. "How exactly doesn't he pay attention to you when the kids are there?" Lofas demanded. The woman said he would not sleep with her and often he went off alone with the children. Lofas made the future stepmother tell him that directly. It was the first time he heard the message clearly without other issues to camouflage her jealousy. With the communication channels open, the two began to know what each wanted from the other.

After remarriage, people arrive in a panic. "We love each other, but the kids are tearing us apart," they say. When Lofas explains that this is typical, but reparable, anxiety lowers.

The New York City foundation has also launched weekend workshops for professionals. The workshop format includes a let's-clean-house-a-bit session because many counselors are themselves steppeople who have not worked out the tangles in their own feelings about living in a stepfamily. "They don't have to solve all their problems," explains Lofas. "But being aware that the problems exist can temper what they do with a client."

Therapists are aware of their past failure with the stepfamily and are filling the gaps—eagerly. In the mid-seventies, at national conferences, professionals began to identify the needs of the stepfamily. By 1978 psychologists, psychiatrists, and social workers had acknowledged that the stepfamily was different. And in 1979, at the American Orthopsychiatric Association annual meeting, a two-day institute brought together professionals whose work in some way touched the life of the stepfamily. Lawyers, educators, psychiatrists, psychologists, sociologists, and social workers recognized the stepfamily as an alternative family form with its own counseling needs. Those attending the overbooked workshop clamored for resources, bibliographies, seminars—anything to help these families, they begged.

But awareness takes sidesteps. One seminar included an interview in which a stepfamily and a therapist talked about how the family members worked in and around all the extra relationships. They painted a rosy picture of their coping, denying anger, jealousy, and unfinished business from the past. During the wrap-up of the seminar, panel members dwelled on this family's problems, discussed how they would intercede, and most made it plain that they still viewed this family as pathological.

By the time the last panel member had spoken, I could barely keep from jumping up and shouting, "This is not a sick family. With all the pressures working against them, they are doing well." Since I was a guest, I kept silent. But the incident bothered me because it revealed how far the helping professions have to go in doffing their blinders and seeing the stepfamily within its own framework.

The institute is now an annual event, overflowing with professionals seeking information about the stepfamily.

A most exciting change is the founding of a national organization to meet the needs of American stepfamilies and the professionals who work with them. The Stepfamily Association of America addresses the specific needs of this family form that are not served by existing community organizations. It provides education and enlightenment through a national network of local chapters, help groups, and survival courses. Its *Stepfamily Bulletin* publication and public relations activities will upgrade the stepfamily's image. The association provides two-day training workshops for professionals who work with stepfamilies; a referral service to those counselors is available to the public. National research, state division, and local chapter development are being coordinated by this national organization dedicated to improving the quality of stepfamily life.

THE MEDIA—TELL IT LIKE IT IS

The media have painted an unrealistic portrait of family living. Television's situation comedies perpetuate the myths of folklore and fairy tales. First came the syrupy "Father Knows Best" and "Ozzie and Harriet" series of the fifties. Then one-parent shows continued the deception; Fred MacMurray played a widower in "My Three Sons" and Brian Keith a bachelor caring for three orphaned relatives in "Family Affair." But how many families have an understanding and dedicated British butler as surrogate mother?

Until recently, TV families were never products of divorce. Our family and the "Brady Bunch" emerged at about the same time. Although never called that, they were a stepfamily. But like the "Eight is Enough" stepfamily, the "Brady Bunch" wore a halo of perfection impossible to match. How common is the stepfamily that has an ever-efficient Alice to care for the house and children while stepmother attends garden club, takes sewing lessons, remains unfettered and understanding, and—always in cheery concert with Dad—comes up with the right solutions, making everyone happy? No "other parent" seems to exist, and all problems are solved in half an hour.

Early in our marriage we did hire an Alice to be at the house from the time the children came home from school until we returned from work. But while our children drew comparisons to the "Brady Bunch," they observed that we never measured up in other ways. We tested each other, fought, felt guilty, and were jealous and resentful. Family reality may be looking up on the tube, but what is missing is a series about real stepfamilies and what they feel and how they survive.

Even when in 1979 the media focused on the family to launch the International Year of the Child, the stepfamily was slighted. *Newsweek* devoted an entire issue to "Saving the Family" and NBC-TV produced a three-hour documentary, "The American Family." Each touched only briefly on the stepfamily.

Unrealistic portrayals or oversight represent only part of the damage the media inflict. Also destructive is the way writers and politicians, both of them formulators of public opinion, use the stepchild image to conjure up neglect or a state of being less than the best.

This image is commonplace. *The New York Times* provided "Made-for-TV Films—Hollywood's Stepchild Comes of Age." In a new children's book a child is murdered by a stepfather. A writer titled a chapter in his book "Stepchild on the Make," referring to ABC as the weakest and smallest broadcast network. Another writer suggests that my book be entitled *The Stepfamily: The Stepchild of Society*—the ultimate irony. A newspaper review of Christina Crawford's chilling account of child abuse by her mother called it the story of her "life with her stepmother actress." Crawford was not a stepchild; she was adopted as an infant. But since her childhood was tainted with emotional cruelty and neglect, the word that seemed most apt was stepmother.

THEME SONG OF THE LAW—
OBLIGATIONS WITHOUT RIGHTS

As applied to biological parents and children, the law is black and white; for those living in stepfamilies, it is gray and filled with inconsistency and injustice. A legal bond exists between remarrieds, but the legal relationship between a stepparent and a stepchild is like an unassembled jigsaw puzzle with missing pieces. The law does not acknowledge this relationship—not even the obligation or right to financial support. Stepchildren are cared for because how could a married person avoid caring for the children of a mate? But in most states, this relationship lacks a legal base and lasts only as long as the marriage.

When legal incidents do arise in the stepfamily, their resolution is likely to be based on the common-law relationship *in loco parentis*, literally "in place of parent." It is a voluntary assumption by any person willing to maintain, rear, and educate a child as a parent would. Its basis is intent. Does the stepparent intend to be legally subject to the obligations and liabilities of this relationship? If the court decides in the affirmative, and *in loco parentis* is established, the rights and liabilities are as between a parent and child in child support, services, and lawsuits.

But without formal adoption, this is the extent of the legal relationship. From insurance to inheritance, other issues are subject to individual statutes, circumstances, and interpretations. Many statutes specifically exempt stepchildren from any legal rights; others grant different rights under inconsistent circumstances. For example, in Georgia one stepchild was included as a child under the Workers' Compensation Act; but in the same jurisdiction another stepchild was unable to recover under the Wrongful Death Statute even though his stepfather had supported and reared him.[15]

To settle insurance claims, in some cases the *in loco parentis* relationship may determine beneficiaries. Many insurance companies require that beneficiaries be referred to by name. When it comes to the naming of adopted children or stepchildren, John Hancock Mutual Life Insurance Company insists they be named specifically or with phrases that leave little room for doubt—children born of the marriage, children legally adopted by the insured, wife or stepchildren of the insured. Because of ambiguity and misinterpretation, this company stays clear of references to family, lawful children of the insured, or dependents.

The *in loco parentis* relationship holds true for settling welfare cases. Society's controversy seems to center on economics. Should the stepparent's income be included when deciding the amount of assistance to stepchildren? Even if welfare is the only alternative support for a child, few states impose support duty on stepfathers. New York does; and in California, a husband is "not bound for support of his wife's children by a former marriage . . . but if he receives them into his family and supports them, it is presumed he does so as a parent."[16] Where no statutes exist, the *in loco parentis* relationship can create obligations.

Some states stop aid to dependent children (ADC) when a mother remarries. A Syracuse, New York, couple said they lived together for a long time so they could collect assistance. But because they wanted their children to respect marriage and the commitment they had as a family, they married and yielded the ADC monies; to make ends meet, the stepfather works at two jobs. In addition to accepting this financial burden, he sees less of his wife and children—an immediate stress on this low-income stepfamily.

Inheritance is another issue stepfamilies must consider, and here the law neglects stepchildren. Inheritance is not a vested right; no child is entitled to it. Under given circumstances parents can disinherit children in their wills. The problem for stepchildren comes from the law's interpretation of the intent of the words used in a will. Under the law, the term *children*, often used in making collective bequests, does not include stepchildren. If stepparents intend to include their stepchildren, the will must be precise and specific. Only the District of Columbia has a statute that does not distinguish between blood ties and others.[17]

While the courts may use *in loco parentis* to establish facts surrounding a relationship, its status remains voluntary. When death, divorce, or separation ends the relationship between a stepparent and a biological parent, stepchildren do not have to be supported. Likewise, a stepparent may take on a long-term emotional commitment in a stepchild and later be denied the right to rear or visit that child. To date, no law defines custody or visitation rights for stepparents.

Stepparents *have* been granted custody of children. But it is rare, and each case turns on its own facts: motive, length of relationship, the stepparent's role in the child's life, and the nature of the child's relationship with the biological parent. The best interest of the child is the determining factor, but can this ambiguous goal ever provide a right decision? "Judges are becoming more sensitive to the emotional needs of children," explains Richard Ellison, Syracuse University professor of law. "That gives stepparents a better chance of gaining custody. But no law provides it merely because they raised the child."

One way for stepparents to clarify obligations without rights is by adoption. A School of Social Work study from the University of Toronto reveals that one-fourth of Canadian stepfathers adopt their stepchildren. In the United States, one-third of the adoptions of stepchildren are by stepfathers.[18]

At our house, talk about adoption surfaced about a year after our marriage. Two family surnames emphasized the step relationship and often proved confusing. Depending upon whom he felt like, or where his loyalty lay, Jeffrey shifted between using Einstein and Matteson. Twice the school registrar called to ask whether his records should be changed because he had been adopted.

The boys' father was unwilling to give them up legally, and each annual discussion with him yielded an emphatic no. In cases of adoption the biological parent's consent is required. But parents don't give up their children easily—not alcoholics, not child abusers, not prisoners.

Later, as our marriage became chaotic, talk of adoption cooled. More often than not, we wondered what we were doing together in the first place, and two years passed without mention of adoption. Today, Walter admits he expected our relationship to fail and he did not want to support someone else's children. But our marriage survived, and when Walter had reared my sons longer than their biological father had, again he sought adoption. He had long supported the children financially; now, morally he claimed them as his.

Such a strong commitment added solidarity to our family I thought, and Walter's willingness to adopt my sons seemed the ultimate sign of solidity in our relationship. Bill began to waver, and during a summer visit he talked with the children about adoption. Bill would still visit us summers, his love for them would not change, neither would their love for him. We all agreed that nothing would change but their names and their rights under the law. He said to go ahead with the paperwork.

We did. But when the papers were in his hands, again he hesitated. Most certainly his reluctance reflected his internal tug-of-war over yielding his sons, and in our eagerness we overlooked his emotional state. Months later he called to say the papers were signed. Two weeks later he died.

As we dealt with our grief over his loss, the court proceedings were postponed. Six months later, we decided that if we were going to complete the adoption, now was the time because Chris was already sixteen. Again we talked with the boys to see if they harbored any doubts. How children feel about adoption is critical, and they must understand the finality of such a matter. Since neither objected, we proceeded.

Because already we had been a family for more than nine years, the court appearance was routine. Indeed, to the younger boy, enamored of ceremony, it was disappointing. "He didn't even put on his black robe or pound his gavel," Jeff said. "I don't feel any different." Formalizing the adoption did not make Walter a better father to the boys; he treated them generally the same. New names did not make them belong to the family any more than they already did; we had built on that. For us, the symbolism of adoption was important.

Shortly after the court appearance, the relationship between Chris and his new father took a turn for the worse. Part of it was related to Walter's parental demands, seemingly intensified by the adoption. Part of it was adolescent rebellion. But some of it was unresolved grief, and he tested out his new father.

A year ago I asked each of my sons privately how they felt about adoption. Both regretted it. Their feelings have little to do with loving Walter; they do, and have for years. Initially, each talked of disliking the celebrated surname, but after deeper probing both admitted they felt guilty yielding their father's name. They were his only sons, and his death heightened such feelings.

There is virtually no guidance for stepparents on this issue. Could we have accomplished the same thing through our wills? What if our remarriage failed? Did we need this legal status? Many anxieties remained. As stepparents weigh facts and feelings about such a critical decision, they need counseling. Although adoptive parents are screened, counseled, and rechecked before they take on such a serious legal commitment, stepparents breeze through the process under the assumption that because they have lived as a family, adoption is the right thing. Although in New York State we submitted to a mandatory investigation, it involved only superficial questions from a social worker who came to the house.

Legally severing a biological tie can be difficult; losing a father to death is traumatic. My sons suffered both losses more deeply than necessary. Our judgment error about the adoption centered on timing. We should have waited until after their mourning was complete; six months was not long enough. But had their father lived, still the timing was wrong—too late. Already both boys were adolescents, and at this stage they had enough identity problems without the added complication of a name change.

My stepdaughter's difficult decision not to have me adopt her should have provided a clue. Because of my deep emotional bond to Brenda, I wanted the adoption ceremony to include her and the boys. (Bev already was married.) As we talked about it, she flip-flopped. Yes, you are my real mom who raised me, and I would like that. No, I cannot hurt my other mom. Maybe. Because she could not approach the subject with her biological mother, her final decision was no.

Today I understand how right and wise her decision was. Adopting her at nineteen would have added nothing to our love and commitment. Her loyalties rightly belonged to her mother. At that time I could not see that truth, but later she said, "I had no option. I knew you would handle it better if I decided against you."

Adoption is no panacea. This permanent legal change in status does not create a sense of belonging; relationships do that. While it clears the air about inheritance and other legal issues, those who contemplate adopting stepchildren must search their hearts and motives. Adoption creates a new legal tie, but to do so it must sever an old one. Far more serious than losing or gaining custody rights, adoption alters parental rights. But it goes deeper. While it provides a secure legal status, it interferes with the biological kinship system and opens up new psychological issues.

Although adoption is surrounded with psychological implications, the law does not handle this delicately. A thirty-three-year-old Baltimore stepchild, now a stepmother, recalls her shock when as a teenager she discovered her dead mother's name missing from her birth certificate. In its place was that of her stepmother, who had adopted her at six. "I never resented her adopting me, because that was a strong commitment from her," the woman says. "But what right did the law have to remove my mother's name as though she never existed, never bore me?"

As I interviewed this woman, our own adoption proceedings were complete, except for receiving the boys' new birth certificates. When they arrived I tore open the envelope. My heart sank as I understood the depth of that woman's anger. It was as though Bill had not fathered my children. His name was removed, and in its place was Walter's name.

Rather than assuring biological accuracy and providing an extra line for adoptive father, some states prepare new birth certificates, then seal the originals and place them under lock and key. Only a court order can release them. The method is identical for infant adoptions, but the circumstances are vastly different. Such secrecy borders on the absurd; locking up a birth certificate can never erase a stepchild's memory of the biological parent.

"This is one aspect of the law affecting stepfamilies that is just plain silly," says Dr. Ellison. "Its purpose is to restructure and create a new parent-child relationship to resemble that of the natural parent and child. Since everybody knows who the parent is, the process is artificial. The child has a history he knows about, and managing birth certificates in this manner seeks to deny that fact. But the law cannot change until attitudes about the stepfamily do."

This practice can be traced to the confidentiality that once shrouded adoption. But times have changed, and this process requires modification. Research reveals the folly of keeping biological parents a secret: Children who do not know their biological parents often suffer from genealogical bewilderment in their adolescence. Adoption works best when stepparents accept the peculiarities of their substitute role. And although adoption ends childlessness, it does not necessarily relieve the disappointment over infertility.[19]

At the Step Family Foundation in New York City, executive director Jeannette Lofas says she counsels stepfathers not to adopt, and mothers to press for adoption. Her paradoxical advice has practical merits for each individual, but her approach typifies the position of many professionals who feel until research provides facts, no answer is right or wrong on adopting stepchildren. When children are very young, or have been raised by a stepparent for many years, adoption may seem just a formality. But emotions cannot be legislated and, when adoption cuts off ties to the biological parent, complicated psychological processes may damage a once healthy relationship.

At the Step Family Association on the West Coast, psychiatrist John Visher comments, "The importance of blood ties to children must be taken seriously, and they cannot be rendered asunder lightly."

From support to adoption to inheritance, in the eyes of the law the stepfamily's position remains ambiguous. That is changing—slowly, but in an area that will ultimately make a difference. Some of the stepfamily's gravest initial problems can result from unresolved custody battles and divorce resolutions that filter into the remarriage relationships. In early 1980, New York State modeled a bill after a California law that established joint custody as the preferred solution to caring for children of divorce. Four other states mentioned the possibility of such an arrangement in their statutes.

The more the relationships are resolved at the time of divorce, the less the pressure on the new stepfamily as it forms. Those with foresight are making an impact in this area of the law at grass-root levels. One innovative matrimonial lawyer, Joseph L. Steinberg of Hartford, Connecticut, urges an attorney-therapist team approach, seeing such a team as the key to rational, minimally destructive divorce. If we can bring about divorces that leave no residual hostility, he believes, we can minimize the stress of separation.

"Attorneys and therapists often have clients who seem committed to the warfare concept of divorce," says Steinberg. "Our purpose should be to dissuade them from that self-destructive path. By working as a team, we reinforce our capacity to offer a dignified alternative to adversarial divorce.

"Clients are selective informers. They tell lawyers one thing and therapists another. Together, we increase our insights. The attorney-therapist team, protected by the client's written authorization, will know far more than the compartmentalized knowledge of an individual attorney and an isolated therapist."

In clarifying communication channels, Steinberg attempts to prevent the couple from taking adversarial positions and from hiring separate therapists. Individual therapists tend to polarize their patients, the attorney says, increasing the probability of a difficult divorce. He urges all his clients to see a family therapist, not to save the marriage, but because he believes that unless his clients learn what they contributed to the divorce, they will repeat their mistakes when they remarry.

At the University of Connecticut, Steinberg teaches two interdisciplinary courses for students at the School of Social Work and the School of Law, with students working in interdisciplinary teams. "It is pointless to have an emotional solution without an appropriate legal conclusion," he says, "and equally unavailing to have a courtroom decision without a psychological resolution."

10 Crisis: The Crossroads

Bayberry candles scented the rooms. Fresh greens with red velvet bows garlanded the stairs and tabletops. The tree was the grandest ever. But as we sat down to Christmas dinner, the holiday trappings could not hide the stress. Family life had been growing steadily worse, and even on Christmas Day we could not keep out the misery. All day long, Walter had been drinking and I had been nagging. By dinnertime we had quarreled.

Trying to calm things for the children, I set a handsome table and fussed over the meal. But I could not dress up my sadness over our five years of stress and conflict. I garnished the roast leg of lamb and set it in front of Walter to carve.

As I sat at the other end of the table, the children relaxed some. Our family had a theory about hunger and irritability, and we believed that once we ate, things would calm down. But before Walter sharpened the carving knife, we were at it again, arguing. From the stereo, carols proclaimed love and peace and joy. He carved a large, rare slice, raised the knife with the meat hanging over its edge, looked at me for a moment with hatred, and thrust it toward me. I gasped and closed my eyes, wondering if he would kill me.

The knife remained in his hand. Only the meat flew at me, the blood staining my blouse. Bev, who was home from boarding school, screamed and ran from the table. Then Walter dashed from the room, slamming the door behind him, and the children began to cry. It was Christmas, everything was out of control, and our family was coming apart.

Depression is a common Christmas malady, but more was wrong with us than holiday blues. Shattered dreams. Unfulfilled expectations. Broken relationships. We had made most of the classic stepfamily mistakes. Unexplored feelings dulled our hearts and minds until our self-esteem and respect for each other were eroded. But external stresses we did not understand also undermined our relationships and triggered explosions like the holiday dinner.

166

Too much stress had erupted into crisis. When stepfamilies keep their feelings buried and allow their mistakes to accumulate, stress creates a burden under which the family may crack. All families face stress. Some stresses come from inside the family—alcoholism, infidelity, immaturity. Others assault the family from outside—unemployment, social change, poor relationships with the extended family.

For some the instant shock of stepfamily living may erupt in crisis the first year. For others, unresolved problems may slowly simmer to crisis. Stress may relate directly to the special complexity of stepfamily life; or it may be brought on by social change or personal growth, which wreak havoc in all families these days. Sometimes a combination of stresses causes the crisis overload that pushes family members to their emotional limits, a matter clearly evident in the remarriage divorce rate—44 percent.[1] But too often stresses that occur in all families get mixed up with stepfamily stresses.

As compared with other family forms, the extra people in the stepfamily's complicated structure certainly add to the stresses. In *Peoplemaking*, family therapist Virginia Satir identifies four components of family life vital to all successful, nurturing families: self-worth, communication, rules, and a link to society.[2] As we have seen, each of these components is a potential problem for the stepfamily: Having come from lost or failed relationships, family members' sense of self-esteem may be low; complex relationships are a hotbed of crisscrossed communication; to produce one set of rules, the stepfamily needs time to meld diverse ways of doing things; and the stepfamily's link to society has been basically negative.

Rooted in the Greek language, *crisis* means decision or turning point. While it need not signal the end of the stepfamily, it does force change. In Chinese, a crisis can mean a danger or opportunity. Heralding a call to action, crisis overturns old habits and evokes new responses. Most stepfamilies agree that it took a crisis to clarify feelings and build firmer relationships.

SORTING OUT THE ISSUES

In our family, Walter and I moved toward middle age during a time when social change was turning everyone's world topsy-turvy. Journalists Gail Sheehy and Ellen Goodman have since written of such changes. In *Passages* Sheehy showed that as predictable events, the developmental changes adults move through are productive; but when one is unaware of these transitions, chaos ensues. In *Turning Points* Goodman illustrated how social changes affect relationships, leave people less in control of events, and indeed can topple any relationship. Within the stepfamily, social changes and personal growth create unpredictable pressures unless the differences are understood.

Sheehy pigeonholed us as a couple perfectly: The Age 35 Survey and the Age 40 Crucible. Like Priscilla Blum in *Passages*, changing but afraid of changing, I was being repotted, and my husband was letting go of the impossible dream.[3] The women's movement, which had an impact on all families, added yet another challenge to our life.

During my first marriage I had always avoided confronting my feelings. Now, married again, I felt about myself as I had during my first marriage. My identity was hidden. Life, I thought, must have more to offer.

When Walter and I married in 1969, both the times and our heads dictated that marriage spelled out rights and roles between us. It was our unspoken agreement that we would live as we had in our former marriages, only better. But as roles were questioned in society, many mothers and wives headed for the classroom; I did so eagerly. Fathers and husbands began to share childrearing and household tasks; Walter did so resentfully. While intellectually he understood my needs and encouraged me, he saw himself losing ground, giving up rights he had earned.

Thirteen years after my high school graduation, and with responsibility to five children, my journey to adulthood began. With no idea of what I would study, let alone professional goals, I saw the school environment as a setting where I could discover why I felt unfulfilled and what I wanted from life. I fit one of Sheehy's classifications well: I was the nurturer who deferred achievement.[4] Even though going back to school was my first step toward saving myself, it compounded our family problems.

Like most older women students, I played Supermom to the hilt, juggling roles to reduce the guilt for being in the classroom rather than the kitchen. After three years of part-time studies, I discovered journalism school, mixed it with my interest in psychology, and began to shape my niche. As I got more serious about my future, the conflict level at home began to rise. As studies opened my eyes to the world, our couple differences magnified and the gap between his values and mine became more obvious. The chasm widened when Walter was dropping bombs on Vietnamese villages and I was attending peace rallies at the University.

Some of our troubles stemmed from being caught up in what writer Tom Wolfe calls the *Me Decade*. Books by the dozen focused on caring for number one, winning by intimidating others, and freeing ourselves from commitments. Some of them made excellent points, and I was receptive.

Many self-help books implied that to become, to grow, I had to choose between myself and my family. Either-or, I interpreted the messages. To release the real me I would have to put myself first. To rear my family I would have to forfeit personal growth or at least defer it for a while longer. Not so, of course. But, like countless others who jump out of marriages when they encounter conflict, I often got caught up in such thinking. Some take-care-of-me-first benefits ultimately contributed to raising my self-esteem, but until I learned to balance on the fine line between selfishness and intelligent self-interest, I seesawed between the two.

BEYOND FRUSTRATION

Never before had the rules changed so fast. No longer did I greet my husband with a martini; I was studying. To lighten my household load, and to rear independent children, I began to teach them household responsibilities without regard to sex roles. The boys learned to cook and push the vacuum cleaner; the girls chopped firewood and changed spark plugs. Such changes made my husband nervous. What would be next?

To worsen matters, the rules changed in his professional life, too. When he reached senior officer rank, the military retained little of the power and status he had worked toward for twenty-two years. This German-born military man was devastated. His wife was no longer acquiescent, his children questioned his authority and answered back, and his military world had shifted. Unable to adjust, his anxiety led him to destructive behavior toward himself and us.

At times it was easy to project onto the family the fears and anxieties attendant on my personal growth. When I kept the conflict inside, anger ate at me; when I released it, the anger hit my family, especially my stepdaughters, by now competitive and rebellious adolescents. How often I dreamed of what I could be doing if these extra children weren't draining my energy. I could have managed all this with only two children, I rationalized, but not with five.

As resentment fed my guilt, it was easy for the children to manipulate me. Because I was uncertain and insecure about my future, and often even doubted whether I had a right to be changing at all, my guilt level rose to all-time highs. As any clever teenager might, the girls used my confusion to their advantage. If a more effective manipulative device than guilt exists, I am unaware of it. Even my young son got in on the act. I would dash in after class or after work to hear him tease, "What? No milk and homemade cookies like the good old days when you were a mom?" I would laugh and feed him Oreos—and cringe over store-bought cookies. I could intellectualize about my changing role, but I had trouble—a lot of trouble—assimilating the changes and believing they were really okay. Although I was in a transition that would lead to expansion, I did not know it, and anxiety became my companion.

When we feel anxious, it is usually vague and indirect, with no particular source. Anxiety is a baffling emotion equally past-oriented and future-oriented. But more often than not, it is generated from a change in our sense of self, rather than a change in the environment.[5] The mother, and stepmother, I was when we married was worlds apart from the woman I had become five years later. But the changes were so subtle that their only clue was constant anxiety.

The longer the delay in discovering one's own identity, the more poignant and painful it becomes. Like Francie's coming-of-age in Betty Smith's *A Tree Grows in Brooklyn*, my journey to emotional adulthood occurred in tandem with stepparenting. Without a doubt, my late blooming added pressures to our stepfamily. My husband and his children chose a domestic-mommy type; they ended up with a woman developing a professional life.

Where adults are in their development affects how well they can stepparent other people's children. When barriers from unmet needs present internal conflict, frustration reigns. Today, many stepmothers are not only attempting to do their best at this new role but also trying to change their old ones. Such change may breed trouble in the stepfamily because often the other mother stayed at home, and the youngsters remember the after-school cookie and milk routine as part of mothering. That same mother may be working to support herself today, but that information is not part of the child's memory.

As stepmothers change, anxiety about who they are becoming may make them more insecure than ever, and may filter into the stepfamily's internal relationships. When I was busy with studies and new interests and failed to meet my husband's domestic needs, he projected his anger onto Bev; when he failed to be sensitive to my needs, I projected my disappointment onto her. Thus Bev was saddled with the role of scapegoat.

As I developed a sense of value about myself outside the kitchen, I began to be assertive. As the girls mirrored my new attitudes and behavior, they often bore the brunt of their father's frustration because all these changes upset him. Again, we tended to see these as stepfamily problems, when indeed the stress was coming from another source.

While developmental changes create conflict, they can also produce positive effects for stepparents who are serving as extra role models. "As they begin to achieve, such changes may make them stronger, and they begin to set models of competency, struggle, and success," says Dr. Goldenberg. At one point in her studies the psychologist, under severe stress, was threatening to quit her doctoral studies. Her stepson became quite upset and worried that she was serious about quitting. "I looked at him and thought I couldn't possibly quit. He saw me working hard toward something, and I realized how important I had become to him as a model."

ADOLESCENT AVALANCHE

As youngsters attempt to master crucial tasks leading them toward adulthood, for most parents adolescence is a stormy time in a child's life. To establish themselves as independent adults, teenagers must achieve sexual maturity, separate themselves from the family, and find their own identity. Adolescent struggles for independence are characterized by maddening behavior—mood swings, rebellion, brooding, disobedience. Teenagers look forward to leaving home yet fear it. They are bored today and excited tomorrow. They reach out for friendships and crave loneliness. All these are natural ingredients of adolescence, but in the unaware stepparent they trigger resentment.

The vulnerable stepfamily has to deal with the severe stress of adolescence early in its own development. While studies are quick to cite the problems of stepchildren, they overlook the fact that most youngsters who become stepchildren are at or near this most tumultuous time of their lives.

Adolescence can be especially difficult for stepfamilies if youngsters' feelings about their biological parents are still unresolved. This is doubly true for very young stepparents who may indeed have only recently passed through adolescence themselves. A stepparent can make this time more endurable by accepting the adolescent behavior as normal and by not reading rejection and hatred into adolescent actions.

The adults in a stepfamily need team parenting skills in dealing with adolescent children. Otherwise, teenagers can form coalitions and wield incredible power over insecure stepparents.

Clashes with teenagers are common in all families. But in stepfamilies they tend to be more intense because of loyalty conflicts and unresolved feelings about the biological parent without custody. Some youngsters cannot resist taking one last shot at their stepparents as they leave; and, if too much meaning is attached to these events, the hasty departures become crises in themselves.

After rescheduling their appointment in order to see their counselor, a New York couple who had been struggling with their remarriage finally met with me. The husband had just kicked out his fourteen-year-old daughter for failing to obey her stepmother's house rules. When the stepdaughter refused to wear winter boots over her shoes, the conflict reached crisis proportions. Everyone insisted the boots were the issue. But to me, the footwear symbolized a power play, and I recognized the stepmother-stepdaughter-father triangle as the kind we had experienced time and again in our family. Communication between the couple had broken down—as it had between Walter and me—and the teenager used the breach to get her way. Compelled to side with his wife, who was adhering to her rigid rule "so I don't lose control of her," the father gave his daughter an either-or option: She wore the boots, or she had to leave.

The youngster moved across town to live with her stepmother's former husband, who had already enticed the teenager's stepsister to his house with the promise of luxuries the stepfamily could not provide. The parents were upset, but it took counseling to make them see that the real problem was their failure to agree about the rules imposed on the children. Once they did, the teenager came home, eagerly. But it took a crisis to force the change.

Stepchildren may ask for a change of custody during adolescence. As they seek a closer relationship with their other parent, some do so calmly. Meeting the child's shifting developmental needs by using the extended family system can be highly adaptive. But many youngsters move to their other parent's house as a rebellion or power play and leave behind them a trail of bad feelings.

The stress of angry adolescent stepchildren in an upstate New York family brought the stepmother to the brink of a nervous breakdown and her husband to heavy drinking. The couple discussed divorce, but admitted they needed love and affection and would seek it elsewhere, probably in another marriage. "Stepparents bear the brunt of the kids' problems," the stepmother said. "Besides dealing with the day-to-day growing pains, we get all the anger oozing up from their childhoods dumped on us." In spite of the havoc, the adults decided to stay together. But to restore their relationship, they had to reevaluate what they had as well as what they wanted and to set goals. Crisis pushed them toward a stronger marriage.

Sometimes crisis forces individuals to confront themselves. By the time my stepdaughters were well into adolescence I had had to examine my illusions about being their mother. About the time when I began to acknowledge that I felt differently about them and about my sons, they were reopening the relationship with their biological mother. Tied to these young women in a way I did not understand, I began to be fearful about their feeling toward me. Once the girls left the nest, would they desert me?

In *My Mother, My Self*, Nancy Friday explains this fear as reciprocal, and I am convinced that for stepmothers and stepdaughters who have built an emotional bond, the same is true. "Daughters fear they will anger their mothers so much that their mothers will desert them. Mothers fear they will anger their daughters so much that their daughters will desert them. Both women call it guilt. Every woman speaks of it. It is not guilt. It is terror. The terror of losing each other. . . . In the end, the ironic truth is that if you have the courage to let each other go, you may be friends for life."[6]

Steppeople should recognize that strong expectations produce pressures; letting go moves individuals closer to their expectations. "It took me years to relinquish my need for a close relationship with my stepchildren," says Dr. Emily Visher. "But when I was finally able to let this dream go, as if by a miracle the pressure lifted and the warmth of closer relationships began to emerge in ways beyond any expectations I'd ever had."

As adolescence pressures the couple's relationship, becoming a stepchild during adolescence creates a conflict for the youngster, explains Dr. John Visher. "Part of their developmental task at this age is to loosen family ties," he says. "At the same time, the new stepfamily must establish cohesiveness. This can be managed only if the adults allow the teenagers considerable personal space and distance from the family."

If this happens, teenagers can relax and appreciate having extra adult role models, and take advantage of having two emotional havens. Separating themselves from two families is complicated because stepchildren who have been exposed to extra relationships have to sort out two sets of values, beliefs, and attitudes. Even though the two families are not ideal models, they provide clues about what the youngsters want to avoid in life, as well as the attitudes and beliefs to be encompassed. Stepfamilies must recognize that teenagers in all families are breaking away, Dr. Visher says. Inviting but not insisting on family participation by adolescents reduces many tensions because it leaves the choice to the youngsters.

Some older adolescents feel left out or kicked out of the new family. A Syracuse University sophomore says when she stays with her mother and new stepfather in their one-bedroom apartment, she sleeps on the couch and lives out of a suitcase. "I feel like an outsider, an intruder." Visiting her father leaves her just as uncomfortable since he married a divorcée with teenage daughters, all of whom compete with her.

Adolescents sometimes get lost in the shuffle, especially during the early stages of a remarriage. Because they do not need the minding that young children do, less attention is paid to their comings and goings. This is especially true when two sets of parents are actively involved, explains Dr. Irene Goldenberg. "If nobody helps the child to work out the problems that adolescence presents, the child may not be psychologically responsible to either set of parents. When trouble strikes, as it does during this period, the kid goes to the peer group, which usually leads to more trouble."

CRISIS FORCES CHANGE

After my stepdaughters left home, life quieted down at our house—for almost six months. Then the teenage conflict shifted to my oldest son and his stepfather.

As I finished working for my degree, Walter made a midlife career change and returned to college. Such changes create pressures that disturb any family; for us the situation became volatile. Ultimately so much was going on that we could not decipher it all, and we blamed all difficulties on our relationships and our stepfamily. So did the children.

Crisis occurs in the stepfamily when its members can no longer meet their basic needs. According to research, three kinds of stress can set the scene for crisis: shock, exhaustion, and maturation. A sudden death, a burned-out house, an auto accident produces *shock crisis,* forcing painful readjustments. For the stepfamily, the death of a biological parent or a shift in custody may be the trigger. After prolonged stress and conflict, when the usual adapting and coping methods fail, the *crisis of exhaustion* hits. A saturation point. Stepfamilies that have endless conflict with an ex-spouse, lack money to support two sets of children, or disagree over childrearing and discipline may finally crumble under the cumulative effects of such stress.

The *maturational crisis* results when social change and personal development overwhelm people. It may also complicate our passages from one life stage to another.[7] Rearing children in stepfamily while the parents are focusing on their own development as individuals aggravates the stress. The internal strength of the stepfamily determines how serious the crisis becomes. Successful stepfamilies try on new behaviors and adapt; others remain rigid and fight the changes.

Crisis also results from indecision. Denying or delaying the facing of issues leaves few other options. When stresses accumulate, or other issues cloud the problems and the stepfamily makes no attempt to sort them out, indecision causes family breakdown.

Identifying and dealing with stress helps prevent crisis. Because at our house we could isolate the problem, the change of custody for Kurt early in our remarriage was settled quickly. After that we were less lucky, because our stresses resulted from transition and exhaustion. Many stemmed from our ignorance of what to do or how a stepfamily should work, but other stresses were hidden under rationalizations. Mistakes we did not even know we were making were worsened by pressures from the social and personal changes we were encountering. All this stress was ambiguous, affecting our lives on many levels.

Our dinner table had become a battleground. Could it become a peace table? One night I risked interrupting an explosive discussion. "I've got an idea," I said. Anxious to avoid another uproar, everyone tuned in. "Let's all tell one thing about each other we dislike," I suggested, "and then follow it immediately with something we really like." Such revelations! But no one seemed hurt or surprised at the negatives we hurled. We had become experts at hurting one another; and, as in most human relation-ships, too often criticism had replaced recognition. But we were amazed at all the good traits we appreciated in each other. Tears and hugging brought us in touch with these relationships we cherished, yet did not know how to nurture. We started over.

Again our mistakes multiplied, our tension grew, and each of us feared our family was coming apart. To dissolve some of the anxiety this unre-solved fear bred, we invented what the children called yelling contests and played them at supper. There were no rules, no prizes, only relief. With our feelings awry, our angers high, and our fear rampant, one of us would suggest we scream it out. We stood at our chairs and began to scream: bloodcurdling shrieks, shrill screams, guttural bellows, and high-pitched squeaks from the boy whose voice had not yet changed. In unison we screamed until our faces were red and our knuckles were white from holding onto our chairs. Then we stood silent and spent, regaining our composure.

These yelling contests temporarily restored our dignity. Our pent-up angers and hurts dissolved, and as we looked at one another we laughed at ourselves. Although we did not understand the psychobiology of our act, a psychologist says this physical discharge of built-up emotion was reducing our aggression.

The time came when supper exercises no longer worked. We had arrived at the crossroads of crisis—the *saturation* point. Nothing seemed to be working, and none of us were getting our needs met.

How well stepfamilies meet their needs determines how prone they are to crisis. Meeting some needs became difficult at our house, and many of them came under attack. A year after the Christmas dinner disaster, Walter kicked Bev out of the house. The precipitating event reflected adolescent rebellion and a poor parental decision; the action resulted from accumulated frustration. With no skills she could use in supporting herself, Bev moved in with her boyfriend, ultimately married him, and by the time she was twenty-two she had two babies. Her hasty exodus left Walter and me looking askance at each other and at our marriage. Bev's leaving amid crisis and conflict made me feel like the wicked stepmother. And as the other children felt the family coming apart, they, too, were threatened and our family was weakened.

In reality, Bev's departure typified a stage of adolescence when youngsters leave the nest. They don't all starve in the gutter or become emotional misfits. Most grow up. But in our family all of us attached intense meanings to this event. I blamed my husband. The children blamed me. It was our crisis, our turning point. Several stepfamilies talked to me of similar breakouts by their youngsters, which, while not unusual for seventeen- or eighteen-year-olds, upset their families and disturbed the couples' relationships as they blamed each other.

SHATTERED STEPFAMILIES

Most families can pinpoint their crisis point—alcoholism, a battered wife or child, a death—and identify stresses that led to it. But the events that lead a stepfamily toward crisis are often submerged in ambiguity. "It became one step forward and two steps back." "Our communication broke down." "It was always the kids, and we had no relationship."

Because they produce so much stress, many remarriages fail. So many people with so many needs and so many egos strain many remarriages to the breaking point. But many of the failures are caused by psychiatric problems, permanent immaturity, or creative needs that make it impossible for some people to live with others. Inner drives and needs that neither marriage partner understands may dominate a relationship.[8] Or, as more and more women return to school or work, new or dormant needs show up. As the adults grow in different directions the marriage may break under stress, but it is important to avoid blaming these causes of failure on the stepfamily.

Because of the special hopes and dreams attached to the relationships, broken stepfamilies are especially difficult. I met several families whose second marriages failed. Some were involved in a third marriage, providing yet another stepparent for their children. Some said they were unaware their problems were normal—until it was too late; others blamed the stepfamily although personal growth or an immature partner was the problem.

A special sadness surrounded one of these families in upstate New York. As I talked individually with a woman, her second husband, and several of their children, each said their stepfamily had developed a sense of family none had experienced before. They surmounted many difficulties, only to have the marriage crack under the strain when the husband had an affair. One of the teenagers described his heartbreak over watching the marriage break up.

"At first it was tough," the sixteen-year-old said, "because we all did things differently. But we grew to love one another and had such high hopes. When they broke up it was harder on all of us than the first divorce, much harder." With his mother remarried, he has another stepfather he says he respects. But his first stepfather is the man who taught him the values and skills he cherishes.

This family's sadness left me unsettled as I recalled our own waverings toward divorce. I asked Brenda whether she had considered the possibility of having yet another mother. "That was one of my biggest fears when you and Dad fought," she said. "All of us felt that way, I think. It was one thing losing a mother and starting over with you, but I could not have stood it again. I would have given her a worse time, and besides, she would only have been Dad's wife and nothing to me."

When everything fell apart for Walter and me, our only escape seemed to be divorce. But although we threatened each other with it and talked about it, neither of us could tolerate another failed marriage. What is more, although there were times when we didn't like each other much, we seemed to have grown to love each other. We decided to stay together; but to do so, we needed counseling.

WORKING IT THROUGH

By the time we arrived at the last counselor's door, our pent-up guilt and rage made communication impossible. We sat with our arms crossed, our backs toward one another. Walter read book titles in the counselor's bookcase; I could not stop crying. I was filled with guilt and shame and anger, and I admitted it. He could not. Although we came supposedly to save the marriage, I think we both sought the verdict that a divorce would be wise. But this perceptive counselor saw us not at the end of our relationship, but at a critical turning point.

Under the conditions of stress that prevailed in our family for years, I wondered whether our children would be better off if we were divorced. Since children learn as much by what they see as by what we say, would our conflict provide a model for their own marriages? But people must not jump to the conclusion that happy marriages are a birthright, nor are people doomed to repeat the mistakes of another generation.

Still, I was troubled, because in writing about children of divorce, child psychiatrist J. Louise Despert warned that it is not divorce but the emotional situation in the home that determines how children adjust to life. Dr. Despert cites *emotional divorce* as the critical destroyer of children. When discord or a lack of love between a husband and wife is so strong that even chill silences and empty courtesies cannot cover their hatred and disappointment, children suffer great emotional damage that colors their future.[9]

According to one expert in human aggression, relationships depend on fighting, as long as the fighting is fair. Intimates must fight—especially husbands and wives. In Beverly Hills, psychotherapist George Bach teaches clients constructive aggression because fighting reduces the natural tensions and frustrations of two people living together.

Triad fights involving mother, father, and child are more complex and generally are viewed with horror. But while Dr. Bach agrees that conflict can harm youngsters, he thinks it can also help. In *Intimate Enemy* he asks, if children cannot learn to fight at an early age, how can they defend themselves in the world outside the family? "Fighting for growth, fighting for opportunity to explore and learn, is a vital function of growing up. Children learn nothing more important than the art of becoming an independent person. And to become independent, they must learn to fight— and to stand up to—everybody in the family, and in the community, until their sense of self-worth reaches an adult level."[10]

Still, after what our children had been through, how would they fare? I talked about this concern with Dr. Bach's son, Roger, a psychologist, whose own experience in rearing someone else's children has made him acutely aware of the inherent conflict in stepfamilies. Although he admits it's not easy, he prefers family life to single-parent living. As they test out their couple relationship, Roger Bach and his two children live with a woman and her young son. Although his nine-year-old daughter sometimes competes with the woman, their three- and four-year-old sons get along well. Still, even this conflict specialist admits the relationships are difficult.

At the Bach Institute, Roger Bach works with many remarrieds who come in to learn to fight constructively. The issues causing the trouble in stepfamilies are usually between the couple, he finds, "but any family fighting about children is in trouble." Once couples learn to fight fairly and establish intimacy, the triad incidents between stepfamily members are less severe because the primary relationship is more secure. Rather than gang up on the child, the adults team up in support.

A lack of intimacy in the stepfamily seems a major stumbling block to family unity. When people cannot get what they want or need, they fight for it until the fighting causes so much pain they end up in crisis, seeking to bring the relationships to a close, explained Dr. Bach.

"But is crisis or conflict necessary to the stepfamily's integration?" I asked him.

"Conflict is necessary for all human relationships, because without it we become irresponsible," said Dr. Bach. "Without corrective feedback, we become lazy. In your relationship, what you and your husband exposed your kids to is years of intense fighting toward a good outcome. As for your kids, they have witnessed a good, positive lesson—tenacity. Ultimately, it pays for the couple to work hard to survive, because in the long run most find it was worth it."

According to research findings by Mavis Hetherington at the University of Virginia, many divorced couples are remorseful after they let their marriage relationship go.[11] Even those who thought their marriage was terrible believed they could have worked out their marital problems.

When crisis finally forces drastic changes, the question may arise— Which comes first, the kids or the couple? Until the crisis is resolved, for ultimate stability it must be the couple. Quality versus quantity is how psychologist Emily Visher sees it. "Children need to learn there are differences between the love couples feel for each other and the love parents and children feel for one another. And they need to learn that the adults' care for their relationship ultimately is a plus for them."

Several experts suggested saving the marriage. "Once that bond is strong, the couple is in a much better position to help the children," explains Dr. Goldenberg. "A stepfamily couple makes a great investment, and to quit before the payoff is foolhardy."

A psychiatrist who is a stepfather says the couple relationship must be the priority. If the children are put first, he believes many a marriage is essentially over—at least emotionally. "Children are not helped to mature by being shown or told they come first because they grow up with delusions of superiority. A strong relationship is what they will seek in their adult lives, and what they see in the stepfamily serves as a model for their futures."

To surrender the stepfamily's destiny is to deny the potential this family unit carries. Furthermore, starting over again yields similar problems with yet another cast. The typical formerly married with whom another remarriage can be made is likely to be a parent (in 1973, close to 60 percent of all divorcing people had children under eighteen),[12] and a subsequent remarriage is likely to repeat this pattern.

Rebuilding and renegotiating our relationship was our only alternative to divorce. After such turmoil, many remarriages end up in court. We have been survivors. Rebuilding relationships is much more difficult than maintaining them, and we face that challenge daily. But since we lacked the maturity and skills to stepparent differently, we had little choice.

Through all these difficulties, why have we stayed married? The answer to my question was provided for me by one of our daughters. Last year, on our anniversary card, Brenda wrote, "I am happy and grateful to have parents who cared about me and themselves enough to have stayed together through thick and thin to provide me with an ongoing sense of family. I know it was rough, but life for all of us is getting stronger and I'll always love you for this."

// Our Real World

Although Brenda also left home in a chaotic exodus, she never severed her ties to the family as her sister had. Her anger at Walter remained, but her need of family contact and her courage brought Brenda back. Bev avoided us and our celebrations. When Bev was about to turn twenty-one, I shopped for something that would be significant for that magical year. The day was my birthday and, as she had for the three years since she left home, I anticipated that she would ignore it. I wondered why I was stalking the perfect gift when she avoided me. What was in it for me?

In discounting my birthday, Bev had delivered a strong message: I am still hurt and angry at you. After three years of being punished, I thought, This year I'll do the same. But I controlled the childish thought and headed for the lingerie department. For the girls, who had been tomboys when we met, pretty lingerie had become one of my traditional birthday gifts. I chose come lacy underthings and then decided on a good robe, too. As I walked out of the store with more generous gifts than usual, my step lightened.

When I got home, on my desk lay a small, soft package with a message penned on the tissue. "Happy Birthday, Elizabeth. Love, Bev."

It was a simple handmade macramé belt that reflected more than her lack of cash during a difficult time in her life; it reminded me of teaching the children the joys of giving and receiving handmade gifts. The simple string belt suggested: I want to rebuild a relationship with you; this is my first step; now the ball is in your court. The next day I offered a movie and supper out. She accepted.

During that first time together again, we dwelled on the present and where we wanted to take our relationship. But all we knew for sure was how nervous we both were. When I asked her to account for her anxiety, she said, "I don't know about you, but this means too much to me to mess it up again."

"Me, too," I mumbled, thinking of the many times when our relationship had floundered. Without a doubt it had to be refashioned, requiring a new commitment from both of us. We agreed that while forgetting might be difficult, forgiveness was possible.

Because Bev's relationship with her father had not improved, we agreed ours would have to be between Bev and me alone. She and I had pieces to sort out, feelings to resolve. Until we put our relationship on a firm footing, or decided it could never be, her relationship with Walter and with me had to be kept separate. Bev seemed relieved.

A year after the birthday reunion I went to visit my stepson. I wanted to explain what had happened and to try to understand his feelings about me.

Referring to the ten years since he had left our family, I asked, "How have you felt about me during all this, Kurt?"

"I thought you were the reason that I had to leave," he said. "I kind of hated you."

I took a couple of deep breaths and began to speak slowly. "You must have, Kurt. From the beginning you and I had trouble. Your father and I thought the problems would lessen after we married, but they only got worse; and because you clung to me so, I thought you missed your mother. I did not understand your fears. There were so many problems then, you seemed to get swallowed up in the confusion. When I look back I see it wasn't all my fault. But it was never yours. Through Dad, I came into your life and you had no choice about what happened. During that early chaos in our family, we didn't feel we had much choice either, and we sent you to live with your mother. Through the years I assumed you hated me for it, yet when you came to visit you were so pleasant, so polite, that at times I wasn't sure. You and I never talked about it, but I never stopped feeling guilty."

"But we never talked about anything," he said. "After a while I didn't hate you, but there was a hostility coming from you I did not understand. It's not here today."

"I think that was guilt. When I saw you with the rest of the kids, I thought maybe if I had been a better person you could have lived with us, too," I told Kurt. "Did you feel rejected?"

"Lost maybe. I never understood anything that was happening to me," he said. "Why didn't Dad explain it? Why wouldn't he talk to me, tell me what would happen?"

"I think I know the answer, but that's between you and your father. What are you going to do about your relationship with him?"

"I can't talk to him. I still get too upset," the eighteen-year-old said, his voice wavering. "I love him because he's my father, but I don't like him as a person."

Saying it aloud triggered his tears. We talked of our anger, holding each other. I suggested that waiting until later to deal with his father, as he planned, might be unwise. Could he move ahead with other important decisions in his life while he was still mired in hurt and anger? Might resolving some of the issues make him feel better about himself? Perhaps now was the time.

"No, he'll have to come to me first. I've tried before," he reminded me. But if my stepson waited for his father to make the first move, it might never happen. Feeling that Kurt deserved the chance to sort out his life as soon as possible, I encouraged him to take the first step. "You must do it so you can dump this hurt and anger and move on."

Kurt asked why I stayed with his father when he had caused us all such pain. "I've grown to love him. We've been through a lot together and I understand his pain—and shared his mistakes."

Before I left, Kurt drove me to dinner. As my stepson wove expertly in and out of the cosmopolitan traffic, I compared him to my sons and wondered about their future. All three young men lost the security of their original families and close contact with their biological fathers. Could they understand or forgive? It was a good evening. We laughed, reminisced, talked about his future. Later Kurt drove me to a hillside high above the city, a place, he confided, where be brings his girlfriends and drinks beer with his buddies.

As I left his mother's house the next morning, Kurt walked me to the car. When I extended my hand for a farewell handshake, he reached beyond it and kissed me. Then he said: "I want you to know that last night I wrote Dad a letter demanding that we talk soon."

Bev's birthday belt and my visit with Kurt symbolized our starting over. We had no legal ties, and accepting or rejecting the relationships would be easier for us than for blood kin. Yet in ten years we had put down deep roots. There were the worst of times, without a doubt; but there were the best of times, too, and none of us forgot that. These young people are a part of my family, my traditions, my future. And I am a part of theirs.

SECURING THE STEPFAMILY'S FUTURE

Repairing a broken stepfamily, like restoring fine porcelain to such a state that only an expert could detect its cracks, takes patient and tedious work. But, like damaged porcelain, broken relationships can be restored—sometimes becoming stronger than they once were.

Looking back, sorting out the past, and hanging onto parts of it are a valuable part of moving into the future. Leaving the past behind is equally critical. Against great odds the stepfamily makes its special emotional commitment to family life, and the decision to cast it aside should be weighed carefully. Often people drift into conflicts they do not know they are in until everything blows apart. It is impossible to gain a perspective on relationships amid chaos and confusion. It takes time to realize that the crisis is past and that out of conflict has come commitment.

For adults, securing the stepfamily's future means acknowledging shortcomings and dealing with mistakes. It means letting go and realizing that out of what seemed like disaster can come many positive results. It means waiting to see before pronouncing judgment or donning a failure label.

For children, it means stepping back to view their parents and stepparents as human beings who have a past of their own to deal with and who don't know all the answers. Empathizing with parents and taking the responsibility for one's own life make it possible to move into the future without excess emotional baggage. By sorting out and understanding the pieces of the puzzle that is a stepfamily, stepchildren can develop a healthy perspective for the future. In this era of divorce and family reorganization, many youngsters who are now stepchildren will one day become stepparents. Dealing with one's feelings and behavior can diminish the risk of repeating negative patterns in yet another stepfamily.

Almost every social problem of our time has been laid at the door of the broken home and, eventually, the stepfamily. As in my own case, the pain and confusion of being a stepchild may be mixed up with the emotional loss of my original family. Living the role of the poor stepchild is self-destructive because it delays the day of awakening and avoids reality. Dwelling on what was missing and clinging to misperceptions and to memories distorted by time leaves one uprooted and fearful.

Developing a perspective on the reality and fullness of stepfamily living takes time. We need to ponder on all that happened and say to ourselves, Okay, losing my first family was traumatic, but I've learned to live with that loss, and there were many good aspects to growing up in a stepfamily. Such an affirmative view makes the rewards from this extended sphere of relationships more readily identifiable. Being able to look back to identify these advantages is good; understanding the positive side of stepfamily life while living in it is better.

It is time to look at what is right about stepfamily living.

WHAT'S GOOD ABOUT IT?

The fact of being a stepchild is not linked to achievement levels—socially or emotionally. Abraham Lincoln and George Washington were stepchildren. So is Gerald Ford. Jacqueline Kennedy Onassis is a stepchild who became a stepmother. Author Alex Haley had a stepmother, and Nancy Reagan is one. A study of graduate students at Pennsylvania State University who were stepchildren revealed that none differed in stability, self-sufficiency, or dominance from the rest of the college population. While the study documented the distortion of the stepchild stereotype, students also talked of the love, help, and understanding their stepparents provided.[1]

The results of this old study were more recently affirmed by anthropologist Paul Bohannan in San Diego, where he found that stepchildren and children reared by biological fathers were equally well adjusted. And in an analysis of two national surveys about stepfathers and stepchildren, researchers merged the data and found no substantial differences.[2] In looking at social and psychological characteristics that ranged from religion, politics, crime, and delinquency to general interpersonal relationships, personal evaluation, and relationships concerning marriage and the family, they found the experience of living in a stepfamily can be positive, negative, or mixed—just as it can be in the intact biological family.

As remarriage reorganizes family systems, the stepfamily serves as both a repairing and learning center. When they learn to trust again, stepchildren can gain from the two-family world in which they live. The fresh start that stepfamily life offers has made a significant change in many young lives. After a Washington, D.C., attorney's mother was hospitalized, he bounced from relative to relative. Then, when he was seven, he gained a stepmother who helped him adjust without forcing herself on him, and he says it changed his life. Because his biological mother lives, he calls his stepmother by her first name. "But my stepmother is the one who taught me what a stable family life could be like."

When they look back, adults who were stepchildren can reel off lists of what was right about living in a stepfamily. First they recall the sorrow and sadness of broken relationships with their biological parents. Then they recall the positive effects their stepparents had on their lives.

A Sacramento stepdaughter recalled that she and her mother had been loners—readers and stay-at-homes. But when her mother remarried, her stepfather opened new vistas to them as he taught her archery, took them fishing and camping, taught them to enjoy traveling. "And he taught me about taste," she recalls. "My first lesson involved a brass chandelier that he found in an antique store. He showed me why its classic lines passed the test of time."

A Manlius, New York, woman who grew up on a farm says that from her city stepmother she learned about the social graces and about hospitality. An adult stepson in Philadelphia says he never forgot his stepfather's "Abe Lincoln examples" when he returned money to people who overpaid him. A California adolescent says the freedom to call her stepfather Dad makes her feel less "outside the window" from friends who live in traditional families.

MORE MODELS, MORE CHOICES

What starts out as a problem in the stepfamily—too many differences—can become an opportunity. One of the ways children learn about life is by observing their parents and doing what they do. Extra parental figures provide additional close-up models for stepchildren, giving them another way of trying on life and viewing the world. This double exposure may at first be confusing, but as children mature they can select the attitudes and behaviors they will accept into their own lives.

A stepparent may offer a skill, behavior, or value the biological parent lacks. A teenage stepchild living in Syracuse, New York, with his second stepfather says the best thing his first stepfather did for him was to force him to make decisions. "At first I hated him for that. When I'd ask him for help, he'd help me see what my options were and then say, 'Let me know what you decide to do.' I used to get angry when I made bad decisions and had no one to blame," he says. "But now I'm grateful. Some of my friends can't decide anything on their own."

My own second chance at family life through my stepfather opened many doors for me. The move from the farm to the city after Mother remarried was my first step up the social ladder. My stepfather kept us active in church, which provided the base for my spiritual life. An amateur musician, he introduced me to music, now one of my deepest joys. My sense of integrity is rooted in his values. Deception was my father's bedfellow; for my stepfather dishonesty was intolerable. My father was an alcoholic; my stepfather rarely drank. And he reinforced good values my parents already had taught me—hard work, self-discipline, perseverance.

Likewise, a vast difference exists in the personalities and fathering styles of the two men who helped rear my sons. As I drew qualities from two fathers to become the person I am, so will my sons. Recently Chris compared his fathers. "One considers formal education and school all-important; the other taught me to teach myself and learn from life's experiences. One lives by rules and discipline; the other taught me to be flexible and to take life easy. My stepfather taught me hands-on skills, mechanics, woodworking; my father couldn't build a doghouse. My father taught me about nature and a love of the outdoors; my stepfather is afraid of bugs and snakes and won't touch a fishing rod. One showed me how to assert myself in the world and to stand up for my beliefs; the other taught me about personal integrity."

An extra parent figure gives stepchildren another adult sounding board. One teenager said, "I like having two mothers. I can ask the same question of both, get two opinions from people who care about me, and make up my own mind."

In *Rewedded Bliss*, Davidyne Mayleas writes humorously of the time when her sixteen-year-old stepdaughter switched their Saturday-night girl talk from ear piercing and the school play to the pill and contraceptive devices. Would her stepmother, whom she was visiting for the weekend, take her to a doctor for a birth control prescription? Her mother would be furious if she asked her. While telling an amusing tale of the nervous pair's search for the pill, the author points up our lack of an etiquette telling us who fills which of these ambiguous roles. The biological mother disapproved of the gynecological caper, but she accepted it, and her daughter was spared a pregnancy. As for the stepmother, she served as an additional adult to whom the youngster could turn for help.[3]

As assertiveness and rebellion dominate family life during adolescence, two mother or father figures offering diverse options and opinions can become a stabilizing influence. A stepparent can soften a child's relationship with a parent of the same sex. An upstate New York teenager did not get along with her mother, who put her down and devalued her until the girl began to tailor her life to the negative image painted about her. From drugs to promiscuous sex, she pulled herself down. But all the while the girl's stepmother kept telling her, "You're special. But you must treat yourself special and act special." When she began to heed the message, the teenager put her life back together.

Extra parental figures offer new places and experiences. Getting out of one setting to visit their other families in a different setting adds yet another dimension to young lives. "I have the best of both worlds," says a twenty-one-year-old New Hampshire woman. "My mother lives in a Boston suburb and there's so much exciting to do there. My father and stepmother live in a hamlet in New York state where it's picturesque and peaceful. I go there to unwind."

As models, extra parents, brothers, and sisters teach stepchildren that various levels of caring and loving exist. Stepsiblings can teach each other about companionship, give-and-take, sharing. A shift in family position from youngest child to middle child provides a new perspective. From older stepbrothers or stepsisters, younger children can learn skills they might not have encountered otherwise. For an only child who becomes a stepchild, brothers and sisters and a large family are an exciting bonus.

Stepchildren learn early the painful lesson that inequality and injustice exist and that life outside the protection of the family is tough. If they are treated unequally by their stepgrandparents, or feel they are loved unequally by their stepparent, this preview of the reality of the outside world will be less of a shock.

Experiencing a broken family and adjusting to a new one teaches the stepchild another basic lesson of life—flexibility. All children need to learn not only how to get along within their families, but how to deal with those outside it. As demands upon them change, successful people are flexible enough to shift strategies and bend with the winds of change. Because in different families these strategies vary, stepchildren have the advantage of learning a variety of ways of coping and how to fit their behavior to the situation.

Double doses of values and behavior can be confusing and require sorting out. In coming to terms with two sets of rules about life, two ways of doing things, stepchildren must make choices. By doing so, they prepare themselves to step into the future buttressed by the ability to see several points of view. Their exposure to the stepfamily's complex network of relationships may make it easier to accept new people with diverse ideas and values.

Double lessons about marriage and family life supply stepchildren with extra information they can take to future relationships. Having experienced the pain of loss, they know marriage can fail; having lived with the confusion of the stepfamily, they understand the difficulty of remarriage. With this knowledge, stepchildren can consider their own future relationships with deeper understanding. Seeing a remarriage succeed can change a youngster's negative attitude about marriage and have a positive influence on relationships with the opposite sex. As they learn that trouble is normal for all marriages, they may themselves be less eager to quit at the first signs of trouble in their own relationships. And viewing their parents' successful remarriages may end any residual guilt about causing the first family's breakup.

LONG-TERM REWARDS

Special joys come from being a stepparent. Sometimes a difficult and thankless task, the experience can push adults to test their limits and tolerances, to face challenges and deal with emotions that might have remained unexplored. As stepparents have extra chances to savor life's contrasts—setbacks and successes, the bitter with the sweet—personal growth is inevitable.

Not long ago, someone asked if I would want to be a stepmother again. The question forced me to deeper thinking about what was good about it. Become a stepmother to yet another set of children? No. The responsibility to three sets of children has been enough. But would I do it *over* again? Without a doubt. My role as a stepmother has had its rewards. It forced me to confront complex emotional issues that biological mothers rarely explore.

In addition to the personal growth resulting from this exposure, my stepchildren and I exchanged values and skills that have changed our lives. I tended to view life through black and white lenses; they helped me to see shades of gray, to be less rigid and judgmental. My values helped my stepchildren develop a clearer sense of integrity. They taught me to relax, to play, to take life less seriously; I taught them about responsibility and caring for others. Both my stepdaughters show a touch of the gourmet in their cooking but understand that homemaking is only one aspect of their lives; I now play tennis, cross-country ski, bicycle, and welcome new experiences.

Another deep reward of being a stepparent remains the possibility— no promises, for sure—that an intimate relationship may develop with a child to whom you make a deep commitment. To love a child who is yours biologically and have that love reciprocated is one thing; to love and be concerned for a child who has lashed out, rebelled, and refused to communicate, to realize in the end that the child respects you and loves you, is a very special experience.

Stepchildren reap similar rewards. When a stepparent makes a commitment to a stepchild and sticks by it even when the youngster acts shabbily, and when the stepparent grows to love and care about the stepchild, that, too, is very special.

My relationship with Brenda is sealed in trust and respect. My love for her is so strong that at times it is hard to believe we share only an emotional bonding. It makes me understand an adoptive mother's love for her child. Part of our intimate bond reflects our personalities because our values, interests, and beliefs are similar. Brenda and I are as alike as Bev and I are different. During Brenda's adolescence we quarreled and disagreed about nearly everything. But today's commitment to each other came about through caring and resolving the difficulties in our relationship.

Since that meeting with Kurt, we are developing a friendship. It still wobbles, because as he reaches out to me for advice and opinions, he gives me a chance to be his rescuer with money or solutions. This places me in a bind. After my bad start with him as a youngster, it's tempting to help him in order to salve my conscience; and when I turn him down, I wonder whether we will ever become friends. But I think I am being tested, and I intend to earn the respect I seek from him.

The future will determine my relationship with Bev. Perhaps I can be effective as her friend or mentor. This is her choice. Neither of us is willing to let our fragile relationship simply die, but because trust and respect were destroyed, the rebuilding is difficult. There are still times when we get nervous. Will we drift back into our old habits? I fear she may again reject me, but I think that is her fear, too. Although our relationship is fitful and not yet free of fears, it links our past to our more important future with our family.

Most often the benefits are long term. Like the patina on fine sterling becoming more beautiful with age, the rewards of living in a stepfamily deepen with the passage of time. The first few surface scratches seem to mar shiny new silver, but over years the cumulative effect of the scratches is to add luster. Because of the stress and hard work involved, when stepfamily relationships come to fruition, the overcoming of such a challenge warms the heart deeply. Because the task seemed harder, for some it carries even a deeper sense of fulfillment.

Knowing that you mattered in the life of a child stimulates deep positive feelings. Dr. Irene Goldenberg says her knowledge that she had an enormous effect on her stepson, now twenty-seven, makes her glow. He came to their remarriage as a testy thirteen-year-old when she was rearing toddlers, attending school, and working part time. "I used to come home wondering how I could be a failure at so many things at once," she says. "But now I look at my stepson—who just earned his master's degree, is happily married, and holds an important job—and feel thrilled at having helped turn him around. In the long run it was his own doing, but it's good to know I am a part of his happiness and success."

Many stepparents recalled occasions when their stepchildren returned home to tell them how much they were appreciated. Some apologized. Both my stepdaughters provided me with such testimonials, and at important times in my life. When I was overwhelmed with guilt about doing everything wrong, they told me of the things I did right, and how much my being in their lives mattered. Whenever I feel being a stepmother was not worth my investment, I savor those letters and restore my perspective on it all.

Not long ago I was able to thank my stepfather for rearing us and making so many sacrifices for us. I told this patient man—whom as a youngster I fought because of the loyalty conflicts over my own father— that I loved and respected him and that I appreciated all he had done for us. As his eyes misted, for one brief moment I saw what such a simple confession meant to this man who had reared five children who belonged to someone else. He took on the task because he loved my mother; he carried it out with dignity because he is a great man.

No special providence smoothed the way for my family or for the stepfamilies who shared their stories with me. As much as I dreamed of figuring out a fairytale ending for stepfamily relationships, I cannot report one. Each attempt to end in a happy vein reminded me of the despair I felt after every interview in a stepfamily's house where everything seemed to be going wrong. Although I left each doorstep cheerily saying, "It'll be fine," I feared that unless some of these families brought their difficulties under control, they would become a remarriage divorce statistic, leaving their children more confused than ever.

There is no magic ending at our house either. After all the turmoil, we are now working at restructuring our marriage and rebuilding our relationships. In many ways our task is harder than that of new stepfamilies because there is no kidding ourselves, no resort to fantasies, only the hard work of undoing past mistakes.

While I cannot write a happily-ever-after ending to the stepfamily's story, a change reminiscent of fairy tales has happened to me. As I peeled off layers of emotion, I discovered that my identity as a stepchild and as a stepmother often had been based on illusion. This unfettering of what I am not is the beginning of learning who I am and gives me the courage to rebuild important family ties.

Several illusions had to go. Above all, I am not my daughters' mother. It was one thing to have "mothered" the girls, but when I began trying to replace their mother, I left myself open to unnecessary hurts. I may never stop calling these young women my daughters, but that is all right because now I understand the difference. Besides, as the poet Schiller wrote, "It is not flesh and blood, but the heart which makes us fathers and sons."[4]

My husband and I were not cruel and insensitive parents. Many of our failings stemmed from our inability to recognize and accept the difference between first families and stepfamilies. Our energy was directed toward being what our first families had been, or what we thought we should be, rather than what we were: a stepfamily. We also failed to understand that relationships with our children's other parent cannot be denied, but somehow must be integrated into the new stepfamily.

During our remarriage, our own needs often conflicted with the needs of five children from broken families. Caught in this complex network of relationships, awash in stereotypes, and with no guidelines, we did the best we could with what we were at the time. How many parents do not wish they had a second chance? Unable to live up to our idyllic expectations, we labored under the illusion that we had failed. If that had been true, our children would have little to do with us today. Quite the opposite is true.

I was not a wicked stepmother offering my stepchildren poisoned fruit and dressing them in rags. Often I had to make decisions these youngsters disliked. All parents must; it is part of loving and responsibility. Loving my stepchildren differently from my own sons was not rooted in malice, but in the kind of bonding that took place within the relationships.

And my own life as an unhappy and pitiable stepchild? This was the gravest illusion to give up, for in yielding this crutch I took on the responsibility for the direction of my life. I was not a deprived stepchild, eternally scarred. Like millions of children of divorce, my security base was shorn from me at a critical time, and my parents did not understand the importance for children to maintain some sort of relationship with both biological parents. My broken home was neither because of me, as I had imagined, nor because my parents did not love me.

My mother's decision to divorce was wise; even wiser was her remarriage choice. My great luck was to have a wonderful stepfather who gave us a second chance at a full family life, making me more than a mere survivor. All adults are survivors of childhood, seeking to become complete human beings, compensating for personal weaknesses and childhood experiences by being involved in valuable and productive work.[5]

Often my fears have limited me. By giving up illusions of being unloved and unworthy, by relinquishing a label that once protected me but kept me from growing, and by taking the responsibility for my life, I filled my future with hope.

Stepfamily dreams that were built like sand castles on a base of illusion can be reconstructed on a firm foundation of reality, commitment, and love—the mortar of all family life. And where there is love, most things are possible.

Notes

1 Meeting the Clan

1. Paul Glick, U.S. Bureau of the Census, Population Division.
2. Glick, Census Bureau.
3. Jane Howard, *Families*, New York: Simon & Schuster, 1978.
4. Virginia Tufte and Barbara Myerhoff, *Changing Images of the Family*, New Haven: Yale University Press, 1979, pp. 1–3.
5. Glick, Census Bureau.
6. Anne W. Simon, *Stepchild in the Family*, New York: Odyssey Press, 1964, p. 60.
7. Simon, *Stepchild in the Family*, p. 19.
8. Jessie Bernard, *Remarriage: A Study of Marriage*, New York: Dryden Press, 1956, p. 14.
9. Constance R. Ahrons, "The Binuclear Family," *Alternative Lifestyles*, Vol. 2, No. 4, November 1979, pp. 499–515.
10. Davidyne Mayleas, *Rewedded Bliss*, New York: Basic Books, 1978, p. 10.
11. Lucile Duberman, *The Reconstituted Family: A Study of Remarried Couples and Their Children*, Chicago: Nelson-Hall, 1975, p. 58.

2 Getting in Deeper

1. Elisabeth Kübler-Ross, *On Death and Dying*, New York: Macmillan, 1969.
2. Leslie Aldridge Westoff, *The Second Time Around*, New York: Penguin Books, 1977, pp. 26–27.
3. Phyllis Chesler, *Women and Madness*, New York: Doubleday, 1972.
4. Morton and Bernice Hunt, *The Divorce Experience*, New York: McGraw-Hill, 1977, p. 125.
5. Jane Adams, *Sex and the Single Parent*, New York: Coward, McCann and Geoghegan, 1978.
6. K. M. Rosenthal and H. F. Keshet, "The Not Quite Stepmother," *Psychology Today*, July 1978.
7. Morton Hunt, *The World of the Formerly Married*, New York: McGraw-Hill, 1966, p. 130.
8. Hunt, *The Divorce Experience*, p. 244.
9. Paul C. Glick, personal communication. Among persons now fifty years old, 96 percent have ever married. An estimated 38 percent of first marriages of women twenty-five to thirty years of age will end in divorce; 80 percent of persons whose first marriage ends in divorce will remarry; and 44 percent of remarriages after divorce will again end in divorce. These estimates are based on a 1975 study and are unlikely to be updated until 1982, if then. According to Dr. Glick, no decennial census has ever produced figures on the number of stepchildren, and the 1980 census was no exception.

10. Judith S. Wallerstein and Joan B. Kelly, "The Effects of Parental Divorce: Experiences of Them in Early Latency," *American Journal of Orthopsychiatry*, January 1976, pp. 21–23.

11. Lucile Duberman, *The Reconstituted Family: A Study of Remarried Couples and Their Children*, Chicago: Nelson-Hall Publishers, 1975, p. 40.

12. Francis I. Nye and Felix M. Berardo, *The Family: Its Structure and Interaction*, New York: Macmillan, 1973. This carefully documented textbook notes that since divorce rates are higher among the low-income and less-skilled occupations, the remarried have less competence in the crucial provider role and probably less in the child-care and socialization roles. The divorced have a higher rate of divorce, not because they are divorced but because a disproportionate share of them have limited competence in enacting the various family roles.

13. Jessie Bernard, *Remarriage*, New York: Dryden Press, 1956, pp. 58–60.

3   Hooking Up

1. Arnold van Gennep, *The Rites of Passage*, London: Routledge and Kegan Paul, 1960.

2. August B. Hollingshead, "Marital Status and Wedding Behavior," *Marriage and Family Living*, November 1952, pp. 308–11.

3. Jessie Bernard, *Remarriage*, New York: Dryden Press, 1956, p. 42.

4. Anne Simon, *Stepchild in the Family*, New York: Odyssey Press, 1964, pp. 96–101.

5. Donald Anspach, "Kinship and Divorce," *Journal of Marriage and the Family*, May 1976, p. 323.

6. Elizabeth Post, *Etiquette: The Blue Book of Social Usage*, 11th rev. ed., New York: Funk and Wagnalls, 1965.

4   Setting the Stage

1. Ruth Roosevelt and Jeanette Lofas, *Living in Step*, New York: McGraw-Hill, 1977, p. 19.

2. Irene Fast and Albert Cain, "The Stepparent Role: Potential for Disturbances in Family Functioning," *American Journal of Orthopsychiatry*, April 1966, p. 490.

3. Emily Visher and John Visher, "Common Problems of Stepparents and Their Spouses," *American Journal of Orthopsychiatry*, April 1978.

4. Paul Bohannan, "Stepping In," *Psychology Today*, January 1978.

5. Kenneth Walker and Lillian Messinger, "Remarriage After Divorce: Dissolution and Reconstruction of Family Boundaries," *Family Process*, 18:2, 1979.

6. Judith S. Wallerstein and Joan B. Kelly, "California's Children of Divorce," *Psychology Today*, January 1980, pp. 67–76. In this Children of Divorce project the researchers interviewed and reinterviewed members of sixty families. Thirty-four percent of the children were happy and thriving, 29 percent were doing reasonably well, but 37 percent were depressed.

7. Margaret Draughon, "Stepmother's Model of Identification in Relation to Mourning in the Child," *Psychological Reports*, 36:183–189, 1975.

8. Phyllis Stern, "Stepfather Families: Integration Around Child Discipline," *Issues in Mental Health Nursing*, 1:50–56, 1978, pp. 52–53.

9. Stern, "Stepfather Families," p. 51.

5   Settling In

1. Observational learning as a three-stage process involving exposure, acquisition, and acceptance was first researched by Albert Bandura and Richard H. Walters. They

contend that people can learn new ways of acting by watching others, and the observer who is exposed to the behavior in such a manner can process and retain it. Observationally learned responses are not necessarily performed at the first opportunity, they note.

2. Erich Fromm, *The Art of Loving*, New York: Harper & Row, 1974, pp. 41–44.

3. Carl Rogers, *On Becoming a Person*, Boston: Houghton Mifflin, 1961.

4. Jerome Kagan, "Motive in Development," adapted from *Understanding Children*, New York: Harcourt Brace Jovanovich, 1971, in *The Growth of the Child*, pp. 144–47.

5. Kagan, "Motive in Development," p. 147.

6. Rita Rooney, "When Child Adoption Doesn't work," *Parade*, March 4, 1979, pp. 23–26; Louise Raymond, revised by C. T. Dywasuk, *Adoption and After*, New York: Harper & Row, 1974, pp. 137–66.

7. T. Berry Brazelton, "Early Parent-Infant Reciprocity," reprinted from Victor Vaughan III and T. Berry Brazelton, eds., *The Family—Can It Be Saved?* Year Book Medical Publishers, 1976, pp. 133–41.

8. Robert M. Liebert and Michael Spiegler, *Personality: Strategies for the Study of Man*, Illinois: Dorsey Press, 1970, p. 247.

9. Kagan, "Motive in Development," pp. 231–35.

10. Nancie Spann and Owen Spann, *Your Child? I Thought It Was My Child*, Pasadena, Calif.: Ward Ritchie Press, 1977, p. 61.

11. Lucile Duberman, *Reconstituted Family: A Study of Remarried Couples and Their Children*, Chicago: Nelson-Hall, 1975, p. 71.

12. Harold Feldman and Margaret Feldman, "Effect of Parenthood at Three Points in Marriage," unpublished paper, 1978. In a study of married couples, these researchers found there was a decrease in marital happiness with the coming of the first child and an increase in marital happiness at the later stages in life when the children were grown.

6   The Other Parent: Friend or Foe

1. Lucile Duberman, *The Reconstituted Family: A Study of Remarried Couples and Their Children*, Chicago: Nelson-Hall, 1975, pp. 78–79.

2. William J. Goode, *Women in Divorce*, New York: Free Press, 1956, p. 301.

3. Duberman, *The Reconstituted Family*, p. 77. "Negative" means hostility and ill will still exist between the respondent and his or her former spouse. "Positive" attitudes indicate cooperation between them with feelings of warmth and sympathy. "Indifference" means the former mate has no significance or value today; no special like or dislike exists.

4. Nancy Friday, *My Mother, My Self*, New York: Dell Publishing, 1977, pp. 160–201. In the stereotyping of the sexes, men are granted their competitive drives. But women go through life denying they are competitive, while seeing other women's gains as somehow barring them from life's feast.

5. Jessie Bernard, *Remarriage*, New York: Dryden Press, 1956, p. 232.

6. Elaine Walster and G. Walster, *A New Look at Love*, Reading, Mass.: Addison-Wesley, 1978, p. 87.

7. Anne Simon, *Stepchild in the Family*, New York: Odyssey Press, 1964, p. 197.

8. Paula Berke, unpublished master's thesis, University of Southern California, from "When Dad Is Given Custody," *Parade*, Rita Rooney, February 24, 1980. This study, which includes two Los Angeles support groups, reveals that most of the women had married young, had had one or more children a year, had stayed married about ten years, and had divorced by age thirty-two. Most of the mothers said their marriages had developed problems early, and the children had created more pressure.

9. Georgia Dullea, "Is Joint Custody Good for Children?" *New York Times Magazine*, February 3, 1980, p. 34.

10. Joseph Goldstein, Anna Freud, and Albert Solnit, *Beyond the Best Interests of the Child*, New York: Free Press, 1973, p. 38.

11. Dullea, "Is Joint Custody Good for Children?" p. 35.

7 Invisible Enemies

1. Willard Gaylin, *Feelings: Our Vital Signs*, New York: Harper & Row, 1979.

2. Konrad Lorenz, *On Aggression*, New York: Harcourt Brace Jovanovich, 1966, p. 25.

3. Paul Bohannan and Rosemary Erickson, "Stepping In," *Psychology Today*, January 1978.

4. Emily B. Visher and John S. Visher, *Stepfamilies: A Guide to Working with Stepparents and Stepchildren*, New York: Brunner-Mazel, 1979.

5. Gerda Schulman, "Myths That Intrude on the Adaptation of the Stepfamily," *Social Casework*, 49:131–39, 1972.

6. B. L. Kell and J. M. Burow, *Developmental Counseling and Therapy*, Boston: Houghton Mifflin, 1970.

7. J. Louise Despert, *Children of Divorce*, New York: Doubleday, 1962.

8. Harris S. Goldstein, "Reconstituted Families: The Second Marriage and Its Children," *Psychiatric Quarterly*, 48:433–40, 1974.

9. Janice H. Nadler, "The Psychological Stress of the Stepmother," unpublished doctoral dissertation, 1976. Part-time stepmothers, besides having more conflict with their husbands and children than biological mothers, have the most conflict with older stepchildren.

10. *Shorter Oxford English Dictionary*, Oxford: Clarendon Press, 1962, p. 355; *American College Dictionary*, New York: Harper & Row, 1950, p. 246.

11. Jessie Bernard, *Remarriage*, New York: Dryden Press, 1956, pp. 227–36.

12. Theodore Caplow, *Two Against One*, Englewood Cliffs, N.J.: Prentice-Hall, 1968, pp. 62–94.

13. Lucile Duberman, "Step-Kin Relationships," *Journal of Marriage and Family*, May 1973, pp. 285–90. These findings can only be considered tentative because there were too few cases to give them credence. The lack of literature on either sibling or stepsibling relationships makes comparisons impossible.

14. Bernard, *Remarriage*, p. 284.

15. Duberman, "Step-Kin Relationships," pp. 55–57.

16. Morton Hunt, *The Divorce Experience*, New York: McGraw-Hill, 1977. Eventually five out of six divorced men and three out of four divorced women remarry, some not until ten to twenty years after divorce.

17. Gaylin, *Feelings: Our Vital Signs*, p. 52.

18. Gershen Kaufman, "The Meaning of Shame: Toward a Self-Affirming Identity," *Journal of Counseling Psychology*, vol. 21, no. 6, 1974, pp. 568–74.

19. Erik H. Erikson, *Childhood and Society*, New York: Norton, 1950, pp. 252–53.

20. Gaylin, *Feelings*, pp. 56–67.

21. Kaufman, "The Meaning of Shame," p. 568.

8 Shadows from Stepchild Land

1. Jerome Kagan, "The Parental Love Trap," *Psychology Today*, August 1978.

2. Pär Lagerkvist, *The Eternal Smile and Other Stories*, New York: Random House, 1954, p. 58.

3. Judith S. Wallerstein and Joan B. Kelly, *Surviving the Break-Up*, New York: Basic Books, 1980.

4. Thomas S. Langer and Stanley T. Michael, *Life Stress and Mental Health*, Illinois: Free Press, 1963, pp. 169–70. This is limited to the upper-class and middle-class families in the study.

5. Jerome Kagan, *The Growth of the Child*, New York: Norton, 1978, p. 212.

6. Kagan, *The Growth of the Child*, p. 232. Although naturally jealous when a new brother or sister arrives, the firstborn has no way to rationalize that resentment. Babies are entitled to extra attention, but when the anger cannot be justified, the firstborn is predisposed to guilt.

7. Constance Ahrons, "The Continuing Co-Parental Relationship Between Divorced Spouses," and Elinor Rosenberg, "Opening Doors to Children of Divorce: The Divorced Family as a Defacto Extended Family System," unpublished papers presented at American Orthopsychiatric Association annual meeting, Toronto, April 1980.

8. Langer and Michael, *Life Stress*, pp. 175–76.

9. Kagan, *The Growth of the Child*, p. 220.

10. Helen Hyman, story adaptations of *A Treasury of the World's Greatest Fairytales*, Danbury, Ct.: Danbury Press, 1972.

11. Bruno Bettelheim, *The Uses of Enchantment*, New York: Vintage, 1977, pp. 6–11 and 273–76.

12. Michel Radomisli, from an unpublished paper "Stereotypes, Stepmothers and Splitting," given at the American Psychiatric Association annual meeting, Atlanta, 1978.

13. Matina Horner, "Sex Differences in Achievement Motivation and Performance in Competitive and Non-Competitive Situations," unpublished doctoral dissertation, University of Minnesota, 1968.

To explain why women hadn't acted like men in two decades of achievement motivation studies, Horner argued that women had a "motive to avoid success in intellectual competence or leadership potential," because they viewed femininity and achievement as desirable but mutually exclusive ends. Horner's conclusions captured the popular and professional imagination, and the media reported her findings widely. Since then, scores of psychologists and students have done variations of her study. This follow-up research suggests that the motive to avoid success may have little to do with achieving success and that men fear success as much as women do.

14. *The International Webster New Encyclopedic Dictionary*, Chicago: English Language Institute of America, 1975, p. 796.

15. Margery Williams, *The Velveteen Rabbit*, New York: Avon, 1975.

9   Nobody Understands

1. Paul Bohannan, *Divorce and After*. New York: Doubleday, 1971, pp. 113–23. This phenomenon of quasi-kin relationships has not been studied, structurally or statistically. But since it has become a regular occurrence in American life, studies of divorce and remarriage must take it into account.

2. Evelyn Duvall, *In-Laws: Pro and Con*. New York: Association Press, 1964.

3. Richard Kalish and Emily Visher, "Grandparents of Divorce and Remarriage," unpublished paper presented at American Orthopsychiatric Association annual meeting, Toronto, April 1980.

4. Bohannan, *Divorce and After*.

5. Donald F. Anspach, "Kinship and Divorce," *Journal of Marriage and Family*, May 1976, pp. 323–30. This study reports that how often children see the kin of their absent father relates to their contact with him. Thus, the father is the link between his kin and his children.

6. Robert B. Hill, *The Strength of Black Families*. New York: Emerson Hall, 1971. Robert Hill serves as the research director of the National Urban League. Beyond kinship bonds, the other strengths of black families he identifies are the adaptability of family roles and strong work, achievement, and religious orientation.

7. Hill, *The Strength of Black Families*, pp. 6–7.

8. William J. Goode, *Women in Divorce*, New York: Free Press, 1965, p. 242.

9. Benjamin Schlesinger and Evelyn Stasiuk, "Children of Divorced Parents in Second Marriages," in *Children of Separation and Divorce*, New York: Grossman, 1972, p. 32; Emily Visher and John S. Visher, *Stepfamilies: A Guide to Working with Step-parents and Stepchildren*. New York: Brunner-Mazel, 1979.

10. Audrey J. Clarkin and John F. Clarkin, "Intervention with Children of Divorce Within the School System," unpublished paper presented at the American Orthopsychiatric Association annual meeting, Toronto, April 1980.

11. Clarkin and Clarkin, "Intervention with Children of Divorce."

12. Isolina Ricci, "Divorce, Remarriage and the Schools," *Stepfamily Bulletin*, September 1980.

13. Harvey J. Locke, *Predicting Adjustment in Marriage*, New York: Henry Holt, 1951, p. 243. Various studies indicate that church attendance and membership, mutual enjoyment of church activity, sex morals, church sanction of the marriage ceremony, and other indicators are related to good marital adjustment.

14. David O. Moberg, *The Church as a Social Institution*, Englewood Cliffs, N.J.: Prentice-Hall, 1962, pp. 349–67.

15. Bernard Berkowitz, "Legal Incidents of Today's 'Step' Relationship: Cinderella Revisited," *Family Law Quarterly* (4), 1970, p. 209.

16. Berkowitz, "Legal Incidents," p. 221.

17. Dr. Richard Ellison, a Syracuse University professor of law, speculates that this blurred distinction is probably a result of the racial composition of the community. The Washington, D.C., population is predominantly black, and black families maintain extended kinship systems and often "morally adopt" youngsters.

18. Visher and Visher, *Stepfamilies*.

19. Brenda Maddox, *The Half-Parent*, New York: Evans, 1975, p. 159.

10 Crisis: The Crossroads

1. Paul Glick, U.S. Bureau of the Census, Population Division.

2. Virginia Satir, *Peoplemaking*, Palo Alto: Science of Behavior Books, 1972, pp. 3–5.

3. Gail Sheehy, *Passages*, New York: Dutton, 1975, pp. 267–71 and 278–79. Sheehy explains the time push that occurs at this age. If the average couple is to find refreshment in midlife, the earlier roles of breadwinning husband and care-giving wife need renegotiating. She has to face the female's inner timidity problem; he must contend with the male's Atlas complex.

4. Sheehy, *Passages*, p. 217. The life pattern of this woman is to defer or suppress that part of her that yearns for a place in the professional world. Because of the identity confusion that so often characterizes the early part of this pattern, the nurturer has a great deal of inner preparation to do before she can pinpoint her outer goals. Vagueness and apprehension are her companions as she sorts out her life.

5. Willard Gaylin, *Feelings: Our Vital Signs*, New York: Harper & Row, 1979, pp. 22–27.

6. Nancy Friday, *My Mother, My Self*, New York: Dell, 1977, p. 199.

7. T. Thomas McMurrain, *Intervention in Human Crisis*, Atlanta: Humanics Press, 1977, pp. 10–34.

8. Leslie Aldridge Westoff, *The Second Time Around*, New York: Viking Press, 1977, p. 158.

9. J. Louise Despert, *Children of Divorce*, New York: Doubleday, 1953, pp. 7–10.

10. George R. Bach and Peter Wyden, *The Intimate Enemy*, New York: Avon, 1968, p. 275.

11. Mavis Hetherington, author of "The Virginia Longitudinal Study," studied 144 couples over seven years. One year after the divorce, 60 percent of the men and 72 percent of the women felt they had made a mistake in breaking up their relationships.

12. Morton Hunt and Bernice Hunt, *The Divorce Experience*, New York: McGraw-Hill, 1977, p. 14.

11   Our Real World

1. Jessie Bernard, *Remarriage*, New York: Dryden Press, 1956, pp. 307–11.

2. Kenneth Wilson, Louis Zurcher, Diana McAdams, and Russell Curtis, "Stepfathers and Stepchildren: An Exploratory Analysis from Two National Surveys," *Journal of Marriage and the Family*, August 1975, pp. 526–35. The highly emotional quality of divorce and remarriage has encouraged laypersons to conclude that children pay a heavy social and psychological price. But the findings from this national analysis demonstrate that there are no substantial differences in persons from stepfather families.

3. Davidyne Mayleas, *Rewedded Bliss*, New York: Basic Books, 1977, pp. 238–54.

4. Johann Christoph Friedrich von Schiller, "Die Räuber" (1777), in *The Macmillan Book of Proverbs, Maxims and Famous Phrases*, New York: Macmillan, 1948, p. 772.

5. Robert Liebert and Michael Spiegler, *Personality: Strategies for the Study of Man*, Homewood, Ill.: Dorsey Press, 1974.

Selected Bibliography

Adams, Bert N., and Thomas Weirath. *Readings on the Sociology of the Family.* Chicago: Markham, 1971.

Adams, Jane. *Sex and the Single Parent.* New York: Coward, McCann and Geoghegan, 1978.

Ahrons, Constance. "The Binuclear Family." *Alternative Styles,* 2:4, pp. 499–515, November 1979.

Ahrons, Constance. "The Continuing Co-Parental Relationship Between Divorced Spouses." Unpublished paper presented at American Orthopsychiatric Association annual meeting in Toronto, April 1980.

Anspach, Donald F. "Kinship and Divorce." *Journal of Marriage and the Family,* 38:323–30, May 1976.

Atkin, Edith, and Estelle Rubin. *Part-Time Father.* New York: Vanguard Press, 1976.

Auerbach, Stevanne. "From Stepparent to Real Parent." *Parents,* June 1976, pp. 34–41.

Bach, George R., and Peter Wyden. *Creative Aggression.* New York: Avon, 1975.

———. *The Intimate Enemy.* New York: Avon, 1968.

Baum, George, and Andrew Greeley. *The Church as an Institution.* New York: Herder and Herder, 1974.

Berkowitz, Bernard. "Legal Incidents of Today's 'Step' Relationship: 'Cinderella' Revisited." *Family Law Quarterly,* 4:209–29, September 1970.

Bernard, Jessie. *Remarriage: A Study of Marriage.* New York: Dryden Press, 1956.

———. *The Future of Marriage.* New York: World Publishing, 1972.

Bettelheim, Bruno. *The Uses of Enchantment.* New York: Knopf, 1976.

Bitterman, Catherine M. "The Multimarriage Family." *Social Casework,* 49:218–21, April 1968.

Bohannan, Paul. *Divorce and After.* New York: Doubleday, 1970.

Bohannan, Paul, and Rosemary Erickson. "Stepping In." *Psychology Today,* January 1978.

Bowerman, Charles E., and Donald P. Irish. "Some Relationships of Stepchildren to Their Parents." In *Marriage and Family in the Modern World,* edited by Ruth S. Cavan. New York: Thomas Crowell, 1969.

Brazelton, T. Berry. "Early Parent-Infant Reciprocity." *The Family—Can It Be Saved?* New York: Year Book Medical Publishers, 1976.

Caplow, Theodore. *Two Against One: Coalitions in Triads.* Englewood Cliffs, N.J.: Prentice-Hall, 1968.

Catton, William R. "What's in a Name? A Study of Role Inertia." *Journal of Marriage and the Family*, February 1969.

Chesler, Phyllis. *Women and Madness*. New York: Doubleday, 1972.

Clarkin, Audrey J., and John F. Clarkin. "Intervention with Children of Divorce Within the School System," unpublished paper given at the American Orthopsychiatric Association annual meeting. Toronto, April 1980.

Cogswell, Betty E., and Marvin B. Sussman. "Changing Family and Marriage Forms: Complications for Human Service Systems." *Family Coordinator*, 21:4, 505–16, 1972.

Despert, J. Louise. *Children of Divorce*. New York: Doubleday, 1953.

Draughon, Margaret. "Stepmother's Role of Identification in Relation to Mourning in the Child." *Psychological Reports*, 36:183–89, 1975.

Duberman, Lucile. *The Reconstituted Family: A Study of Remarried Couples and Their Children*. Chicago: Nelson-Hall, 1975.

———. "Step-Kin Relationships." *Journal of Marriage and the Family*, 35:283–95, May 1973.

Dullea, Georgia. "Is Joint Custody Good for Children?" *New York Times Magazine*, February 3, 1980.

Duvall, Evelyn. *In-Laws: Pro and Con*. New York: Association Press, 1964.

Einstein, Elizabeth. "Stepfamily Lives." *Human Behavior*, April 1979, pp. 63–68.

Erikson, Erik H. *Childhood and Society*, 2d edition. New York: Norton, 1963.

———. *Identity: Youth and Crisis*. New York: Norton, 1968.

Fast, Irene, and Albert C. Cain. "The Stepparent Role: Potential for Disturbance in Family Functioning." *American Journal of Orthopsychiatry*, 36:485–91, 1966.

Feldman, Harold, and Margaret Feldman. "Effect of Parenthood at Three Points in Marriage," unpublished paper, 1978.

Felsenthal, Helen. "The Developing Self: The Parental Role." In *The Child and His Image*, edited by Kaoru Yamamoto. Boston: Houghton Mifflin, 1972.

Forgione, A. G., and R. S. Surwit. *Fear: Learning to Cope*. New York: Van Nostrand Reinhold, 1978.

Friday, Nancy. *My Mother, My Self: The Daughter's Search for Identity*. New York: Dell Publishing, 1977.

Fromm, Erich. *The Art of Loving*. New York: Harper & Row, 1974.

Gardner, Richard A. *The Parents' Book About Divorce*. New York: Doubleday, 1977.

———. *Psychotherapy with Children of Divorce*. New York: Jason Aronson, 1976.

Gaylin, Willard. *Feelings: Our Vital Signs*. New York: Harper & Row, 1979.

Glick, Paul C. "A Demographer Looks at American Families." *Journal of Marriage and the Family*, 37:15–26, February 1975.

———. "Living Arrangements of Children and Young Adults." Revision of a paper presented at the annual meeting of the Population Association of America, Seattle, April 17–19, 1975.

Goetting, Ann. "The Normative Integration of the Former Spouse Relationship." *Journal of Divorce*, 2:4, Summer 1979.

Goldenberg, Irene, and Herbert Goldenberg. *Family Therapy: An Overview.* Monterey, Calif.: Brooks/Cole, 1980.

Goldstein, H. "Reconstituted Families: The Second Marriage and Its Children." *Psychiatric Quarterly,* 48:433–40.

Goldstein, Joseph, Anna Freud, and Albert Solnit. *Before the Best Interests of the Child.* New York: Free Press, 1980.

——. *Beyond the Best Interests of the Child.* New York: Free Press, 1973.

Goode, William J. *Women in Divorce.* New York: Free Press, 1965.

Goodman, Ellen. *Turning Points.* New York: Doubleday, 1979.

Gordon, Michael, ed. *The American Family in Social-Historical Perspective.* New York: St. Martin's Press, 1978.

Green, Ernest J. *Personal Relationships: An Approach to Marriage and Family.* New York: McGraw-Hill, 1978.

Hetherington, E. Mavis, Martha Cox, and Roger Cox. "Divorced Fathers." *The Family Coordinator,* October 1976.

Hill, Robert B. *The Strengths of Black Families.* New York: Emerson Hall, 1971.

Hollingshead, A. B. "Marital Status and Wedding Behavior." *Marriage and Family Living,* November 1952, pp. 308–11.

Howard, Jane. *Families.* New York: Simon and Schuster, 1978.

Hunt, Morton. *The World of the Formerly Married.* New York: McGraw-Hill, 1966.

Hunt, Morton, and Bernice Hunt. *The Divorce Experience: A New Look at the Formerly Married.* New York: McGraw-Hill, 1977.

Hyman, Helen. Story adaptations of *A Treasury of the World's Greatest Fairytales.* Danbury, Conn.: Danbury Press, 1972.

Jones, Shirley Maxwell. "Divorce and Remarriage: A New Beginning, a New Set of Problems." *Journal of Divorce,* 2:2, Winter 1978.

Justice, Blair, and Rita Justice. *The Broken Taboo: Sex in the Family.* New York: Human Sciences Press, 1979.

Kagan, Jerome. *The Growth of the Child.* New York: Norton, 1978.

——. "The Parental Love Trap." *Psychology Today,* August 1978, pp. 54–91.

Kagan, Jerome, R. B. Kearsley, and P. R. Zelazo. *Infancy: Its Place in Human Development.* Cambridge, Mass.: Harvard University Press, 1978.

Kalish, Richard, and Emily Visher. "Grandparents of Divorce and Remarriage." Unpublished paper presented at American Orthopsychiatric annual meeting. Toronto, April 1980.

Kaufman, Gershen. "The Meaning of Shame: Toward a Self-Affirming Identity." *Journal of Counseling Psychology,* 21:6, 1974.

Kell, B. L., and J. M. Burow. *Developmental Counseling and Therapy.* Boston: Houghton Mifflin, 1970.

Krantzler, Mel. *Creative Divorce.* New York: Evans, 1973.

Kübler-Ross, Elisabeth. *On Death and Dying.* New York: Macmillan, 1969.

Lagerkvist, Pär. *The Eternal Smile and Other Stories.* New York: Random House, 1954.

Landis, J. T. "The Trauma of Children When Parents Divorce." *Marriage and Family Living,* 22:7–13, 1960.

Langer, Thomas S., and Stanley T. Michael. *Life Stress and Mental Health.* New York: Free Press, 1963.

Levinger, George, and Oliver C. Moles. *Divorce and Separation: Context, Causes and Consequences.* New York: Basic Books, 1979.

Liebert, Robert M., and Michael D. Spiegler. *Personality: Strategies for the Study of Man.* Homewood, Ill.: Dorsey Press, revised 1974.

Locke, Harvey J. *Predicting Adjustment in Marriage: A Comparison of a Divorced and a Happily Married Group.* New York: Henry Holt, 1951.

Lorenz, Konrad. *On Aggression.* New York: Harcourt, Brace, 1966.

McCormick, Mona. *Stepfathers: What the Literature Reveals.* La Jolla, Calif.: Western Behavioral Sciences Institute, 1974.

McMurrain, T. Thomas. *Intervention in Human Crisis.* Atlanta: Humanics Press, 1977.

Maddox, Brenda. *The Half-Parent.* New York: Evans, 1975.

Magrab, Phyllis. "For the Sake of the Children: A Review of the Psychological Effects of Divorce." *Journal of Divorce,* Spring 1978, pp. 233–45.

Maslow, Abraham. *Motivation and Personality.* 2d edition. New York: Harper & Row, 1970.

Mayleas, Davidyne. *Rewedded Bliss.* New York: Basic Books, 1977.

Messinger, Lillian. "Remarriage Between Divorced People with Children from Previous Marriages: A Proposal for Preparation for Remarriage." *Journal of Marriage and Family Counseling,* 2:193–200, April 1976.

Moberg, David O. *The Church as a Social Institution.* Englewood Cliffs, N.J.: Prentice-Hall, 1962.

Monahan, Thomas P. "How Stable Are Remarriages?" *American Journal of Sociology,* 58:280–88, November 1952.

Mowatt, Marian H. "Group Psychotherapy for Stepfathers and Their Wives." *Psychotherapy: Theory, Research and Practice,* 9:4, Winter 1972.

Nadler, Janice H. "The Psychological Stress of the Stepmother." Unpublished doctoral dissertation, California School of Professional Psychology, 1976.

Noble, June, and William Noble. *How to Live with Other People's Children.* New York: Hawthorne, 1979.

Nolan, J. F. "The Impact of Divorce on Children." *Conciliation Courts Review,* 15:2, December 1977.

Norton, Arthur J., and Paul C. Glick. "Marital Instability: Past, Present and Future." *Journal of Social Issues,* 32, November 1, 1976.

Nye, F. I., and F. M. Berardo. *The Family: Its Structure and Interaction.* New York: Macmillan, 1973.

Parad, Howard J., ed. *Crisis Intervention: Selected Readings.* Family Services Association, 1965.

Perkins, Terry F., and James P. Kahan. "An Empirical Comparison of Natural-Father and Stepfather Family Systems." *Family Process,* 18:2, 175–83, June 1979.

Piers, Gerhart, and Milton B. Singer. *Shame and Guilt: A Psychoanalytic and Cultural Study.* Springfield, Ill.: Charles C. Thomas, 1953.

Post, Elizabeth. *Etiquette: The Blue Book of Social Usage,* 11th rev. ed. New York: Funk & Wagnalls, 1965.

Radomisli, Michel. "Stereotypes, Stepmothers and Splitting." From an unpublished paper presented at the American Psychiatric Association annual meeting. Atlanta, 1978.

Rallings, E. M. "The Special Role of Stepfather." *The Family Coordinator*, October 1976.

Ransom, Jane W., Stephen Schlesinger, and Andre Derdeyb. "A Stepfamily in Formation." *American Journal of Orthopsychiatry*, 49:1, 36ff, January 1979.

Raphael, Phyllis. "The Stepmother Trap." *McCalls*, February 1978.

Raymond, Louise. *Adoption and After*. Revised by Colette Taube Dywasuk. New York: Harper & Row, 1974.

Ricci, Isolina. "Divorce, Remarriage and the Schools." *Stepfamily Bulletin*, September 1980.

———. *Mom's House, Dad's House: Making Joint Custody Work*. New York: Macmillan, 1980.

Rogers, Carl. *Becoming Partners*. New York: Delacorte Press, 1972.

———. *On Becoming a Person*. Boston: Houghton Mifflin, 1961.

Roman, Mel, and William Haddad. "The Case for Joint Custody." *Psychology Today*, September 1978, pp. 96–105.

Rooney, Rita. "When Dad Is Given Custody." *Parade*, February 24, 1980, pp. 4–5.

Roosevelt, Ruth, and Jeannette Lofas. *Living in Step*. New York: McGraw-Hill, 1977.

Rosenbaum, Jean, and Veryl Rosenbaum. *Stepparenting: A Sympathetic Guide to Living with Other People's Children*. New York: Dutton, 1977.

Rosenberg, Elinor. "Opening Doors to Children of Divorce: The Divorced Family as a Defacto Extended Family System." Unpublished paper presented at American Orthopsychiatric Association annual meeting. Toronto, April 1980.

Rosenthal, Kristine M., and Harry F. Keshet. "The Not-Quite Stepmother." *Psychology Today*, July 1978, pp. 83–101.

Rossi, Alice. "Transition to Parenthood." *Journal of Marriage and the Family*. 30:26–39, February 1968.

———, Jerome Kagan, and Tamara Hareven, eds. *The Family*. New York: Norton, 1978.

Salk, Lee. "You and Your Stepchildren." *Harper's Bazaar*, June 1975, pp. 108–81.

Satir, Virginia. *Peoplemaking*. Palo Alto, Calif.: Science and Behavior Books, 1972.

Schlesinger, Benjamin, and Eugene Stasiuk. "Children of Divorced Parents in Second Marriages." In *Children of Separation and Divorce*, edited by Irving Stuart and Lawrence Abt. New York: Grossman, 1972, pp. 32ff.

Schulman, Gerda. "Myths That Intrude on the Adaptation of the Stepfamily." *Social Casework*, 53:131–39, 1972.

Sheehy, Gail. *Passages*. New York: Dutton, 1975.

Shorter, Edward. *The Making of the Modern Family*. New York: Basic Books, 1975.

Simon, Anne W. *Stepchild in the Family*. New York: Odyssey Press, 1964.

Spann, Nancie, and Owen Spann. *Your Child? I Thought It Was My Child*. Pasadena, Calif.: Ward Ritchie Press, 1977.

Stark, Gail. "Seven on a Honeymoon." *Parents Magazine*, 46:445, May 1971.

Steinzor, Bernard. *When Parents Divorce.* New York: Pantheon, 1969.

Stern, Phyllis. "Stepfather Families: Integration Around Child Discipline." *Issues in Mental Health Nursing*, 1:50–56, 1978.

Stinnett, Nick, and Craig Wayne Birdsong. *The Family and Alternate Life Styles.* Chicago: Nelson-Hall, 1978.

Teismann, Mark W. "Jealousy: Systematic, Problem-Solving Therapy with Couples." *Family Process*, June 1969, pp. 151–60.

Tufte, Virginia, and Barbara Myerhoff, eds. *Changing Images of the Family.* New Haven: Yale University Press, 1979.

Turow, Rita. *Daddy Doesn't Live Here Any More.* Matteson, Ill.: Great Lakes Living Press, 1977.

van Gennep, Arnold. *The Rites of Passage.* London: Routledge & Kegan Paul, 1960.

Visher, Emily B., and John S. Visher. *Stepfamilies: A Guide to Working with Stepparents and Stepchildren.* New York: Brunner-Mazel, 1979.

———. "Common Problems of Stepparents and Their Spouses." *American Journal of Orthopsychiatry*, April 1978, pp. 252–61.

Walker, Kenneth N., and Lillian Messinger. "Remarriage After Divorce: Dissolution and Reconstruction of Family Boundaries." *Family Process*, 18:2, pp. 185ff., June 1979.

Walker, Kenneth N., Joy Rogers, and Lillian Messinger. "Remarriage After Divorce: A Review." *Social Casework*, 58:276ff., May 1977.

Walker, Libby, et al. "An Annotated Bibliography of the Remarried, the Living Together, and Their Children." *Family Process*, June 1969, pp. 193ff.

Wallerstein, Judith S., and Joan B. Kelly. "The Effects of Parental Divorce: Experiences of the Child in Early Latency." *American Journal of Orthopsychiatry*, 40(1):20ff., January 1976.

———. "California's Children of Divorce." *Psychology Today*, January 1980, pp. 67–76.

———. "The Effects of Parental Divorce: The Adolescent Experience." *Journal of the Academy of Child Psychiatry*, 14:4, Autumn 1975.

———. "The Effects of Parental Divorce: Experiences of the Child in Later Latency." *American Journal of Orthopsychiatry*, 46:256–69, April 1976.

———. *Surviving the Break-up: How Children Actually Cope with Divorce.* New York: Basic Books, 1980.

Walster, Elaine, and G. Walster. *A New Look at Love.* Reading, Mass.: Addison-Wesley, 1978.

Walters, James, and Nick Stinnett. "Parent-Child Relationships: A Decade Review of Research." *Journal of Marriage and the Family*, 33:82, 1971.

Westoff, Leslie Aldridge. *The Second Time Around: Remarriage in America.* New York: Penguin Books, 1978.

Whiteside, Mary F., and Lynn S. Auerbach. "Can the Daughter of My Father's New Wife Be My Sister?" *Journal of Divorce*, Spring 1978, pp. 271–83.

Williams, Margery. *The Velveteen Rabbit.* New York: Avon, 1975.

Wilson, K., et al. "Stepfathers and Stepchildren: An Exploratory Analysis from Two National Surveys." *Journal of Marriage and Family*, 37:526–36, August 1975.

Index